INSIDE OS/2

GORDON LETWIN
Chief Architect, Systems Software, Microsoft®

Foreword by Bill Gates

PUBLISHED BY

Microsoft Press
A Division of Microsoft Corporation
16011 NE 36th Way, Box 97017, Redmond, Washington 98073-9717

Library of Congress Cataloging in Publication Data

Letwin, Gordon.
Inside OS/2.

Includes index.
1. MS OS/2 (Computer operating system) I. Title.
II. Title: Inside OS/Two.
QA76.76.063L48   1988   005.4'46   87-31579
ISBN 1-55615-117-9

Printed and bound in the United States of America

1 2 3 4 5 6 7 8 9 MLML 8 9 0 9 8

Distributed to the book trade in the
United States by Harper & Row.

Distributed to the book trade in
Canada by General Publishing Company, Ltd.

Distributed to the book trade outside the
United States and Canada by Penguin Books Ltd.

Penguin Books Ltd., Harmondsworth, Middlesex, England
Penguin Books Australia Ltd., Ringwood, Victoria, Australia
Penguin Books N.Z. Ltd., 182-190 Wairau Road, Auckland 10, New Zealand

British Cataloging in Publication Data available

Editor: Patricia Pratt

Dedication

To R.P.W.

Contents

Acknowledgments

Although a book can have a single author, a work such as OS/2 necessarily owes its existence to the efforts of a great many people. The architecture described herein was hammered out by a joint Microsoft/IBM design team: Ann, Anthony, Carolyn, Ed, Gordon, Jerry, Mark, Mike, Ray, and Ross. This team accomplished a great deal of work in a short period of time.

The bulk of the credit, and my thanks, go to the engineers who designed and implemented the code and made it work. The size of the teams involved throughout the project prevents me from listing all the names here. It's hard for someone who has not been involved in a software project of this scope to imagine the problems, pressure, chaos, and "reality shifts" that arise in a never-ending stream. These people deserve great credit for their skill and determination in making OS/2 come to pass.

Thanks go to the OS/2 development staffers who found time, in the heat of the furnace, to review and critique this book: Ian Birrell, Ross Cook, Rick Dewitt, Dave Gilman, Vic Heller, Mike McLaughlin, Jeff Parsons, Ray Pedrizetti, Robert Reichel, Rajen Shaw, Anthony Short, Ben Slivka, Pete Stewart, Indira Subramanian, Bryan Willman, and Mark Zbikowski.

I'd like to give special thanks to Mark Zbikowski and Aaron Reynolds, the "gurus of DOS." Without their successes there would never have been an opportunity for a product such as OS/2.

And finally I'd like to thank Bill Gates for creating and captaining one hell of a company, thereby making all this possible.

Foreword

OS/2 is destined to be a very important piece of software. During the next 10 years, millions of programmers and users will utilize this system. From time to time they will come across a feature or a limitation and wonder why it's there. The best way for them to understand the overall philosophy of the system will be to read this book. Gordon Letwin is Microsoft's architect for OS/2. In his very clear and sometimes humorous way, Gordon has laid out in this book why he included what he did and why he didn't include other things.

The very first generation of microcomputers were 8-bit machines, such as the Commodore Pet, the TRS-80, the Apple II, and the CPM 80 based machines. Built into almost all of them was Microsoft's BASIC Interpreter. I met Gordon Letwin when I went to visit Heath's personal computer group (now part of Zenith). Gordon had written his own BASIC as well as an operating system for the Heath system, and he wasn't too happy that his management was considering buying someone else's. In a group of about 15 people, he bluntly pointed out the limitations of my BASIC versus his. After Heath licensed my BASIC, I convinced Gordon that Microsoft was the place to be if you wanted your great software to be popular, and so he became one of Microsoft's first 10 programmers. His first project was to single-handedly write a compiler for Microsoft BASIC. He put a sign on his door that read

> Do not disturb, feed, poke, tease...the animal

and in 5 months wrote a superb compiler that is still the basis for all our BASIC compilers. Unlike the code that a lot of superstar programmers write, Gordon's source code is a model of readability and includes precise explanations of algorithms and why they were chosen.

When the Intel 80286 came along, with its protected mode completely separate from its compatible real mode, we had no idea how we were going to get at its new capabilities. In fact, we had given up until Gordon came up with the patented idea described in this book that has been referred to as "turning the car off and on at 60 MPH." When we first explained the idea to Intel and many of its customers, they were sure it wouldn't work. Even Gordon wasn't positive it would work until he wrote some test programs that proved it did.

Gordon's role as an operating systems architect is to overview our designs and approaches and make sure they are as simple and as elegant as possible. Part of this job includes reviewing people's code. Most programmers enjoy having Gordon look over their code and point out how it could be improved and simplified. A lot of programs end up about half as big after Gordon has explained a better way to write them. Gordon doesn't mince words, however, so in at least one case a particularly sensitive programmer burst into tears after reading his commentary. Gordon isn't content to just look over other people's code. When a particular project looks very difficult, he dives in. Currently, Gordon has decided to personally write most of our new file system, which will be dramatically faster than our present one. On a recent "vacation" he wrote more than 50 pages of source code.

This is Gordon's debut as a book author, and like any good designer he has already imagined what bad reviews might say. I think this book is both fun and important. I hope you enjoy it as much as I have.

BILL GATES

Introduction

Technological breakthroughs develop in patterns that are distinct from patterns of incremental advancements. An incremental advancement—an improvement to an existing item—is straightforward and unsurprising. An improvement is created; people see the improvement, know what it will do for them, and start using it.

A major advance without closely related antecedents—a technological breakthrough—follows a different pattern. The field of communication is a good example. Early in this century, a large infrastructure existed to facilitate interpersonal communication. Mail was delivered twice a day, and a variety of efficient services relayed messages. A businessman dictated a message to his secretary, who gave it to a messenger service. The service carried the message to its nearby destination, where a secretary delivered it to the recipient.

Into this environment came a technological breakthrough—the telephone. The invention of the telephone was a breakthrough, not an incremental advance, because it provided an entirely new way to communicate. It wasn't an improvement over an existing method. That it was a breakthrough development impeded its acceptance. Most business people considered it a newfangled toy, of little practical use. "What good does it do me? By the time I dictate the message, and my secretary writes it down and gives it to the mailroom, and they phone the addressee's mailroom, and the message is copied—perhaps incorrectly—and delivered to the addressee's secretary, it would have been as fast to have it delivered by messenger! All my correspondents are close by, and, besides, with messengers I don't have to pay someone to sit by the telephone all day in case a message comes in."

This is a classic example of the earliest stages of breakthrough technology—potential users evaluate it by trying to fit it into present work patterns. Our example businessman has not yet realized that he needn't write the message down anymore and that it needn't be copied down at the destination. He also doesn't realize that the reason his recipients are close by is that they have to be for decent messenger delivery. The telephone relaxed this requirement, allowing more efficient locations near factories and raw materials or where office space was cheaper. But it was necessary for the telephone to be accepted before these advantages could be realized.

Another impedance to the acceptance of a breakthrough technology is that the necessary new infrastructure is not in place. A telephone did little good if your intended correspondent didn't have one. The nature of telephones required a standard; until that standard was set, your correspondent might own a phone, but it could be connected to a network unreachable by you. Furthermore, because the technology was in its infancy, the facilities were crude.

These obstacles were not insurmountable. The communications requirements of some people were so critical that they were willing to invent new procedures and to put up with the problems of the early stages. Some people, because of their daring or ambition, used the new system to augment their existing system. And finally, because the new technology was so powerful, some used it to enhance the existing technology. For example, a messenger service might establish several offices with telephone linkage between them and use the telephones to speed delivery of short messages by phoning them to the office nearest the destination, where they were copied down and delivered normally. Using the telephone in this fashion was wasteful, but where demand for the old service was high enough, any improvement, however "wasteful," was welcome.

After it has a foot in the door, a breakthrough technology is unstoppable. After a time, standards are established, the bugs are worked out, and, most important, the tool changes its users. Once the telephone became available, business and personal practices developed in new patterns, patterns that were not considered before because they were not possible. Messenger services used to be fast enough, but only because, before the telephone, the messenger service was the fastest technology available. The telephone changed the life-style of its users.

This change in the structure of human activity explains why an intelligent person could say, "Telephones are silly gadgets," and a few years later say, "Telephones are indispensable." This change in the tool user—caused by the tool itself—also makes predicting the ultimate effect of the new technology difficult. Extrapolating from existing trends is wildly inaccurate because the new tool destroys many practices and creates wholly unforeseen ones. It's great fun to read early, seemingly silly predictions of life in the future and to laugh at the predictors, but the predictors were frequently intelligent and educated. Their only mistake was in treating the new development as an incremental advance rather than as a breakthrough technology. They saw how the new development would improve their current practices, but they couldn't see how it would replace those practices.

Digital computers are an obvious breakthrough technology, and they've shared the classic three-stage pattern: "exotic toys," "limited use," and "indispensable." Mainframe computers have gone the full route, in the milieu of business and scientific computing. IBM's initial estimate of the computer market was a few dozen machines. But, as the technology and the support infrastructure grew, and as people's ways of working adapted to computers, the use of computers grew—from the census bureau, to life insurance companies, to payroll systems, and finally to wholly new functions such as MIS (Management Information Sciences) systems and airline reservation networks.

Microcomputers are in the process of a similar development. The "exotic toy" stage has already given way to the "limited use" stage. We're just starting to develop standards and infrastructure and are only a few years from the "indispensable" stage. In anticipation of this stage, Microsoft undertook the design and the development of OS/2.

Although studying the mainframe computer revolution helps in trying to predict the path of the microcomputer revolution, microcomputers are more than just "cheap mainframes." The microcomputer revolution will follow the tradition of breakthroughs, creating new needs and new uses that cannot be anticipated solely by studying what happened with mainframe systems.

This book was written because of the breakthrough nature of the microcomputer and the impact of the coming second industrial revolution. The designers of OS/2 tried to anticipate, to the greatest extent possible, the demands that would be placed on the system when the tool—the personal computer—and the tool user reached their new equilibrium. A knowledge of MS-DOS and a thorough reading of the OS/2 reference manuals will not, in themselves, clarify the key issues of the programming environment that OS/2 was written to support. This is true not only because of the complexity of the product but because many design elements were chosen to provide services that—from a prebreakthrough perspective—don't seem needed and solve problems that haven't yet arisen.

Other books provide reference information and detailed how-to instructions for writing OS/2 programs. This book describes the underlying architectural models that make up OS/2 and discusses how those models are expected to meet the foreseen and unforeseen requirements of the oncoming office automation revolution. It focuses on the general issues, problems, and solutions that all OS/2 programs encounter regardless of the programming and interface models that a programmer may employ.

As is often the case in a technical discussion, everything in OS/2 is interconnected in some fashion to everything else. A discussion on the shinbone naturally leads to a discussion of the thighbone and so on. The author and the editor of this book have tried hard to group the material into a logical progression without redundancy, but the very nature of the material makes complete success at this impossible. It's often desirable, in fact, to repeat material, perhaps from a different viewpoint or with a different emphasis. For these reasons, the index references every mention of an item or a topic, however peripheral. Having too many references (including a few worthless ones) is far better than having too few references. When you're looking for information about a particular subject, I recommend that you first consult the contents page to locate the major discussion and then peruse the index to pick up references that may appear in unexpected places.

Part I

The Project

1

History of the Project

Microsoft was founded to realize a vision of a microcomputer on every desktop—a vision of the second industrial revolution. The first industrial revolution mechanized physical work. Before the eighteenth century, nearly all objects were created and constructed by human hands, one at a time. With few exceptions, such as animal-powered plowing and cartage, all power was human muscle power. The second industrial revolution will mechanize routine mental work. Today, on the verge of the revolution, people are still doing "thought work," one piece at a time.

Certain tasks—those massive in scope and capable of being rigidly described, such as payroll calculations—have been automated, but the majority of "thought work" is still done by people, not by computers. We have the computer equivalent of the plow horse, but we don't have the computer equivalent of the electric drill or the washing machine.

Of course, computers cannot replace original thought and creativity (at least, not in the near future) any more than machines have replaced design and creativity in the physical realm. But the bulk of the work in a white-collar office involves routine manipulation of information. The second industrial revolution will relieve us of the "grunt work"—routine data manipulation, analysis, and decisions—freeing us to deal only with those situations that require human judgment.

Most people do not recognize the inevitability of the second industrial revolution. They can't see how a computer could do 75 percent of their work because their work was structured in the absence of computers. But, true to the pattern for technological breakthroughs, the tremendous utility of the microcomputer will transform its users and the way they do their work.

For example, a great deal of work is hard to computerize because the input information arrives on paper and it would take too long to type it all in. Ten years ago, computer proponents envisioned the "paperless office" as a solution for this problem: All material would be generated by computer and then transferred electronically or via disk to other computers. Offices are certainly becoming more paperless, and the arrival of powerful networking systems will accelerate this, but paper continues to be a very useful medium. As a result, in recent years growth has occurred in another direction—incorporating paper as a computer input and output device. Powerful laser printers, desktop publishing systems, and optical scanners and optical character recognition will make it more practical to input from and output to paper.

Although the founders of Microsoft fully appreciate the impact of the second industrial revolution, nobody can predict in detail how the revolution will unfold. Instead, Microsoft bases its day-to-day decisions on dual sets of goals: short-term goals, which are well known, and a long-term goal—our vision of the automated office. Each decision has to meet our short-term goals, and it must be consonant with our long-term vision, a vision that becomes more precise as the revolution progresses.

When 16-bit microprocessors were first announced, Microsoft knew that the "iron" was now sufficiently powerful to begin to realize this vision. But a powerful computer environment requires both strong iron and a sophisticated operating system. The iron was becoming available, but the operating system that had been standard for 8-bit microprocessors was inadequate. This is when and why Microsoft entered the operating system business: We knew that we needed a powerful operating system to realize our vision and that the only way to guarantee its existence and suitability was to write it ourselves.

1.1   **MS-DOS version 1.0**

MS-DOS got its start when IBM asked Microsoft to develop a disk operating system for a new product that IBM was developing, the IBM Personal Computer (PC). Microsoft's only operating system product at that time was XENIX, a licensed version of AT&T's UNIX® operating system. XENIX/UNIX requires a processor with memory management and protection facilities. Because the 8086/8088 processors had neither and because XENIX/UNIX memory requirements—modest by minicomputer standards of the day—were nonetheless large by microcomputer standards, a different operating system had to be developed.

CP/M-80, developed by Digital Research,® Incorporated (DRI), had been the standard 8-bit operating system, and the majority of existing microcomputer software had been written to run on CP/M-80. For this reason, Microsoft decided to make MS-DOS version 1.0 as compatible as possible with CP/M-80. The 8088 processor would not run the existing CP/M-80 programs, which were written for the 8080 processor, but because 8080 programs could be easily and semiautomatically converted to run on the 8088, Microsoft felt that minimizing adaptation hassles by minimizing operating system incompatibility would hasten the acceptance of MS-DOS on the IBM PC.

A major software product requires a great deal of development time, and IBM was in a hurry to introduce its PC. Microsoft, therefore, looked around for a software product to buy that could be built onto to create MS-DOS version 1.0. Such a product was found at Seattle Computer Products. Tim Paterson, an engineer there, had produced a CP/M-80 "clone," called SCP-DOS, that ran on the 8088 processor. Microsoft purchased full rights to this product and to its source code and used the product as a starting point in the development of MS-DOS version 1.0.

MS-DOS version 1.0 was released in August 1981. Available only for the IBM PC, it consisted of 4000 lines of assembly-language source code and ran in 8 KB of memory. MS-DOS version 1.1 was released in 1982 and worked with double-sided 320 KB floppy disks.

Microsoft's goal was that MS-DOS version 1.0 be highly CP/M compatible, and it was. Ironically, it was considerably more compatible than DRI's own 8088 product, CP/M-86. As we shall see later, this CP/M compatibility, necessary at the time, eventually came to cause Microsoft engineers a great deal of difficulty.

1.2   **MS-DOS version 2.0**

In early 1982, IBM disclosed to Microsoft that it was developing a hard disk-based personal computer, the IBM XT. Microsoft began work on MS-DOS version 2.0 to provide support for the new disk hardware. Changes were necessary because MS-DOS, in keeping with its CP/M-80 compatible heritage, had been designed for a floppy disk environment. A disk could contain only one directory, and that directory could contain a maximum of 64 files. This decision was reasonable when first made because floppy disks held only about 180 KB of data.

For the hard disk, however, the 64-file limit was much too small, and using a single directory to manage perhaps hundreds of files was

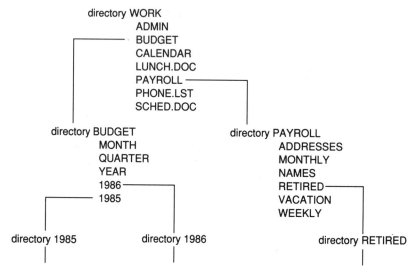

Figure 1-1.
A directory tree hierarchy. Within the WORK directory are five files (ADMIN, CALENDAR, LUNCH.DOC, PHONE.LST, SCHED.DOC) and two subdirectories (BUDGET, PAYROLL). Each subdirectory has its own subdirectories.

clumsy. Therefore, the MS-DOS version 2.0 developers—Mark Zbikowski, Aaron Reynolds, Chris Peters, and Nancy Panners—added a hierarchical file system. In a hierarchical file system a directory can contain other directories and files. In turn, those directories can contain a mixture of files and directories and so on. A hierarchically designed system starts with the main, or "root," directory, which itself can contain (as seen in Figure 1-1 on the preceding page) a tree-structured collection of files and directories.

1.3   **MS-DOS version 3.0**

MS-DOS version 3.0 was introduced in August 1984, when IBM announced the IBM PC/AT. The AT contains an 80286 processor, but, when running DOS, it uses the 8086 emulation mode built into the chip and runs as a "fast 8086." The chip's extended addressing range and its protected mode architecture sit unused.[1]

MS-DOS version 3.1 was released in November 1984 and contained networking support. In January 1986, MS-DOS version 3.2—a minor revision—was released. This version supported 3½-inch floppy disks and contained the formatting function for a device in the device driver. In 1987, MS-DOS version 3.3 followed; the primary enhancement of this release was support for the IBM PS/2 and compatible hardware.

1.4   **MS-DOS version 4.0**

Microsoft started work on a multitasking version of MS-DOS in January 1983. At the time, it was internally called MS-DOS version 3.0. When a new version of the single-tasking MS-DOS was shipped under the name MS-DOS version 3.0, the multitasking version was renamed, internally, to MS-DOS version 4.0. A version of this product—a multitasking, real-mode only MS-DOS—was shipped as MS-DOS version 4.0. Because MS-DOS version 4.0 runs only in real mode, it can run on 8088 and 8086 machines as well as on 80286 machines. The limitations of the real mode environment make MS-DOS version 4.0 a specialized

---

1. Products such as Microsoft XENIX/UNIX run on the PC/AT and compatibles, using the processor's protected mode. This is possible because XENIX/UNIX and similar systems had no preexisting real mode applications that needed to be supported.

product. Although MS-DOS version 4.0 supports full preemptive multitasking, system memory is limited to the 640 KB available in real mode, with no swapping.[2] This means that all processes have to fit into the single 640 KB memory area. Only one MS-DOS version 3.x compatible real mode application can be run; the other processes must be special MS-DOS version 4.0 processes that understand their environment and cooperate with the operating system to coexist peacefully with the single MS-DOS version 3.x real mode application.

Because of these restrictions, MS-DOS version 4.0 was not intended for general release, but as a platform for specific OEMs to support extended PC architectures. For example, a powerful telephone management system could be built into a PC by using special MS-DOS version 4.0 background processes to control the telephone equipment. The resulting machine could then be marketed as a ''compatible MS-DOS 3 PC with a built-in superphone.''

Although MS-DOS version 4.0 was released as a special OEM product, the project—now called MS-DOS version 5.0—continued. The goal was to take advantage of the protected mode of the 80286 to provide full general purpose multitasking without the limitations—as seen in MS-DOS version 4.0—of a real-mode only environment. Soon, Microsoft and IBM signed a Joint Development Agreement that provided for the design and development of MS-DOS version 5.0 (now called CP/DOS). The agreement is complex, but it basically provides for joint development and then subsequent joint ownership, with both companies holding full rights to the resulting product.

As the project neared completion, the marketing staffs looked at CP/DOS, nee DOS 5, nee DOS 4, nee DOS 3, and decided that it needed...you guessed it...a name change. As a result, the remainder of this book will discuss the design and function of an operating system called OS/2.

---

2. It is not feasible to support general purpose swapping without memory management hardware that is unavailable in 8086 real mode.

2

Goals and
Compatibility
Issues

OS/2 is similar to traditional multitasking operating systems in many
ways: It provides multitasking, scheduling, disk management, memory
management, and so on. But it is also different in many ways, because a
personal computer is very different from a multiuser minicomputer.
The designers of OS/2 worked from two lists: a set of goals and a set of
compatibility issues. This chapter describes those goals and compatibility issues and provides the context for a later discussion of the
design itself.

2.1 Goals

The primary goal of OS/2 is to be the ideal office automation operating
system. The designers worked toward this goal by defining the following intermediate and, seemingly, contradictory goals:

- To provide device-independent graphics drivers without introducing any significant overhead.

- To allow applications direct access to high-bandwidth peripherals
  but maintain the ability to virtualize or apportion the usage of
  those peripherals.

- To provide multitasking without reducing the performance and response available from a single-tasking system.

- To provide a fully customized environment for each program and its descendants yet also provide a standard environment that is unaffected by other programs in the system.

- To provide a protected environment to ensure system stability yet one that will not constrain applications from the capabilities they have under nonprotected systems.

2.1.1 Graphical User Interface

By far the fastest and easiest way people receive information is through the eye. We are inherently visual creatures. Our eyes receive information rapidly; they can "seek" to the desired information and "zoom" their attention in and out with small, rapid movements of the eye muscles. A large part of the human brain is dedicated to processing visual information. People abstract data and meaning from visual material—from text to graphics to motion pictures—hundreds of times faster than from any other material.

As a result, if an office automation system is to provide quantities of information quickly and in a form in which it can be easily absorbed, a powerful graphics capability is essential. Such capabilities were rare in earlier minicomputer operating systems because of the huge memory and compute power costs of high-resolution displays. Today's microcomputers have the memory to contain the display information, they have the CPU power to create and manipulate that information, and they have no better use for those capabilities than to support powerful, easy-to-use graphical applications.

Graphics can take many forms—pictures, tables, drawings, charts—perhaps incorporating color and even animation. All are powerful adjuncts to the presentation of alphanumeric text. Graphical applications don't necessarily employ charts and pictures. A WYSIWYG (What You See Is What You Get) typesetting program may display only text, but if that text is drawn in graphics mode, the screen can show any font, in any type size, with proportional spacing, kerning, and so on.

The screen graphics components of OS/2 need to be device independent; that is, an application must display the proper graphical "picture" without relying on the specific characteristics of any particular graphical display interface board. Each year the state of the art in displays gets better; it would be extremely shortsighted to tie applications to a particular display board, for no matter how good it is, within a couple of years it will be obsolete.

The idea is to encapsulate device-specific code by requiring that each device come with a software package called a device driver. The application program issues commands for a generic device, and the device driver then translates those commands to fit the characteristics of the actual device. The result is that the manufacturer of a new graphics display board needs to write an appropriate device driver and supply it with the board. The application program doesn't need to know anything about the device, and the device driver doesn't need to know anything about the application, other than the specification of the common interface they share. This common interface describes a virtual display device; the general technique of hiding a complicated actual situation behind a simple, standard interface is called "virtualization."

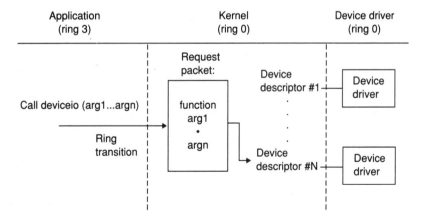

Figure 2-1.
Traditional device driver architecture. When an application wants to do device I/O, it calls the operating system, which builds a device request packet, determines the target device, and delivers the packet. The device driver's response follows the opposite route through the kernel back to the application.

Figure 2-1 shows the traditional operating system device driver architecture. Applications don't directly call device drivers because device drivers need to execute in the processor's privilege mode to manipulate their device; the calling application must run in normal mode. In the language of the 80286/80386 family of processors, privilege mode is called ring 0, and normal mode is called ring 3. The operating system usually acts as a middleman: It receives the request, validates it, deals with issues that arise when there is only one device but multiple applications are using it, and then passes the request to the device driver. The device driver's response or return of data takes the reverse path, winding its way through the operating system and back to the application program.

This approach solves the device virtualization problem, but at a cost in performance. The interface between the application and the device driver is narrow; that is, the form messages can take is usually restricted. Commonly, the application program is expected to build a request block that contains all the information and data that the device driver needs to service the request; the actual call to the operating system is simply "pass this request block to the device driver." Setting up this block takes time, and breaking it down in the device driver again takes time. More time is spent on the reply; the device driver builds, the operating system copies, and the application breaks down. Further time is spent calling down through the internal layers of the operating system, examining and copying the request block, routing to the proper device driver, and so forth. Finally, the transition between rings (privilege and normal mode) is also time-consuming, and two such transitions occur—to privilege mode and back again.

Such a cost in performance was acceptable in nongraphics-based systems because, typically, completely updating a screen required only 1920 (or fewer) bytes of data. Today's graphics devices can require 256,000 bytes or more per screen update, and future devices will be even more demanding. Furthermore, applications may expect to update these high-resolution screens several times a second.[1]

---

1. It's not so much the amount of data that slows the traditional device driver model, but the number of requests and replies. Disk devices work well through the traditional model because disk requests tend to be large (perhaps 40,000 bytes). Display devices tend to be written piecemeal—a character, a word, or a line at a time. It is the high rate of these individual calls that slows the device driver model, not the number of bytes written to the screen.

OS/2 needed powerful, device-independent graphical display support that had a wide, efficient user interface—one that did not involve ring transitions, the operating system, or other unnecessary overhead. As we'll see later, OS/2 meets this requirement by means of a mechanism called dynamic linking.

2.1.2   Multitasking

To be really useful, a personal computer must be able to do more than one chore at a time—an ability called multitasking. We humans multitask all the time. For example, you may be involved in three projects at work, be halfway through a novel, and be taking Spanish lessons. You pick up each task in turn, work on it for a while, and then put it down and work on something else. This is called serial multitasking. Humans can also do some tasks simultaneously, such as driving a car and talking. This is called parallel multitasking.

In a serial multitasking computer environment, a user can switch activities at will, working for a while at each. For example, a user can leave a word-processing program without terminating it, consult a spreadsheet, and then return to the waiting word-processing program. Or, if someone telephones and requests an appointment, the user can switch from a spreadsheet to a scheduling program, consult the calendar, and then return to the spreadsheet.

The obvious value of multitasking makes it another key requirement for OS/2: Many programs or applications can run at the same time. But multitasking is useful for more than just switching between applications: Parallel multitasking allows an application to do work by itself—perhaps print a large file or recalculate a large spreadsheet—while the user works with another application. Because OS/2 supports full multitasking, it can execute programs in addition to the application(s) the user is running, providing advanced services such as network mail without interrupting or interfering with the user's work.[2]

---

2. Present-day machines contain only one CPU, so at any instant only one program can be executing. At this microscopic level, OS/2 is a serial multitasking system. It is not considered serial multitasking, however, because it performs preemptive scheduling. At any time, OS/2 can remove the CPU from the currently running program and assign it to another program. Because these rescheduling events may occur many times a second at totally unpredictable places within the running programs, it is accurate to view the system as if each program truly runs simultaneously with other programs.

2.1.3 **Memory Management**

Multitasking is fairly easy to achieve. All that's necessary is a source of periodic hardware interrupts, such as a clock circuit, to enable the operating system to effect a "context switch," or to reschedule. To be useful, however, a multitasking system needs an effective memory management system. For example, a user wants to run two applications on a system. Each starts at as low a memory location as possible to maximize the amount of memory it can use. Unfortunately, if the system supports multitasking and the user tries to run both applications simultaneously, each attempts to use the same memory cells, and the applications destroy each other.

A memory management system solves this problem by using special hardware facilities built into 80286/80386 processors (for example, IBM PC/AT machines and compatibles and 80386-based machines).[3] The memory management system uses the hardware to virtualize the memory of the machine so that each program appears to have all memory to itself.

Memory management is more than keeping programs out of each other's way. The system must track the owner or user(s) of each piece of memory so that the memory space can be reclaimed when it is no longer needed, even if the owner of the memory neglects to explicitly release it. Some operating systems avoid this work by assuming that no application will ever fail to return its memory when done or by examining the contents of memory and ascertaining from those contents whether the memory is still being used. (This is called "garbage collection.") Neither alternative was acceptable for OS/2. Because OS/2 will run a variety of programs written by many vendors, identifying free memory by inspection is impossible, and assuming perfection from the applications themselves is unwise. Tracking the ownership and usage of memory objects can be complex, as we shall see in our discussion on dynamic link libraries.

Finally, the memory management system must manage memory overcommit. The multitasking capability of OS/2 allows many applications to be run simultaneously; thus, RAM must hold all these programs and their data. Although RAM becomes cheaper every year,

---

3. Earlier 8086/8088 processors used in PCs, PC/XTs, and similar machines lack this hardware. This is why earlier versions of MS-DOS didn't support multitasking and why OS/2 won't run on such machines.

buying enough to hold all of one's applications at one time is still prohibitive. Furthermore, although RAM prices continue to drop, the memory requirements of applications will continue to rise. Consequently, OS/2 must contain an effective mechanism to allocate more memory to the running programs than in fact physically exists. This is called memory overcommit.

OS/2 accomplishes this magic with the classic technique of swapping. OS/2 periodically examines each segment of memory to see if it has been used recently. When a request is made for RAM and none is available, the least recently used segment of memory (the piece that has been unused for the longest time) is written to a disk file, and the RAM it occupied is made available. Later, if a program attempts to use the swapped-out memory, a "memory not present" fault occurs. OS/2 intercepts the fault and reloads the memory information from the disk into memory, swapping out some other piece of memory, if necessary, to make room. This whole process is invisible to the application that uses the swapped memory area; the only impact is a small delay while the needed memory is read back from the disk.

The fundamental concepts of memory overcommit and swapping are simple, but a good implementation is not. OS/2 must choose the right piece of memory to swap out, and it must swap it out efficiently. Not only must care be taken that the swap file doesn't grow too big and consume all the free disk space but also that deadlocks don't occur. For example, if all the disk swap space is filled, it may be impossible to swap into RAM a piece of memory because no free RAM is available, and OS/2 can't free up RAM because no swap space exists to write it out to. Naturally, the greater the load on the system, the slower the system will be, but the speed degradation must be gradual and acceptable, and the system must never deadlock.

The issues involved in memory management and the memory management facilities that OS/2 provides are considerably more complex than this overview. We'll return to the subject of memory management in detail in Chapter 9.

2.1.4 Protection

I mentioned earlier that OS/2 cannot trust applications to behave correctly. I was talking about memory management, but this concern generalizes into the next key requirement: OS/2 must protect applications from the proper or improper actions of other applications that may be running on the system.

Because OS/2 will run applications and programs from a variety of vendors, every user's machine will execute a different set of applications, running in different ways on different data. No software vendor can fully test a product in all possible environments. This makes it critical that an error on the part of one program does not crash the system or some other program or, worse, corrupt data and *not* bring down the system. Even if no data is damaged, system crashes are unacceptable. Few users have the background or equipment even to diagnose which application caused the problem.

Furthermore, malice, as well as accident, is a concern. Microsoft's vision of the automated office cannot be realized without a system that is secure from deliberate attack. No corporation will be willing to base its operations on a computer network when any person in that company—with the help of some "cracker" programs bought from the back of a computer magazine—can see and change personnel or payroll files, billing notices, or strategic planning memos.

Today, personal computers are being used as a kind of super-sophisticated desk calculator. As such, data is secured by traditional means—physical locks on office doors, computers, or file cabinets that store disks. Users don't see a need for a protected environment because their machine is physically protected. This lack of interest in protection is another example of the development of a breakthrough technology. Protection is not needed because the machine is secure and operates on data brought to it by traditional office channels. In the future, however, networked personal computers will become universal and will act both as the processors and as the source (via the network) of the data. Thus, in this role, protection is a key requirement and is indeed a prerequisite for personal computers to assume that central role.

2.1.5 Encapsulation

When a program runs in a single-tasking system such as MS-DOS version 3.x, its environment is always constant—consisting of the machine and MS-DOS. The program can expect to get the same treatment from the system and to provide exactly the same interaction with the user each time it runs. In a multitasking environment, however, many programs can be running. Each program can be using files and devices in different ways; each program can be using the mouse, each program can have the screen display in a different mode, and so on. OS/2 must encapsulate, or isolate, each program so that it "sees" a uniform environment each time it runs, even though the computer environment itself may be different each time.

2.1.6   Interprocess Communication (IPC)

In a single-tasking environment such as MS-DOS version 3.x, each program stands alone. If it needs a particular service not provided by the operating system, it must provide that service itself. For example, every application that needs a sort facility must contain its own.

Likewise, if a spreadsheet needs to access values from a database, it must contain the code to do so. This extra code complicates the spreadsheet program, and it ties the program to a particular database product or format. A user might be unable to switch to a better product because the spreadsheet is unable to understand the new database's file formats.

A direct result of such a stand-alone environment is the creation of very large and complex "combo" packages such as Lotus Symphony. Because every function that the user may want must be contained within one program, vendors supply packages that attempt to contain everything.

In practice, such chimeric programs tend to be large and cumbersome, and their individual functional components (spreadsheets, word processors, and databases, for example) are generally more difficult to use and less sophisticated than individual applications that specialize in a single function.

The stand-alone environment forces the creation of larger and more complex programs, each of which typically understands only its own file formats and works poorly, if at all, with data produced by other programs. This vision of personal computer software growing monstrous until collapsing from its own weight brings about another OS/2 requirement: Applications must be able to communicate, easily and efficiently, with other applications.

More specifically, an application must be able to find (or name) the application that provides the information or service that the client needs, and it must be able to establish efficient communication with the provider program without requiring that either application have specific knowledge of the internal workings of the other. Thus, a spreadsheet program must be able to communicate with a database program and access the values it needs. The spreadsheet program is therefore not tied to any particular database program but can work with any database system that recognizes OS/2 IPC requests.

Applications running under OS/2 not only retain their full power as individual applications but also benefit from cross-application communication. Furthermore, the total system can be enhanced by upgrading an application that provides services to others. When a new, faster, or more fully featured database package is installed, not only is the user's database application improved but the database functions of the spreadsheet program are improved as well.

The OS/2 philosophy is that no program should reinvent the wheel. Programs should be written to offer their services to other programs and to take advantage of the offered services of other programs. The result is a maximally effective and efficient system.

2.1.7 Direct Device Access

Earlier, we discussed the need for a high-performance graphical interface and the limitations of the traditional device driver architecture. OS/2 contains a built-in solution for the screen graphical interface, but what about other, specialized devices that may require a higher bandwidth interface than device drivers provide? The one sure prediction about the future of a technological breakthrough is that you can't fully predict it. For this reason, the final key requirement for OS/2 is that it contain an ''escape hatch'' in anticipation of devices that have performance needs too great for a device driver model.

OS/2 provides this expandability by allowing applications direct access to hardware devices—both the I/O ports and any device memory. This must be done, of course, in such a way that only devices which are intended to be used in this fashion can be so accessed. Applications are prevented from using this access technique on devices that are being managed by the operating system or by a device driver. This facility gives applications the ability to take advantage of special nonstandard hardware such as OCRs (Optical Character Readers), digitizer tablets, Fax equipment, special purpose graphics cards, and the like.

2.2 Compatibility Issues

But OS/2 has to do more than meet the goals we've discussed: It must be compatible with 8086/8088 and 80286 architecture, and it must be compatible with MS-DOS. By far the easiest solution would have been to create a new multitasking operating system that would not be compatible with MS-DOS, but such a system is unacceptable. Potential users may be excited about the new system, but they won't buy it until applications are available. Application writers may likewise be excited, but they won't adapt their products for it until the system has sold enough copies to gain significant market share. This "catch 22" means that the only people who will buy the new operating system are the developers' mothers, and they probably get it at a discount anyway.

2.2.1 Real Mode *vs* Protect Mode

The first real mode compatibility issue relates to the design of the 80286 microprocessor—the "brain" of an MS-DOS computer. This chip has two incompatible modes—real (compatibility) mode and protect mode. Real mode is designed to run programs in exactly the same manner as they run on the 8086/8088 processor. In other words, when the 80286 is in real mode, it "looks" to the operating system and programs exactly like a fast 8088.

But the designers of the 80286 wanted it to be more than a fast 8088. They wanted to add such features as memory management, memory protection, and the ring protection mechanism, which allows the operating system to protect one application from another. They weren't able to do this while remaining fully compatible with the earlier 8088 chip, so they added a second *mode* to the 80286—protect mode. When the processor is running in protect mode, it provides these important new features, but it will not run most programs written for the 8086/8088.

In effect, an 80286 is two separate microprocessors in one package. It can act like a very fast 8088—compatible, but with no new capabilities—or it can act like an 80286—incompatible, but providing new features. Unfortunately, the designers of the chip didn't appreciate the importance of compatibility in the MS-DOS marketplace, and they designed the 80286 so that it can run in either mode but can't switch back and forth at will.[4] In other words, an 80286 was designed to run only old 8086/8088 programs, *or* it can run only new 80286 style programs, but never both at the same time.

In summary, OS/2 was required to do something that the 80286 was not designed for—execute both 8086/8088 style (real mode) and 80286 style (protect) mode programs at the same time. The existence of this book should lead you to believe that this problem was solved, and indeed it was.

2.2.2   Running Applications in Real (Compatibility) Mode

Solving the real mode *vs* protect mode problem, however, presented other problems. In general, the problems came about because the real mode programs were written for MS-DOS versions 2.x or 3.x, both of which are single-tasking environments.

Although MS-DOS is normally spoken of as an operating system, it could just as accurately be called a "system executive." Because it runs in an unprotected environment, applications are free to edit interrupt vectors, manipulate peripherals, and in general take over from MS-DOS wherever they wish. This flexibility is one reason for the success of MS-DOS; if MS-DOS doesn't offer the service your program needs, you can always help yourself. Developers were free to explore new possibilities, often with great success. Most applications view MS-DOS as a program loader and as a set of file system subroutines, interfacing directly with the hardware for all their other needs, such as intercepting interrupt vectors, editing disk controller parameter tables, and so on.

It may seem that if a popular application "pokes" the operating system and otherwise engages in unsavory practices that the authors or users of the application will suffer because a future release, such as OS/2, may not run the application correctly. To the contrary, the market dynamics state that the application has now set a standard, and it's the operating system developers who suffer because they must support that standard. Usually, that "standard" operating system interface is not even known; a great deal of experimentation is necessary to

---

4. The 80286 initializes itself in real mode. There is a command to switch from real mode to protect mode, but there is no command to switch back.

discover exactly which undocumented side effects, system internals, and timing relationships the application is dependent on.

Offering an MS-DOS–compatible Applications Program Interface (API) provides what we call level 1 compatibility. Allowing applications to continue to manipulate system hardware provides level 2 compatibility. Level 3 issues deal with providing an execution environment that supports the hidden assumptions that programs written for a single-tasking environment may make. Three are discussed below by way of illustration.

2.2.2.1   Memory Utilization

The existing real mode applications that OS/2 must support were written for an environment in which no other programs are running. As a result, programs typically consume all available memory in the system in the belief that, since no other program is around to use any leftover memory, they might as well use it all. If a program doesn't ask for all available memory at first, it may ask for the remainder at some later time. Such a subsequent request could never be refused under MS-DOS versions 2.x and 3.x, and applications were written to depend on this. Therefore, such a request must be satisfied under OS/2 to maintain full compatibility.

Even the manner of a memory request depends on single-tasking assumptions. Programs typically ask for all memory in two steps. First, they ask for the maximum amount of memory that an 8088 can provide—1 MB. The application's programmer knew that the request would be refused because 1 MB is greater than the 640 KB maximum supported by MS-DOS; but when MS-DOS refuses the request, it tells the application exactly how much memory is available. Programs then ask for *that* amount of memory. The programmer knew that MS-DOS would not refuse the second memory request for insufficient memory because when MS-DOS responded to the first request it told the application exactly how much memory was available. Consequently, programmers rarely included a check for an "insufficient memory" error from the second call.

This shortcut introduces problems in the OS/2 multitasking environment. When OS/2 responded to the first too-large request, it would return the amount of memory available *at that exact moment*. Other programs are simultaneously executing; by the time our real mode program makes its second request, some more memory may have been given out, and the second request may also be too large. It won't do any good for OS/2 to respond with an error code, however, because the real mode application does not check for one (it was written in the belief that it is impossible to get such a code on the second call). The upshot is that even if OS/2 refused the second call the real mode application would assume that it had been given the memory, would use it, and in the process would destroy the other program(s) that were the true owners of that memory.

Obviously, OS/2 must resolve this and similar issues to support the existing base of real mode applications.

2.2.2.2   File Locking

Because multitasking systems run more than one program at the same time, two programs may try to write or to modify the same file at the same time. Or one may try to read a file while another is changing that file's contents. Multitasking systems usually solve this problem by means of a *file-locking* mechanism, which allows one program to temporarily prevent other programs from reading and/or writing a particular file.

An application may find that a file it is accessing has been locked by some other application in the system. In such a situation, OS/2 normally returns a "file locked" error code, and the application typically gives up or waits and retries the operation later. OS/2 cannot return a "file locked" error to an old-style real mode application, though, because when the application was written (for MS-DOS versions 2.x or 3.x) no such error code existed because no such error was possible. Few real mode applications even bother to check their read and write operations for error codes, and those that do wouldn't "understand" the error code and wouldn't handle it correctly.

OS/2 cannot compromise the integrity of the file-locking mechanism by allowing the real mode application to ignore locks, but it cannot report that the file is locked to the application either. OS/2 must determine the proper course of action and then take that action on behalf of the real mode application.

2.2.2.3 **Network Piggybacking**

Running under MS-DOS version 3.1, an application can use an existing network virtual circuit to communicate with an application running on the server machine to which the virtual circuit is connected. This is called "piggybacking" the virtual circuit because the applications on each end are borrowing a circuit that the network redirector established for other purposes. The two sets of programs can use a single circuit for two different purposes without confusion under MS-DOS version 3.1 because of its single-tasking nature. The redirector only uses the circuit when the application calls MS-DOS to perform a network function. Because the CPU is inside MS-DOS, it can't be executing the application software that sends private messages, which leaves the circuit free for use by the redirector.

Conversely, if the application is sending its own private messages— piggybacking—then it can't be executing MS-DOS, and therefore the redirector code (which is built into MS-DOS) can't be using the virtual circuit.

This is no longer the case in OS/2. OS/2 is a multitasking system, and one application can use the redirector at the same time that the real mode application is piggybacking the circuit. OS/2 must somehow interlock access to network virtual circuits so that multiple users of a network virtual circuit do not conflict.

2.2.3 **Popular Function Compatibility**

We've discussed some issues of binary compatibility, providing applications the internal software interfaces they had in MS-DOS. This is because it is vitally important that existing applications run correctly, unchanged, under the new operating system.[5] OS/2 also needs to provide functional compatibility; it has to allow the creation of protect mode applications that provide the functions that users grew to know and love in real mode applications.

This can be difficult because many popular applications (for example, "terminate and stay resident loadable helper" routines such as

---

5. An extremely high degree of compatibility is required for virtually any application to run because a typical application uses a great many documented and undocumented interfaces and features of the earlier system. If any one of those interfaces is not supplied, the application will not run correctly. Consequently, we cannot provide 90 percent compatibility and expect to run 90 percent of existing applications; 99.9 percent compatibility is required for such a degree of success.

SideKick) were written for a single-tasking, unprotected environment without regard to the ease with which their function could be provided in a protected environment. For example, a popular application may implement some of its features by patching (that is, editing) MS-DOS itself. This cannot be allowed in OS/2 (the reason is discussed in Chapter 4), so OS/2 must provide alternative mechanisms for protect mode applications to provide services that users have grown to expect.

2.2.4   Downward Compatibility

So far, our discussion on compatibility has focused exclusively on *upward compatibility*—old programs must run in the new system but not vice versa. Downward compatibility—running new programs under MS-DOS—is also important. Developers are reluctant to write OS/2-only applications until OS/2 has achieved major penetration of the market, yet this very unavailability of software slows such penetration. If it's possible to write applications that take advantage of OS/2's protect mode yet also run unchanged under MS-DOS version 3.x, ISVs (Independent Software Vendors) can write their products for OS/2 without locking themselves out of the existing MS-DOS market.

2.2.4.1   Family API

To provide downward compatibility for applications, OS/2 designers integrated a Family[6] Applications Program Interface (Family API) into the OS/2 project. The Family API provides a standard execution environment under MS-DOS version 3.x and OS/2. Using the Family API, a programmer can create an application that uses a subset of OS/2 functions (but a superset of MS-DOS version 3.x functions) and that runs in a binary compatible fashion under MS-DOS version 3.x and OS/2. In effect, some OS/2 functions can be retrofitted into an MS-DOS version 3.x environment by means of the Family API.

2.2.4.2   Network Server-Client Compatibility

Another important form of upward and downward compatibility is the network system. You can expect any OS/2 system to be on a network, communicating not only with MS-DOS 3.x systems but, one day, with a new version of OS/2 as well. The network interface must be simultaneously upwardly and downwardly compatible with all past and future versions of networking MS-DOS.

---

6. *Family* refers to the MS-DOS/OS/2 family of operating systems.

3

The OS/2
Religion

Religion, in the context of software design, is a body of beliefs about design rights and design wrongs. A particular design is praised or criticized on the basis of fact—it is small or large, fast or slow—and also on the basis of religion—it is good or bad, depending on how well it obeys the religious precepts. Purpose and consistency underlie the design religion as a whole; its influence is felt in every individual judgment.

The purpose of software design religion is to specify precepts that designers can follow when selecting an approach from among the many possibilities before them. A project of the size and scope of OS/2 needed a carefully thought out religion because OS/2 will dramatically affect this and future generations of operating systems. It needed a strong religion for another reason: to ensure consistency among wideranging features implemented by a large team of programmers. Such consistency is very important; if one programmer optimizes design to do A well, at the expense of doing B less well, and another programmer—in the absence of religious guidance—does the opposite, the end result is a product that does neither A nor B well.

This chapter discusses the major architectural dogmas of the OS/2 religion: maximum flexibility, a stable environment, localization of errors, and the software tools approach.

3.1 **Maximum Flexibility**

The introduction to this book discusses the process of technological breakthroughs. I have pointed out that one of the easiest predictions about breakthroughs is that fully predicting their course is impossible. For example, the 8088 microprocessor is designed to address 1 MB of memory, but the IBM PC and compatible machines are designed so that addressable memory is limited to 640 KB. When this decision was made, 640 KB was ten times more memory than the then state-of-the-art 8080 machines could use; the initial PCs were going to ship with 16 KB in them, and it seemed to all concerned that 640 KB was overly generous. Yet it took only a few years before 640 KB became the typical memory complement of a machine, and within another year that amount of memory was viewed as pitifully small.

OS/2's design religion addresses the uncertain future by decreeing that—to the extent compatible with other elements in the design religion—OS/2 shall be as flexible as possible. The tenet of flexibility is that each component of OS/2 should be designed as if massive changes will occur in that area in a future release. In other words, the current component should be designed in a way that does not restrict new features and in a way that can be easily supported by a new version of OS/2, one that might differ dramatically in internal design.

Several general principles result from a design goal of flexibility. All are intended to facilitate change, which is inevitable in the general yet unpredictable in the specific:

1. All OS/2 features should be sufficiently elemental (simple) that they can be easily supported in any future system, including systems fundamentally different in design from OS/2. Either the features themselves are this simple, or the features are built using base features that are this simple. The adjective *simple* doesn't particularly refer to externals—a small number of functions and options—but to internals. The internal operating system infrastructure necessary to provide a function should be either very simple or so fundamental to the nature of operating systems that it is inevitable in future releases.

   By way of analogy, as time travelers we may be able to guess very little about the twenty-first century, but we do know that people will still need to eat. The cuisine of the twenty-first century may be unguessable, but certainly future kitchens will contain facilities to cut and heat food. If we bring food that needs only those two operations, we'll find that even if there's nothing to our liking on the twenty-first-century standard menu the kitchen can still meet our needs.

We've seen how important upward compatibility is for computer operating systems, so we can rest assured that the future MS-DOS "kitchen" will be happy to make the necessary effort to support old programs. All we have to do today is to ensure that such support is possible. Producing a compatible line of operating system releases means more than looking backward; it also means looking forward.

2. All system interfaces need to support expansion in a future release. For example, if a call queries the status of a disk file, then in addition to passing the operating system a pointer to a structure to fill in with the information, the application must also pass in the length of that structure. Although the current release of the operating system returns N bytes of information, a future release may support new kinds of disk files and may return M bytes of information. Because the application tells the operating system, via the buffer length parameter, which version of the information structure that the application understands (the old short version or the new longer version), the operating system can support both old programs and new programs simultaneously.

In general, all system interfaces should be designed to support the current feature set without restraining the addition of features to the interfaces in future releases. Extra room should be left in count and flag arguments for future expansion, and all passed and returned structures need either to be self-sizing or to include a size argument.

One more interface deserves special mention—the file system interface. Expanding the capabilities of the file system, such as allowing filenames longer than eight characters, is difficult because many old applications don't know how to process filenames that are longer than eight characters or they regard the longer names as illegal and reject them. OS/2 solves this and similar problems by specifying that all filenames supplied to or returned from the operating system be zero-terminated strings (ASCIIZ strings) of arbitrary length.

Programmers are specifically cautioned against parsing or otherwise "understanding" filenames. Programs should consider file system pathnames as "magic cookies" to be passed to and from the operating system, but not to be parsed by the program. The details of this interface and other expandable interfaces are discussed in later chapters.

3. OS/2 needs to support the addition of functions at any time. The implementation details of these functions need to be hidden from the client applications so that those details can be changed at any time. Indeed, OS/2 should disguise even the source of a feature. Some APIs are serviced by kernel code, others are serviced by subroutine libraries, and still others may be serviced by other processes running in the system. Because a client application can't tell the difference, the system designers are free to change the implementation of an API as necessary. For example, an OS/2 kernel API might be considerably changed in a future release. The old API can continue to be supported by the creation of a subroutine library routine. This routine would take the old form of the API, convert it to the new form, call the OS/2 kernel, and then backconvert the result. Such a technique allows future versions of OS/2 to support new features while continuing to provide the old features to existing programs. These techniques are discussed in detail in Chapter 7, Dynamic Linking.

4. Finally, to provide maximum flexibility, the operating system should be extensible and expandable in a piecemeal fashion out in the field. In other words, a user should be able to add functions to the system—for example, a database engine—or to upgrade or replace system components—such as a new graphics display driver—without a new release from Microsoft. A microcomputer design that allows third-party hardware additions and upgrades in the field is called an *open system*. The IBM PC line is a classic example of an open system. A design that contains no provisions for

such enhancements is called a *closed system*. The earliest version of the Apple Macintosh is an example. At first glance, MS-DOS appears to be a closed software system because it contains no provisions for expansion. In practice, its unprotected environment makes MS-DOS the king of the open software systems because every application is free to patch the system and access the hardware as it sees fit. Keeping a software system open is as important as keeping a hardware system open. Because OS/2 is a protected operating system, explicit features, such as dynamic linking, are provided to allow system expansion by Microsoft, other software vendors, and users themselves. The topic of open systems is discussed more fully in Chapter 7.

3.2 A Stable Environment

An office automation operating system has to provide its users—the application programs and the human operator—with a stable environment. Every application should work the same way each time it's run; and each time an application is given the same data, it should produce the same result. The normal operation of one application should not affect any other application. Even a program error (bug) should not affect other programs in the system. Finally, if a program has bugs, the operating system should detect those bugs whenever possible and report them to the user. These certainly are obvious goals, but the nature of present-day computers makes them surprisingly difficult to achieve.

3.2.1 Memory Protection

Modern computers are based on the Von Neumann design—named after John Von Neumann, the pioneering Hungarian-born American mathematician and computer scientist. A Von Neumann computer consists of only two parts: a memory unit and a processing unit. The memory unit contains both the data to be operated on and the instructions (or program) that command the processing unit. The processing unit reads instructions from memory; these instructions may tell it to issue further reads to memory to retrieve data, to operate on data retrieved earlier, or to store data back into memory.

A Von Neumann computer does not distinguish between instructions and data; both are stored in binary code in the computer's memory. Individual programs are responsible for keeping track of which memory locations hold instructions and which hold data, and each program uses the memory in a different way. Because the computer does not distinguish between instructions and data, a program may operate on its own instructions exactly as it operates on data. A program can read, modify, and write computer instructions at will.[1]

This is exactly what OS/2 does when it is commanded to run a program: It reads the program into memory by treating it as data, and then it causes the data in those locations to be executed. It is even possible for a program to dynamically "reprogram" itself by manipulating its own instructions.

Computer programs are extremely complex, and errors in their logic can cause the program to unintentionally modify data or instructions in memory. For example, a carelessly written program might contain a command buffer 80 bytes in size because it expects no commands longer than 80 bytes. If a user types a longer command, perhaps in error, and the program does not contain a special check for this circumstance, the program will overwrite the memory beyond the 80-byte command buffer, destroying the data or instructions placed there.[2]

In a single-tasking environment such as MS-DOS, only one application runs at a time. An error such as our example could damage memory belonging to MS-DOS, the application, or memory that is not in use. In practice (due to memory layout conventions) MS-DOS is rarely damaged. An aberrant program typically damages itself or modifies memory not in use. In any case, the error goes undetected, the program produces an incorrect result, or the system crashes. In the last two cases, the user loses work, but it is clear which application is in error—the one executing at the time of the crash. (For completeness, I'll point out that it is possible for an aberrant application to damage MS-DOS subtly enough so that the application itself completes correctly, but the

---

1. This is a simplification. OS/2 and the 80286 CPU contain features that do distinguish somewhat between instructions and data and that limit the ability of programs to modify their own instructions. See 9.1 Protection Model for more information.

2. This is a simplified example. Rarely would a present-day, well-tested application contain such a naive error, but errors of this type—albeit in a much more complex form—exist in nearly all software.

next time an application runs, it fails. This is rare, and the new application generally fails immediately upon startup; so after a few such episodes with different applications, the user generally identifies the true culprit.)

As we have seen, errors in programs are relatively well contained in a single-tasking system. MS-DOS cannot, unfortunately, correct the error, nor can it very often detect the error (these tasks can be shown to be mathematically impossible, in the general case). But at least the errors are contained within the aberrant application; and should errors in data or logic become apparent, the user can identify the erring application. When we execute a second program in memory alongside the first, the situation becomes more complicated.

The first difficulty arises because the commonest error for a program to make is to use memory that MS-DOS has not allocated to it. In a single-tasking environment these memory locations are typically unused, but in a multitasking environment the damaged location(s) probably belong to some other program. That program will then either give incorrect results, damage still other memory locations, crash, or some combination of these. In summary, a memory addressing error is more dangerous because there is more in memory to damage and that damage will have a more severe effect.

The second difficulty arises, not from explicit programming errors, but from conflicts in the normal operation of two or more co-resident programs that are in some fashion incompatible. A simple example is called "hooking the keyboard vector" (see Figure 3-1 on the following page).

In this case, an application modifies certain MS-DOS memory locations so that when a key is pressed the application code, instead of the MS-DOS code, is notified by the hardware. Applications do this because it allows them to examine certain keyboard events, such as pressing the shift key without pressing any other key, that MS-DOS does not pass on to applications which ask MS-DOS to read the keyboard for them. It works fine for one application to "hook" the keyboard vector; although hooking the keyboard vector modifies system memory locations that don't belong to the application, the application generally gets away with it successfully. In a multitasking environment, however, a second application may want to do the same trick, and the

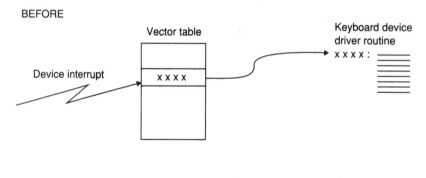

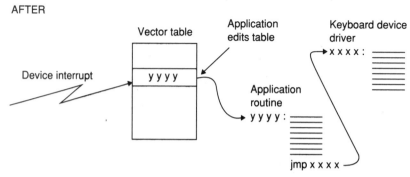

Figure 3-1.
Hooking the keyboard vector.

system probably won't function correctly. The result is that a stable environment requires memory protection. An application must not be allowed to modify, accidentally or deliberately, memory that isn't assigned to that application.

3.2.2 Side-Effects Protection

A stable environment requires more than memory protection; it also requires that the system be designed so that the execution of one application doesn't cause side effects for any other application. Side effects can be catastrophic or they can be unremarkable, but in all cases they violate the tenet of a stable environment.

For example, consider the practice of hooking the keyboard interrupt vector. If one application uses this technique to intercept keystrokes, it will intercept all keystrokes, even those intended for some other application. The side effects in this case are catastrophic—the hooking application sees keystrokes that aren't intended for it, and the other applications don't get any keystrokes at all.

Side effects can plague programs even when they are using official system features if those features are not carefully designed. For example, a mainframe operating system called TOPS-10 contains a program that supports command files similar to MS-DOS .BAT files, and it also contains a program that provides delayed offline execution of commands. Unfortunately, both programs use the same TOPS-10 facility to do their work. If you include a .BAT file in a delayed command list, the two programs will conflict, and the .BAT file will not execute.

OS/2 deals with side effects by virtualizing to the greatest extent possible each application's operating environment. This means that OS/2 tries to make each application "see" a standard environment that is unaffected by changes in another application's environment. The effect is like that of a building of identical apartments. When each tenant moves in, he or she gets a standard environment, a duplicate of all the apartments. Each tenant can customize his or her environment, but doing so doesn't affect the other tenants or their environments.

Following are some examples of application environment issues that OS/2 virtualizes.

- Working Directories. Each application has a *working* (or *current*) *directory* for each disk drive. Under MS-DOS version 3.x, if a child process changes the working directory for drive C and then exits, the working directory for drive C remains changed when the parent process regains control. OS/2 eliminates this side effect by maintaining a separate list of working directories for each process in the system. Thus, when an application changes its working directories, the working directories of other applications in the system remain unchanged.

- Memory Utilization. The simple act of memory consumption produces side effects. If one process consumes all available RAM, none is left for the others. The OS/2 memory management system uses memory overcommit (swapping) so that the memory needs of each application can be met.

- Priority. OS/2 uses a priority-based scheduler to assign the CPU to the processes that need it. Applications can adjust their priority and that of their child processes as they see fit. However, the very priority of a task causes side effects. Consider a process that tells

OS/2 that it must run at a higher priority than any other task in the system. If a second process makes the same request, a conflict occurs: Both processes cannot be the highest priority in the system. In general, the priority that a process wants for itself depends on the priorities of the other processes in the system. The OS/2 scheduler contains a sophisticated absolute/relative mechanism to deal with these conflicts.

■ File Utilization. As discussed earlier, one application may modify the files that another application is using, causing an unintended side effect. The OS/2 file-locking mechanism prevents unintended modifications, and the OS/2 record-locking mechanism coordinates intentional parallel updates to a single file.

■ Environment Strings. OS/2 retains the MS-DOS concept of environment strings: Each process has its own set. A child process *inherits* a copy of the parent's environment strings, but changing the strings in this copy will not affect the original strings in the parent's environment.

■ Keyboard Mode. OS/2 applications can place the keyboard in one of two modes—*cooked* or *raw*. These modes tell OS/2 whether the application wants to handle, for example, the backspace character (raw mode) or whether it wants OS/2 to handle the backspace character for it (cooked mode). The effect of these calls on subsequent keyboard read operations would cause side effects for other applications reading from the keyboard, so OS/2 maintains a record of the cooked/raw status of each application and silently switches the mode of the keyboard when an application issues a keyboard read request.

3.3 Localization of Errors

A key element in creating a stable environment is localizing errors. Humans always make errors, and human creations such as computer programs always contain errors. Before the development of computers, routine human errors were usually limited in scope. Unfortunately, as the saying goes, a computer can make a mistake in 60 seconds that it would take a whole office force a year to make. Although OS/2 can do little to prevent such errors, it needs to do its best to localize the errors.

Localizing errors consists of two activities: minimizing as much as possible the impact of the error on other applications in the system, and maximizing the opportunity for the user to understand which of the many programs running in the computer caused the error. These two activities are interrelated in that the more successful the operating system is in restricting the damage to the domain of a single program, the easier it is for the user to know which program is at fault.

The most important aspect of error localization has already been discussed at length—memory management and protection. Other error localization principles include the following:

- No program can crash or hang the system. A fundamental element of the OS/2 design religion is that no application program can, accidentally or even deliberately, crash or hang the system. If a failing application could crash the system, obviously the system did not localize the error! Furthermore, the user would be unable to identify the responsible application because the entire system would be dead.

- No program can make inoperable any screen group other than its own. As we'll see in later chapters of this book, sometimes design goals, design religions, or both conflict. For example, the precept of no side effects conflicts with the requirement of supporting keyboard macro expander applications. The sole purpose of such an application is to cause a side effect—specifically to translate certain keystroke sequences into other sequences. OS/2 resolves this conflict by allowing applications to examine and modify the flow of data to and from devices (see Chapter 16) but in a controlled fashion. Thus, an aberrant keyboard macro application that starts to "eat" all keys, passing none through to the application, can make its current screen group unusable, but it can't affect the user's ability to change screen groups.

    Note that keyboard monitors can intercept and consume any character or character sequence *except* for the keystrokes that OS/2 uses to switch screen groups (Ctrl-Esc and Alt-Esc). This is to prevent aberrant keyboard monitor applications from accidentally locking the user into his or her screen group by consuming and discarding the keyboard sequences that are used to switch from screen groups.

- Applications cannot intercept general protection (GP) fault errors. A GP fault occurs when a program accesses invalid memory locations or accesses valid locations in an invalid way (such as writing into read-only memory areas). OS/2 always terminates the operation and displays a message for the user. A GP fault is evidence that the program's logic is incorrect, and therefore it cannot be expected to fix itself or trusted to notify the user of its ill health.

The OS/2 design does allow almost any other error on the part of an application to be detected and handled by that application. For example, "Illegal filename" is an error caused by user input, not by the application. The application can deal with this error as it sees fit, perhaps correcting and retrying the operation. An error such as "Floppy disk drive not ready" is normally handled by OS/2 but can be handled by the application. This is useful for applications that are designed to operate unattended; they need to handle errors themselves rather than waiting for action to be taken by a nonexistent user.

3.4 Software Tools Approach

In Chapter 2 we discussed IPC and the desirability of having separate functions contained in separate programs. We discussed the flexibility of such an approach over the "one man band" approach of an all-in-one application. We also touched on the value of being able to upgrade the functionality of the system incrementally by replacing individual programs. All these issues are *software tools* issues.

Software tools refers to a design philosophy which says that individual programs and applications should be like tools: Each should do one job and do it very well. A person who wants to turn screws and also drive nails should get a screwdriver and a hammer rather than a single tool that does neither job as well.

The tools approach is used routinely in nonsoftware environments and is taken for granted. For example, inside a standard PC the hardware and electronics are isolated into functional components that communicate via interfaces. The power supply is in a box by itself; its interface is the line cord and some power connectors. The disk drives are separate from the rest of the electronics; they interface via more connectors. Each component is the equivalent of a software application: It does one job and does it well. When the disk drive needs power, it doesn't build in a power supply; it uses the standard interface to the power supply module—the power "specialist" in the system.

Occasionally, the software tools approach is criticized for being inefficient. People may argue that space is wasted and time is lost by packaging key functions separately; if they are combined, the argument goes, nothing is wasted. This argument is correct in that some RAM and CPU time is spent on interface issues, but it ignores the gains involved in "sending out the work" to a specialist rather than doing it oneself. One could argue, for example, that if I built an all-in-one PC system I'd save money because I wouldn't have to buy connectors to plug everything together. I might also save a little by not having to buy buffer chips to drive signals over those connectors. But in doing so, I'd lose the advantage of being able to buy my power supply from a very high-volume and high-efficiency supplier—someone who can make a better, cheaper supply, even *with* the cost of connectors, than my computer company can.

Finally, the user gains from the modular approach. If you need more disk capability, you can buy one and plug it in. You are not limited to one disk maker but rather can choose the one that's right for your needs—expensive and powerful or cheap and modest. You can buy third-party hardware, such as plug-in cards, that the manufacturer of your computer doesn't make. All in all, the modest cost of a few connectors and driver chips is paid back manyfold, both in direct system costs (due to the efficiency of specialization) and in the additional capability and flexibility of the machine.

As I said earlier, the software tools approach is the software equivalent of an *open system*. It's an important part of the OS/2 religion: Although the system doesn't *require* a modular tools approach from applications programs, it should do everything in its power to facilitate such systems, and it should itself be constructed in that fashion.

Part II

The Architecture

4

Multitasking

I have discussed the goals and compatibility issues that OS/2 is intended to meet, and I have described the design religion that was established for OS/2. The following chapters discuss individual design elements in some detail, emphasizing not only how the elements work and are used but the role they play in the system as a whole.

In a *multitasking* operating system, two or more programs can execute at the same time. Some benefits of such a feature are obvious: You (the user) can switch between several application programs without saving work and exiting one program to start another. When the telephone rings, for example, you can switch from the word processor application you are using to write a memo and go to the application that is managing your appointment calendar or to the spreadsheet application that contains the figures that are necessary to answer your caller's query.

This type of multitasking is similar to what people do when they're not working with a computer. You may leave a report half read on your desk to address a more pressing need, such as answering the phone. Later, perhaps after other tasks intervene, you return to the report. You don't terminate a project and return your reference materials to the bookshelf, the files, and the library to answer the telephone; you merely switch your attention for a while and later pick up where you left off.

This kind of multitasking is called *serial multitasking* because actions are performed one at a time. Although you probably haven't thought of it this way, you've spent much of your life serially multitasking. Every day when you leave for work, you suspend your home life and resume your work life. That evening, you reverse the process. You serially multitask a hobby—each time picking it up where you left off last time and then leaving off again. Reading the comics in a daily newspaper is a prodigious feat of human serial multitasking—you switch from one to another of perhaps 20 strips, remembering for each what has gone on before and then waiting until tomorrow for the next installment. Although serial multitasking is very useful, it is not nearly as useful as *full multitasking*—the kind of multitasking built into OS/2.

Full multitasking on the computer involves doing more than one thing—running more than one application—at the same time. Humans do a little of this, but not too much. People commonly talk while they drive cars, eat while watching television, and walk while chewing gum. None of these activities requires one's full concentration though. Humans generally can't fully multitask activities that require a significant amount of concentration because they have only one brain.

For that matter, a personal computer has only one "brain"—one CPU.[1] But OS/2 can switch this CPU from one activity to another very rapidly—dozens or even hundreds of times a second. All executing programs seem to be running at the same time, at least on the human scale of time. For example, if five programs are running and each in turn gets 0.01 second of CPU time (that is, 10 milliseconds), in 1 second each program receives 20 *time slices*. To most observers, human or other computer software, all five programs appear to be running simultaneously but each at one-fifth its maximum speed. We'll return to the topic of time slicing later; for now, it's easiest—and, as we shall see, best—to pretend that all executing programs run simultaneously.

The full multitasking capabilities of OS/2 allow the personal computer to act as more than a mere engine to run applications; the personal computer can now be a *system* of services. The user can interact with a spreadsheet program, for example, while a mail application is receiving network messages that the user can read later. At the same time, other programs may be downloading data from a mainframe computer or spooling output to a printer or a plotter. The user may have explicitly initiated some of these activities; a program may have initiated others. Regardless, they all execute simultaneously, and they all do their work without requiring the user's attention or intervention.

---

1. Although multiple-CPU computers are well known, personal computers with multiple CPUs are uncommon. In any case, this discussion applies, with the obvious extensions, to multiple-CPU systems.

Full multitasking is useful to programs themselves. Earlier, we discussed the advantages of a tools approach—writing programs so that they can offer their services to other programs. The numerous advantages of this technique are possible only because of full multitasking. For example, if a program is to be able to invoke another program to sort a data file, the sort program must execute at the same time as its client program. It wouldn't be very useful if the client program had to terminate in order for the sort program to run.

Finally, full multitasking is useful within a program itself. A thread is an OS/2 mechanism that allows more than one path of execution through a particular application. (Threads are discussed in detail later; for now it will suffice to imagine that several CPUs can be made to execute the same program simultaneously.) This allows individual applications to perform more than one task at a time. For example, if the user tells a spreadsheet program to recalculate a large budget analysis, the program can use one thread to do the calculating and another to prompt for, read, and obey the user's next command. In effect, multiple operations overlap during execution and thereby increase the program's responsiveness to the user.

OS/2 uses a time-sliced, priority-based preemptive scheduler to provide full multitasking. In other words, the OS/2 scheduler *preempts*—takes away—the CPU from one application at any time the scheduler desires and assigns the CPU another application. Programs don't surrender the CPU when they feel like it; OS/2 preempts it. Each program in the system (more precisely, each thread in the system) has its own priority. When a thread of a higher priority than the one currently running wants to run, the scheduler preempts the running thread in favor of the higher priority one. If two or more runnable threads have the same highest priority, OS/2 runs each in turn for a fraction of a second—a *time slice*.

The OS/2 scheduler does not periodically look around to see if the highest priority thread is running. Such an approach wastes CPU time and slows response time because a higher priority thread must wait to run until the next scheduler scan. Instead, other parts of the system call the scheduler when they think that a thread other than the one running should be executed.

4.1 **Subtask Model**

The terms *task* and *process* are used interchangeably to describe the direct result of executing a binary (.EXE) file. A process is the unit of ownership under OS/2, and processes own resources such as memory, open files, connections to dynlink libraries, and semaphores. Casual users would call a process a ''program''; and, in fact, under MS-DOS all programs and applications consist of a single process. OS/2 uses the terms *task* or *process* because a single application program under OS/2 may consist of more than one process. This section describes how this is done.

First, some more terminology. When a process creates, or *execs*, another process, the creator process is called the *parent* process, and the created process is called the *child* process. The parent of the parent is the child's *grandparent* and so on. As with people, each process in the system has or had a parent.[2] Although we use genealogical terms to describe task relationships, a child task, or process, is more like an agent or employee of the parent task. Employees are hired to do work for an employer. The employer provides a workplace and access to the information employees need to do their jobs. The same is generally true for a child task. When a child task is created, it *inherits* (or receives a copy of) a great deal of the parent task's environment. For example, it inherits, or takes on, the parent's base scheduling priority and its screen group. The term *inherit* is a little inappropriate because the parent task has not died. It is alive and well, going about its business.

The most important items a child task inherits are its parent's open file handles. OS/2 uses a *handle* mechanism to perform file I/O, as do MS-DOS versions 2.0 and later. When a file is opened, OS/2 returns a handle—an integer value—to the process. When a program wants to read from or write to a file, it gives OS/2 the file handle. Handles are not identical among processes. For example, the file referred to by handle 6 of one process bears no relationship to the file referred to by another process's handle 6, unless one of those processes is a child of the other. When a parent process creates a child process, the child process, by default, inherits each of the parent's open file handles. For example, a parent process has the file \WORK\TEMPFILE open on

---

2. Obviously, during boot-up OS/2 creates an initial parentless process by ''magic,'' but this is ancient history by the time any application may run, so the anomaly may be safely ignored.

handle 5; when the child process starts up, handle 5 is open and references the \WORK\TEMPFILE file.

This undoubtedly seems brain damaged if you are unfamiliar with this model. Why is it done in this crazy way? What use does the child process have for these open files? What's to keep the child from mucking up the parent's files? All this becomes clearer when the other piece of the puzzle is in place—the *standard file handles.*

4.1.1   Standard File Handles

Many OS/2 functions use 16-bit integer values called handles for their interfaces. A handle is an object that programmers call a "magic cookie"—an arbitrary value that OS/2 provides the application so that the application can pass the value back to OS/2 on subsequent calls. Its purpose is to simplify the OS/2 interface and speed up the particular service. For example, when a program creates a system semaphore, it is returned a semaphore handle—a magic cookie—that it uses for subsequent request and release operations. Referring to the semaphore via a 16-bit value is much faster than passing around a long filename. Furthermore, the magic in magic cookie is that the meaning of the 16-bit handle value is indecipherable to the application. OS/2 created the value, and it has meaning only to OS/2; the application need only retain the value and regurgitate it when appropriate. An application can never make any assumptions about the values of a magic cookie.

File handles are an exceptional form of handle because they are not magic cookies. The handle value, in the right circumstances, is meaningful to the application and to the system as a whole. Specifically, three handle values have special meaning: handle value 0, called STDIN (for *standard input*); handle value 1, called STDOUT (*standard output*); and handle value 2, called STDERR (*standard error*). A simple program—let's call it NUMADD—will help to explain the use of these three handles. NUMADD will read two lines of ASCII text (each containing a decimal number), convert the numbers to binary, add them, and then convert the results to an ASCII string and write out the result. Note that we're confining our attention to a simple non-screen-oriented program that might be used as a tool, either directly by a programmer or by another program (see Figure 4-1 and Listing 4-1 on the following page).

Figure 4-1.
Program NUMADD operation—interactive.

```
#include <stdio.h>              /* defines stdin and stdout */

main()
{
    int value1, value2, sum;

    fscanf (stdin, "%d", &value1);
    fscanf (stdin, "%d", & value2);
    sum = value1 + value2;
    fprintf (stdout, "%d\n", sum);
}
```

Listing 4-1.
Program NUMADD.

By convention, all OS/2 programs read input from STDIN and write output to STDOUT. Any error messages are written to STDERR. The program itself does not open these handles; it inherits them from the parent process. The parent may have opened them itself or inherited them from its own parent. As you can see, NUMADD would not contain **DosOpen** calls; instead, it would start immediately issuing **fscanf** calls on handle 0 (STDIN), which in turn issues **DosRead** calls, and, when ready, directly issue **fprintf** calls to handle 1 (STDOUT), which in turn issues **DosWrites**.

Figure 4-2 and Listing 4-2 show a hypothetical application, NUMARITH. NUMARITH reads three text lines. The first line contains an operation character, such as a plus (+) or a minus (−); the second and third lines contain the values to be operated upon. The author of this program doesn't want to reinvent the wheel; so when the program NUMARITH encounters a + operation, it executes NUMADD to do the work. As shown, the parent process NUMARITH has its STDIN connected to the keyboard and its STDOUT connected to the screen device drivers.[3] When NUMADD executes, it reads input from the keyboard via STDIN. After the user types the two numbers, NUMADD displays the result on the screen via STDOUT. NUMARITH has invoked NUMADD to do some work for it, and

---

3. CMD.EXE inherited these handles from its own parent. This process is discussed later.

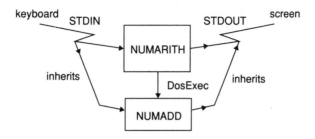

Figure 4-2.
Program NUMARITH operation—interactive.

```
#include <stdio.h>

/**     Numarith - Perform ASCII Arithmetic
*
*       Numarith reads line triplets:
*
*               operation
*               value1
*               value2
*
*       performs the specified operation (+, -, *, /) on
*       the two values and prints the result on stdout.
*/

main ()
{
        char operation;

        fscanf (stdin, "%c", &operation);

        switch (operation) {

            case '+':  execl ("numadd",  0);
                        break;

            case '-':  execl ("numsub", 0);
                        break;

            case '*':  execl ("nummul", 0);
                        break;

            case '/':  execl ("numdiv", 0);
                        break;

        }

}
```

Listing 4-2.
Program NUMARITH.

NUMADD has silently and seamlessly acted as a part of NUMARITH. The employee metaphor fits well here. NUMADD acted as an employee of NUMARITH, making use of NUMARITH's I/O streams, and as a result the contribution of the NUMADD employee to the NUMARITH company is seamless.

Figure 4-3 shows a similar situation. In this case, however, NUMARITH's STDIN and STDOUT handles are open on two files, which we'll call DATAIN and DATAOUT. Once again, NUMADD does its work seamlessly. The input numbers are read from the command file on STDIN, and the output is properly intermingled in the log file on STDOUT. The key here is that this NUMADD is exactly the same program that ran in Listing 4-2; NUMADD *contains no special code to deal with this changed situation.* In both examples, NUMADD simply reads from STDIN and writes to STDOUT; NUMADD neither knows nor cares where those handles point. Exactly the same is true for the parent. NUMARITH doesn't know and doesn't care that it's working from files instead of from the screen; it simply uses the STDIN and STDOUT handles that it inherited from its parent.

This is the single most important concept in the relationship and inheritance structure between processes. The reason a process inherits so

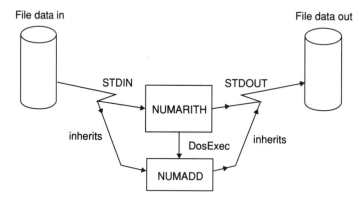

Figure 4-3.
Program NUMARITH operation—from files.

much from its parent is so that the parent can set up the tool's environment—make it read from the parent's STDIN or from a file or from an
anonymous pipe (see 4.1.2 Anonymous Pipes). This gives the parent
the flexibility to use a tool program as it wishes, and it frees the tool's
author from the need to be "all things to all people."

Of equal importance, the inheritance architecture provides *nesting
encapsulation* of child processes. NUMARITH's parent process
doesn't know and doesn't need to know how NUMARITH does its job.
NUMARITH can do the additions itself, or it can invoke NUMADD
as a child, but the architecture encapsulates the details of
NUMARITH's operation so that NUMADD's involvement is hidden
from NUMARITH's parent. Likewise, the decision of NUMARITH's
parent to work from a file or from a device or from a pipe is encapsulated (that is, hidden) from NUMARITH and from any child processes
that NUMARITH may execute to help with its work. Obviously, this
architecture can be extended arbitrarily: NUMADD can itself execute
a child process to help NUMADD with its work, and this would silently and invisibly work. Neither NUMARITH nor its parent would know
or need to know anything about how NUMADD was doing its work.
Other versions can replace any of these applications at any time. The
new versions can invoke more or fewer child processes or be changed
in any other way, and their client (that is, parent) processes are
unaffected. The architecture of OS/2 is tool-based; as long as the function of a tool remains constant (or is supersetted), its implementation is
irrelevant and can be changed arbitrarily.

The STDIN, STDOUT, and STDERR architecture applies to all
programs, even those that only use VIO, KBD, or the presentation manager and that never issue operations on these handles. See Chapter 14,
Interactive Programs.

4.1.2   Anonymous Pipes

NUMADD and NUMARITH are pretty silly little programs; a moment's consideration will show how the inheritance architecture applies to more realistic programs. An example is the TREE program that
runs when the TREE command is given to CMD.EXE. TREE inherits

the STDIN and STDOUT handles, but it does not use STDIN; it merely writes output to STDOUT. As a result, when the user types TREE at a CMD.EXE prompt, the output appears on the screen. When TREE appears in a batch file, the output appears in the LOG file or on the screen, depending on where STDOUT is pointing.

This is all very useful, but what if an application wants to further process the output of the child program rather than having the child's output intermingled with the application's output? OS/2 does this with *anonymous pipes*. The adjective *anonymous* distinguishes these pipes from a related facility, *named pipes*, which are not implemented in OS/2 version 1.0.

An anonymous pipe is a data storage buffer that OS/2 maintains. When a process opens an anonymous pipe, it receives two file handles—one for writing and one for reading. Data can be written to the write handle via the **DosWrite** call and then read back via the read handle and the **DosRead** call. An anonymous pipe is similar to a file in that it is written and read via file handle operations, but an anonymous pipe and a file are significantly different. Pipe data is stored only in RAM buffers, not on a disk, and is accessed only in FIFO (First In First Out) fashion. The **DosSeek** operation is illegal on pipe handles.

An anonymous pipe is of little value to a single process, since it acts as a simple FIFO (First In First Out) storage buffer of limited size and since the data has to be copied to and from OS/2's pipe buffers when **DosWrite**s and **DosRead**s are done. What makes an anonymous pipe valuable is that child processes inherit file handles. A parent process can create an anonymous pipe and then create a child process, and the child process inherits the anonymous pipe handles. The child process can then write to the pipe's write handle, and the parent process can read the data via the pipe's read handle. Once we add the **DosDupHandle** function, which allows handles to be renumbered, and the standard file handles (STDIN, STDOUT, and STDERR), we have the makings of a powerful capability.

Let's go back to our NUMARITH and NUMADD programs. Suppose NUMARITH wants to use NUMADD's services but that NUMARITH wants to process NUMADD's results itself rather than having them appear in NUMARITH's output. Furthermore, assume that NUMARITH doesn't want NUMADD to read its arguments from

NUMARITH's input file; NUMARITH wants to supply NUMADD's arguments itself. NUMARITH can do this by following these steps:

1. Create two anonymous pipes.

2. Preserve the item pointed to by the current STDIN and STDOUT handles (the item can be a file, a device, or a pipe) by using **DosDupHandle** to provide a duplicate handle. The handle numbers of the duplicates may be any number as long as it is not the number of STDIN, STDOUT, or STDERR. We know that this is the case because **DosDupHandle** assigns a handle number that is not in use, and the standard handle numbers are always in use.

3. Close STDIN and STDOUT via **DosClose**. Whatever object is "on the other end" of the handle is undisturbed because the application still has the object open on another handle.

4. Use **DosDupHandle** to make the STDIN handle a duplicate of one of the pipe's input handles, and use **DosDupHandle** to make the STDOUT handle a duplicate of the other pipe's output handle.

5. Create the child process via **DosExecPgm**.

6. Close the STDIN and STDOUT handles that point to the pipes, and use **DosDupHandle** and **DosClose** to effectively rename the objects originally described by STDIN and STDOUT back to those handles.

The result of this operation is shown in Figure 4-4. NUMADD's STDIN and STDOUT handles are pointing to two anonymous pipes, and the parent process is holding the other end of those pipes. The parent process used **DosDupHandle** and **DosClose** to effectively "rename" the STDIN and STDOUT handles temporarily so that the

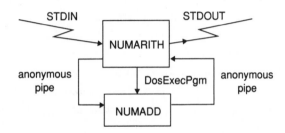

Figure 4-4.
Invoking NUMADD via an anonymous pipe.

child process can inherit the pipe handles rather than its parent's STDIN and STDOUT. At this point the parent, NUMARITH, can write input values into the pipe connected to NUMADD's STDIN and read NUMADD's output from the pipe connected to NUMADD's STDOUT.

If you compare Figure 4-4 with Listing 4-2, Figure 4-2, and Figure 4-3, you see another key feature of this architecture: NUMADD has no special code or design to allow it to communicate directly with NUMARITH. NUMADD functions correctly whether working from the keyboard and screen, from data files, or as a tool for another program. The architecture is fully recursive: If NUMADD invokes a child process to help it with its work, everything still functions correctly. Whatever mechanism NUMADD uses to interact with its child/tool program is invisible to NUMARITH. Likewise, if another program uses NUMARITH as a tool, that program is not affected by whatever mechanism NUMARITH uses to do its work.

This example contains one more important point. Earlier I said that a process uses **DosRead** and **DosWrite** to do I/O over a pipe, yet our NUMADD program uses **fscanf** and **fprintf**, two C language library routines. **fscanf** and **fprintf** themselves call **DosRead** and **DosWrite**, and because a pipe handle is indistinguishable from a file handle or a device handle for these operations, not only does NUMADD work unchanged with pipes, but the library subroutines that it calls work as well. This is another example of the principle of encapsulation as expressed in OS/2,[4] in which the differences among pipes, files, and devices are hidden behind, or encapsulated in, a standardized handle interface.

4.1.3 Details, Details

While presenting the "big picture" of the OS/2 tasking and tool architecture, I omitted various important details. This section discusses them, in no particular order.

STDERR (handle value 2) is an output handle on which error messages are written. STDERR is necessary because STDOUT is a program's normal output stream. For example, suppose a user types:

DIR filename >logfile

---

4. And in UNIX, from which this aspect of the architecture was adapted.

where the file *filename* does not exist. If STDERR did not exist as a separate entity, no error message would appear, and logfile would apparently be created. Later, when the user attempted to examine the contents of the file, he or she would see the following message:

FILE NOT FOUND

For this reason, STDERR generally points to the display screen, and applications rarely redirect it.

The special meanings of STDIN, STDOUT, and STDERR are not hard coded into the OS/2 kernel; they are *system conventions*. All programs should follow these conventions at all times to preserve the flexibility and utility of OS/2's tool-based architecture. Even programs that don't do handle I/O on the STD handles must still follow the architectural conventions (see Chapter 14, Interactive Programs). However, the OS/2 kernel code takes no special action nor does it contain any special cases in support of this convention. Various OS/2 system utilities, such as CMD.EXE and the presentation manager, do contain code in support of this convention.

I mentioned that a child process inherits all its parent's file handles unless the parent has explicitly marked a handle ''no inherit.'' The use of STDIN, STDOUT, and STDERR in an inherited environment has been discussed, but what of the other handles?

Although a child process inherits all of its parent's file handles, it is usually interested only in STDIN, STDOUT, and STDERR. What happens to the other handles? Generally, nothing. Only handle values 0 (STDIN), 1 (STDOUT), and 2 (STDERR) have explicit meaning. All other file handles are merely magic cookies that OS/2 returns for use in subsequent I/O calls. OS/2 doesn't guarantee any particular range or sequence of handle values, and applications should never use or rely on explicit handle values other than the STD ones.

Thus, for example, if a parent process has a file open on handle N and the child process inherits that handle, little happens. The child process won't get the value N back as a result of a **DosOpen** because the handle is already in use. The child will never issue operations to handle N because it didn't open any such handle and knows nothing of its existence. Two side effects can result from inheriting ''garbage'' handles. One is that the object to which the handle points cannot be closed until both the parent and the child close their handles. Because the child knows nothing of the handle, it won't close it. Therefore, a handle close issued by a parent won't be effective until the child and all of that child's descendant processes (which in turn inherited the handle) have terminated. If another application needs the file or device, it is unavailable because a child process is unwittingly holding it open.

The other side effect is that each garbage handle consumes an entry in the child's handle space. Although you can easily increase the default maximum of 20 open handles, a child process that intends to open only 10 files wouldn't request such an increase. If a parent process allows the child to inherit 12 open files, the child will run out of available open file handles. Writing programs that always raise their file handle limit is not good practice because the garbage handles are extra overhead and the files-held-open problem remains. Instead, parent programs should minimize the number of garbage handles they allow child processes to inherit.

Each time a program opens a file, it should do so with the **DosOpen** request with the ''don't inherit'' bit set if the file is of no specific interest to any child programs. If the bit is not set at open time, it can be set later via **DosSetFHandState**. The bit is per-handle, not per-file; so if a process has two handles open on the same file, it can allow one but not the other to be inherited. Don't omit this step simply because you don't plan to run any child processes; unbeknownst to you, dynlink library routines may run child programs on your behalf. Likewise, in dynlink programs the ''no inherit'' bit should be set when file opens are issued because the client program may create child processes.

Finally, do not follow the standard UNIX practice of blindly closing file handles 3 through 20 during program initialization. Dynlink subsystems are called to initialize themselves for a new client before control is passed to the application itself. If subsystems have opened files during that initialization, a blanket close operation will close those files and cause the dynlink package to fail. All programs use dynlink subsystems, whether they realize it or not, because both the OS/2 interface package and the presentation manager are such subsystems. Accidentally closing a subsystem's file handles can cause bizarre and inexplicable problems. For example, when the VIO subsystem is initialized, it opens a handle to the screen device. A program that doesn't call VIO may believe that closing this handle is safe, but it's not. If a handle write is done to STDOUT when STDOUT points to the screen device, OS/2 calls VIO on behalf of the application—with potentially disastrous effect.

I discussed how a child process, inheriting its parent's STDIN and STDOUT, extracts its input from the parent's input stream and intermingles its output in the parent's output stream. What keeps the parent process from rereading the input consumed by the child, and what keeps the parent from overwriting the output data written by the child? The answer is in the distinction between duplicated or inherited handles to a file and two handles to the same file that are the result of two separate opens.

Each time a file is opened, OS/2 allocates a handle to that process and makes an entry in the process's handle table. This entry then points to the System File Table (SFT) inside OS/2. The SFT contains the *seek pointer* to the file—the spot in the file that is currently being read from or written to. When a handle is inherited or duplicated, the new handle points to the same SFT entry as the original. Thus, for example, the child's STDIN handle shares the same seek pointer as the parent's STDIN handle. When our example child program NUMADD read two lines from STDIN, it advanced the seek pointer of its own STDIN and that of its parent's STDIN (and perhaps that of its grandparent's STDIN and so forth). Likewise, when the child writes to STDOUT, the seek pointer advances on STDOUT so that subsequent writing by the parent appends to the child's output rather than overwriting it.

This mechanism has two important ramifications. First, in a situation such as our NUMARITH and NUMADD example, the parent process must refrain from I/O to the STD handles until the child process has completed so that the input or output data doesn't intermingle. Second, the processes must be careful in the way they buffer data to and from the STD handles.

Most programs that read data from STDIN do so until they encounter an EOF (End Of File). These programs can buffer STDIN as they wish. A program such as NUMARITH, in which child processes read some but not all of its STDIN data, cannot use buffering because the read-ahead data in the buffer might be the data that the child process was to read. NUMARITH can't "put the data back" by backing up the STDIN seek pointer because STDIN might be pointing to a device (such as the keyboard) or to a pipe that cannot be seeked. Likewise, because NUMADD was designed to read only two lines of input, it also must read STDIN a character at a time to be sure it doesn't "overshoot" its two lines.

Programs must also be careful about buffering STDOUT. In general, they can buffer STDOUT as they wish, but they must be sure to flush out any buffered data before they execute any child processes that might write to STDOUT.

Finally, what if a parent process doesn't want a child process to inherit STDIN, STDOUT, or STDERR? The parent process should not mark those handles "no inherit" because then those handles will not be open when the child process starts. The OS/2 kernel has no built-in recognition of the STD file handles; so if the child process does a **DosOpen** and handle 1 is unopened (because the process's parent set "no inherit" on handle 1), OS/2 might open the new file on handle 1. As a result, output that the child process intends for STDOUT appears in the other file that unluckily was assigned handle number 1.

If for some reason a child process should not inherit a STD handle, the parent should use the **DosDupHandle**/rename technique to cause that handle to point to the NULL device. You do this by opening a handle on the NULL device and then moving that handle to 0, 1, or 2 with **DosDupHandle**. This technique guarantees that the child's STD handles will all be open.

The subject of STDIN, STDOUT, and handle inheritance comes up again in Chapter 14, Interactive Programs.

4.2 PIDs and Command Subtrees

The PID (process identification) is a unique code that OS/2 assigns to each process when it is created. The number is a magic cookie. Its value has no significance to any process; it's simply a name for a process. The PID may be any value except 0. A single PID value is never assigned to two processes at the same time. PID values are reused but not "rapidly." You can safely remember a child's PID and then later attempt to affect that child by using the PID in an OS/2 call. Even if the child process has died unexpectedly, approximately 65,000 processes would have to be created before the PID value might be reassigned; even a very active system takes at least a day to create, execute, and terminate that many processes.

I've discussed at some length the utility of an architecture in which child programs can create children and those children can create grandchildren and so on. I've also emphasized that the parent need not know the architecture of a child process—whether the child process creates children and grandchildren of its own. The parent *need* not know and indeed *should* not know because such information may make the parent dependent on a particular implementation of a child or grandchild program, an implementation that might change. Given that a parent process starting up a child process can't tell if that child creates its own descendants, how can the parent process ask the system if the work that the child was to do has been completed? The system could tell the parent whether the child process is still alive, but this is insufficient. The child process may have farmed out all its work to one or more grandchildren and then terminated itself before the actual work was started. Furthermore, the parent process may want to change the priority of the process(es) that it has created or even terminate them because an error was detected or because the user typed Ctrl-C.

All these needs are met with a concept called the *command subtree*. When a child process is created, its parent is told the child's PID. The PID is the name of the single child process, and when taken as a command subtree ID, this PID is the name of the entire tree of descendant processes of which the child is the root. In other words, when used as a command subtree ID, the PID refers not only to the child process but also to any of its children and to any children that they may have and so on. A single command subtree can conceivably contain dozens of processes (see Figure 4-5 on the following page and Figure 4-6 on page 59).

Some OS/2 functions, such as **DosCWait** and **DosKillProcess**, can take either PID or command subtree values, depending on the subfunction requested. When the PID form is used, only the named process is affected. When the command subtree form is used, the named process and all its descendants are affected. *This is true even if the child process no longer exists* or if the family tree of processes contains holes as a result of process terminations.

No statute of limitations applies to the use of the command subtree form. That is, even if child process X died a long time ago, OS/2 still allows references to the command subtree X. Consequently, OS/2 places one simple restriction on the use of command subtrees so that it isn't forced to keep around a complete process history forever: Only the

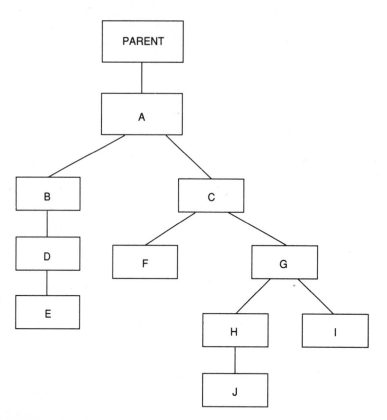

Figure 4-5.
Command subtree. A is the root of (one of) the parent's command subtrees. B and C are the root of two of A's subtrees and so on.

direct parent of process X can reference the command subtree X. In other words, X's grandparent process can't learn X's PID from its parent and then issue command subtree forms of commands; only X's direct parent can. This puts an upper limit on the amount and duration of command subtree information that OS/2 must retain; when a process terminates, information pertaining to its command subtrees can be discarded. The command subtree concept is recursive. OS/2 discards information about the terminated process's own command subtrees, but if any of its descendant processes still exist, the command subtree information pertaining to their child processes is retained. And those surviving descendants are still part of the command subtree belonging to the terminated process's parent process.[5]

---

5. Assuming that the parent process itself still exists. In any case, all processes are part of a nested set of command subtrees belonging to all its surviving ancestor processes.

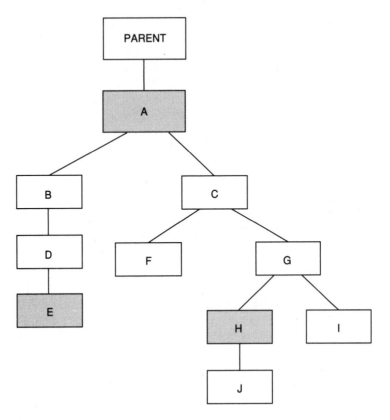

Figure 4-6.
Command subtree. The shaded processes have died, but the subtrees remain. PARENT
can still use subtree A to affect all remaining subprocesses. Likewise, an operation by C
on subtree G will affect process J.

4.3 **DosExecPgm**

To execute a child process, you use the **DosExecPgm** call. The form of
the call is shown in Listing 4-3.

```
extern unsigned far pascal DOSEXECPGM (
        char far                *OBJNAMEBUF,
        unsigned                OBJNAMEBUFL,
        unsigned                EXECTYPE,
        char far                *ARGSTRING,
        char far                *ENVSTRING,
        struct ResultCodes far  *CODEPID,
        char far                *PGMNAME);
```

Listing 4-3.
DosExecPgm call.

The *obj namebuf* arguments provide an area where OS/2 can return a character string if the **DosExecPgm** function fails. In MS-DOS version 2.0 and later, the EXEC function was quite simple: It loaded a file into memory. Little could go wrong: file not found, file bad format, insufficient memory, to name some possibilities. A simple error code sufficed to diagnose problems. OS/2's dynamic linking facility is much more complicated. The earliest prototype versions of OS/2 were missing these *obj namebuf* arguments, and engineers were quickly frustrated by the error code "dynlink library load failed." "Which library was it? The application references seven of them! But all seven of those libraries are alive and well. Perhaps it was a library that one of *those* libraries referenced. But which libraries *do* they reference? Gee, I dunno..." For this reason, the object name arguments were added. The buffer is a place where OS/2 returns the name of the missing or defective library or other load object, and the length argument tells OS/2 the maximum size of the buffer area. Strings that will not fit in the area are truncated.

The exectype word describes the form of the **DosExecPgm**. The values are as follows.

0: Execute the child program synchronously. The thread issuing the **DosExecPgm** will not execute further until the child process has finished executing. The thread returns from **DosExecPgm** when the child process itself terminates, not when the command subtree has terminated. This form of **DosExecPgm** is provided for ease in converting MS-DOS version 3.x programs to OS/2. It is considered obsolete and should generally be avoided. Its use may interfere with proper Ctrl-C and Ctrl-Break handling (see Chapter 14, Interactive Programs).

1: Execute the program asynchronously. The child process begins executing as soon as the scheduler allows; the calling thread returns from the **DosExecPgm** call immediately. You cannot assume that the child process *has* received CPU time before the parent thread returns from the **DosExecPgm** call; neither can you assume that the child process *has not* received such CPU service. This form instructs OS/2 not to bother remembering the child's termination code for a future **DosCWait** call. It is used when the parent process doesn't care what the result code of the child may be or when or if it completes, and it frees the parent from the necessity of issuing **DosCWait** calls. Programs executing other programs as tools would rarely use this form. This form might be used by a system utility, for example, whose job is to fire off certain programs once an hour but not to take any action or notice should any of those programs fail. Note that, unlike the *detach* form described below, the created process is still recorded as a child of the executing parent. The parent can issue a **DosCWait** call to determine whether the child subtree is still executing, although naturally there is no return code when the child process does terminate.

2: This form is similar to form 1 in that it executes the child process asynchronously, but it instructs OS/2 to retain the child process's exit code for future examination by **DosCWait**. Thus, a program can determine the success or failure of a child process. The parent process should issue an appropriate **DosCWait** "pretty soon" because OS/2 version 1.0 maintains about 2600 bytes of data structures for a dead process whose parent is expected to **DosC-Wait** but hasn't yet done so. To have one of these structures lying around for a few minutes is no great problem, but programs need to issue **DosCWait**s in a timely fashion to keep from clogging the system with the carcasses of processes that finished hours ago.

   OS/2 takes care of all the possible timing considerations, so it's OK to issue the **DosCWait** before or after the child process has completed. Although a parent process can influence the relative assignment of CPU time between the child and parent processes by setting its own and its child's relative priorities, there is no reliable way of determining which process will run when. Write your program in such a way that it doesn't matter if the child completes before or after the **DosCWait**, or use some form of IPC to synchronize the execution of parent and child processes. See 4.4 **DosCWait** for more details.

3: This form is used by the system debugger, CodeView. The system architecture does not allow one process to latch onto another arbitrary process and start examining and perhaps modifying the target process's execution. Such a facility would result in a massive side effect and is contrary to the tenet of encapsulation in the design religion. Furthermore, such a facility would prevent OS/2 from ever providing an environment secure against malicious programs. OS/2 solves this problem with the **DosPtrace** function, which peeks, pokes, and controls a child process. This function is allowed to affect only processes that were executed with this special mode value of 3.

4: This form executes the child process asynchronously but also detaches it from the process issuing the **DosExecPgm** call. A detached process does not inherit the parent process's screen group; instead, it executes in a special invalid screen group. Any attempt to do screen, keyboard, or mouse I/O from within this screen group returns an error code. The system does not consider a detached process a child of the parent process; the new process has no connection with the creating process. In other words, it's parentless. This form of **DosExecPgm** is used to create daemon programs that execute without direct interaction with the user.

The EnvString argument points to a list of ASCII text strings that contain environment values. OS/2 supports a separate environment block for each process. A process typically inherits its parent's environment strings. In this case, the EnvPointer argument should be NULL, which tells OS/2 to supply the child process with a copy of the parent's environment strings (see Listing 4-4).

```
PATH=C:\DOS;C:\EDITORS;C:\TOOLS;C:\XTOOLS;C:\BIN;C:\UBNET
INCLUDE=\include
TERM=h19
INIT=c:\tmp
HOME=c:\tmp
USER=c:\tmp
TEMP=c:\tmp
TERM=ibmpc
LIB=c:\lib
PROMPT=($p)
```

Listing 4-4.
A typical environment string set.

The environment strings are normally used to customize a particular execution environment. For example, suppose a user creates two screen groups, each running a copy of CMD.EXE. Each CMD.EXE is a direct child of the presentation manager, which manages and creates screen groups, and each is also the ancestor of all processes that will run in its particular screen group. If the user is running utility programs that use the environment string "TEMP=<dirname>" to specify a directory to hold temporary files, he or she may want to specify different TEMP= values for each copy of CMD.EXE. As a result, the utilities that use TEMP= will access the proper directory, depending on which screen group they are run in, because they will have inherited the proper TEMP= environment string from their CMD.EXE ancestor. See Chapter 10, Environment Strings, for a complete discussion.

Because of the inheritable nature of environment strings, parent processes that edit the environment list should remove or edit only those strings with which they are involved; any unrecognized strings should be preserved.

4.4 DosCWait

When a process executes a child process, it usually wants to know when that child process has completed and whether the process succeeded or failed. **DosCWait**, the OS/2 companion function to **DosExecPgm**, returns such information. Before we discuss **DosCWait** in detail, two observations are in order. First, although each **DosExecPgm** call starts only a single process, it's possible—and not uncommon—for that child process to create its own children and perhaps they their own and so on. A program should not assume that its child process won't create subchildren; instead, programs should use the command-subtree forms of **DosCWait**. One return code from the direct child process (that is, the root of the command subtree) is sufficient because if that direct child process invokes other processes to do work for it the direct child is responsible for monitoring their success via **DosCWait**. In other words, if a child process farms out some of its work to a grandchild process and that grandchild process terminates in error, then the child process should also terminate with an error return.

Second, although we discuss the process's child, in fact processes can have multiple child processes and therefore multiple command subtrees at any time. The parent process may have interconnected the child processes via anonymous pipes, or they may be independent of one another. Issuing separate **DosCWait**s for each process or subtree is unnecessary. The form of the **DosCWait** call is shown in Listing 4-5 on the following page.

```
extern unsigned far pascal DOSCWAIT (
      unsigned                ACTIONCODE,
      unsigned                WAITOPTION,
      struct ResultCodes far  *RESULTWORD,
      unsigned far            *PIDRETURN,
      unsigned                PID);
```

Listing 4-5.
DosCWait function.

Three of the arguments affect the scope of the command: **Action-Code, WaitOption,** and **PID**. It's easiest to show how these interact by arranging their possible values into tables.

DosCWait forms: Command Subtrees

These forms of **DosCWait** operate on the entire command subtree, which may, of course, consist of only one child process. We recommend these forms because they will continue to work correctly if the child process is changed to use more or fewer child processes of its own.

ActionCode	WaitOption	ProcessId	Action
1	0	n	Wait until the command subtree has completed and then return the direct child's termination code.
1	1	n	If the command subtree has completed, return the direct child's termination code. Otherwise, return the ERROR_WAIT_NO_CHILDREN error code.

DosCWait forms: Individual Processes

These forms of **DosCWait** are used to monitor individual child processes. The processes must be direct children; grandchild or unrelated processes cannot be **DosC-Wait**ed. Use these forms only when the child process is part of the same application or software package as the parent process; the programmer needs to be certain that she or he can safely ignore the possibility that grandchild processes might still be running after the direct child has terminated.*

ActionCode	WaitOption	ProcessId	Action
0	0	0	**DosCWait** returns as soon as a direct child process terminates. If a child process had already terminated at the time of this call, it will return immediately.

(continued)

DosCWait forms: Individual Processes *(Continued)*

ActionCode	WaitOption	ProcessId	Action
0	0	N	**DosCWait** returns as soon as the direct child process *N* terminates. If it had already terminated at the time of the call, **DosCWait** returns immediately.
0	1	0	**DosCWait** checks for a terminated direct child process. If one is found, its status is returned. If none is found, an error code is returned.
0	1	N	**DosCWait** checks the status of the direct child process *N*. If it is terminated, its status is returned. If it is still running, an error code is returned.

* It is in itself not an error to collect a child process's termination code via **DosCWait** while that child still has living descendant processes. However, such a case generally means that the child's work, whatever that was, is not yet complete.

DosCWait forms: Not Recommended

ActionCode	WaitOption	ProcessId	Action
1	0	0	**DosCWait** waits until a direct child has terminated and then waits until all of that child's descendants have terminated. It then returns the direct child's exit code. This form does *not* wait until the first command subtree has terminated; it selects a command subtree based on the first direct child that terminates, and then it waits as long as necessary for the remainder of that command subtree, even if other command subtrees meanwhile complete.

(continued)

DosCWait forms: Not Recommended *(Continued)*

ActionCode	WaitOption	ProcessId	Action
1	1	0	This form returns ERROR_ CHILD_NOT_COMPLETE if any process in any of the caller's subtrees is still executing. If all subtrees have terminated, this form returns with a direct child's exit code. If no direct child processes have unwaited exit codes, the code ERROR_WAIT_ NO_CHILDREN is returned.

4.5 Control of Child Tasks and Command Subtrees

A parent process has only limited control over its child processes because the system is designed to minimize the side effects, or cross talk, between processes. Specifically, a parent process can affect its command subtrees in two ways: It can change their CPU priority, and it can terminate (kill) them. Once again, the command subtree is the recommended form for both commands because that form is insensitive to the operational details of the child process.

4.5.1 DosKillProcess

A parent process may initiate a child process or command subtree and then decide to terminate that activity before the process completes normally. Often this comes about because of a direct user command or because the user typed Ctrl-Break. See Chapter 14, Interactive Programs, for special techniques concerning Ctrl-Break and Ctrl-C.

DosKillProcess flags each process in the command subtree (or the direct child process if that form is used) for termination. A process flagged for termination normally terminates as soon as all its threads leave the system (that is, as soon as all its threads return from all system calls). The system aborts calls that might block for more than a second or two, such as those that read a keyboard character, so that the process can terminate quickly. A process can intercept SIGKILL to delay termination longer, even indefinitely. Delaying termination inordinately via **SetSignalHandler**/SIGKILL is very bad practice and is considered a bug rather than a feature.

4.5.2 **DosSetPrty**

A child process inherits its parent's process priority when the **DosEx-ecPgm** call is issued. After the **DosExecPgm** call, the parent can still change the process priority of the command subtree or of only the direct child process. The command subtree form is recommended; if the child process's work deserves priority N, then any child processes that it executes to help in that work should also run at priority N.

5

Threads and Scheduler/ Priorities

5.1 Threads

Computers consist of a CPU (central processing unit) and RAM (random access memory). A computer program consists of a sequence of instructions that are placed, for the most part, one after the other in RAM. The CPU reads each instruction in sequence and executes it. The passage of the CPU through the instruction sequence is called a *thread of execution*. All versions of MS-DOS executed programs, so they necessarily supported a thread of execution. OS/2 is unique, however, in that it supports multiple threads of execution within a single process. In other words, a program can execute in two or more spots in its code at the same time.

Obviously, a multitasking system needs to support multiple threads in a systemwide sense. Each process necessarily must have a thread; so if there are ten processes in the system, there must be ten threads. Such an existence of multiple threads in the system is invisible to the programmer because each program executes with only one thread. OS/2 is different from this because it allows an individual program to execute with multiple threads if it desires.

Because threads are elements of processes and because the process is the unit of resource ownership, all threads that belong to the same process share that process's resources. Thus, if one thread opens a file on file handle X, all threads in that process can issue **DosRead**s or **DosWrite**s to that handle. If one thread allocates a memory segment, all threads in that process can access that memory segment. Threads are analogous to the employees of a company. A company may consist of a single employee, or it may consist of two or more employees that divide the work among them. Each employee has access to the company's resources—its office space and equipment. The employees themselves, however, must coordinate their work so that they cooperate and don't conflict. As far as the outside world is concerned, each employee speaks for the company. Employees can terminate and/or more can be hired without affecting how the company is seen from outside. The only requirement is that the company have at least one employee. When the last employee (thread) dies, the company (process) also dies.

Although the process is the unit of resource ownership, each thread does "own" a small amount of private information. Specifically, each thread has its own copy of the CPU's register contents. This is an obvious requirement if each thread is to be able to execute different instruction sequences. Furthermore, each thread has its own copy of the floating point registers. OS/2 creates the process's first thread when the program begins execution. Any additional threads are created by means of the **DosCreateThread** call. Any thread can create another thread. All threads in a process are considered siblings; there are no parent-child relationships. The initial thread, thread 1, has some special characteristics and is discussed below.

5.1.1 Thread Stacks

Each thread has its own stack area, pointed to by that thread's SS and SP values. Thread 1 is the process's primal thread. OS/2 allocates it stack area in response to specifications in the .EXE file. If additional threads are created via the **DosCreateThread** call, the caller specifies a stack area for the new thread. Because the memory in which each thread's stack resides is owned by the process, any thread can modify this memory; the programmer must make sure that this does not happen. The size of the segment in which the stack resides is explicitly specified; the size of a thread's stack is not. The programmer can place a thread's stack in its own segment or in a segment with other data values, including other thread stacks. In any case, the programmer must ensure sufficient room for each thread's needs. Each thread's stack must have at least 2 KB free in addition to the thread's other needs at all times. This extra space is set aside for the needs of dynamic link routines, some of which consume considerable stack space. All threads must maintain this stack space reserve even if they are not used to call dynamic link routines. Because of a bug in many 80286 processors, stack segments must be preallocated to their full size. You cannot overrun a stack segment and then assume that OS/2 will grow the segment; overrunning a stack segment will cause a stack fault, and the process will be terminated.

5.1.2   Thread Uses

Threads have a great number of uses. This section describes four of them. These examples are intended to be inspirations to the programmer; there are many other uses for threads.

5.1.2.1   Foreground and Background Work

Threads provide a form of multitasking within a single program; therefore, one of their most obvious uses is to provide simultaneous foreground and background[1] processing for a program. For example, a spreadsheet program might use one thread to display menus and to read user input. A second thread could execute user commands, update the spreadsheet, and so on.

This arrangement generally increases the perceived speed of the program by allowing the program to prompt for another command before the previous command is complete. For example, if the user changes a cell in a spreadsheet and then calls for recalculation, the "execute" thread can recalculate while the "command" thread allows the user to move the cursor, select new menus, and so forth. The spreadsheet should use RAM semaphores to protect its structures so that one thread can't change a structure while it is being manipulated by another thread. As far as the user can tell, he or she is able to overlap commands

---

1. Here I mean foreground and background in the sense of directly interacting with the user, not as in foreground and background screen groups.

without restriction. In actuality, the previous command is usually complete before the user can finish entering the new command. Occasionally, however, the new command is delayed until the first has completed execution. This happens, for example, when the user of a spreadsheet deletes a row right after saving the spreadsheet to disk. Of course, the performance in this worst case situation is no worse than a standard single-thread design is for all cases.

5.1.2.2 Asynchronous Processing

Another common use of threads is to provide asynchronous elements in a program's design. For example, as a protection against power failure, you can design an editor so that it writes its RAM buffer to disk once every minute. Threads make it unnecessary to scatter time checks throughout the program or to sit in polling loops for input so that a time event isn't missed while blocked on a read call. You can create a thread whose sole job is periodic backup. The thread can call **DosSleep** to sleep for 60 seconds, write the buffer, and then go back to sleep for another 60 seconds.

The asynchronous event doesn't have to be time related. For example, in a program that communicates over an asynchronous serial port, you can dedicate a thread to wait for the modem carrier to come on or to wait for a protocol time out. The main thread can continue to interact with the user.

Programs that provide services to other programs via IPC can use threads to simultaneously respond to multiple requests. For example, one thread can watch the incoming work queue while one or more additional threads perform the work.

5.1.2.3 Speed Execution

You can use threads to speed the execution of single processes by overlapping I/O and computation. A single-threaded process can perform computations or call OS/2 for disk reads and writes, but not both at the same time. A multithreaded process, on the other hand, can compute one batch of data while reading the next batch from a device.

Eventually, PCs containing multiple 80386 processors will become available. An application that uses multiple threads may execute faster by using more than one CPU simultaneously.

5.1.2.4 Organizing Programs

Finally, you can use threads to organize and simplify the structure of a program. For example, in a program for a turnkey security/alarm system, you can assign a separate thread for each activity. One thread can watch the status of the intrusion switches; a second can send commands to control the lights; a third can run the telephone dialer; and a fourth can interface with each control panel.

This structure simplifies software design. The programmer needn't worry that an intrusion switch is triggering unnoticed while the CPU is executing the code that waits on the second key of a two-key command. Likewise, the programmer doesn't have to worry about talking to two command consoles at the same time; because each has its own thread and local (stack) variables, multiple consoles can be used simultaneously without conflict.

Of course, you can write such a program without multiple threads; a rat's nest of event flags and polling loops would do the job. Much better would be a family of co-routines. But best, and simplest of all, is a multithreaded design.

5.1.3 Interlocking

The good news about threads is that they share a process's data, files, and resources. The bad news is that they share a process's data, files, and resources—and that sometimes these items must be protected against simultaneous update by multiple threads. As we discussed earlier, most OS/2 machines have a single CPU; the "random" preemption of the scheduler, switching the CPU among threads, gives the illusion of the simultaneous execution of threads. Because the scheduler is deterministic and priority based, scheduling a process's threads is certainly not random; but good programming practice requires that it be considered so. Each time a program runs, external events will perturb the scheduling of the threads. Perhaps some other, higher priority task needs the CPU for a while. Perhaps the disk arm is in a different position, and a disk read by one thread takes a little longer this time than it did the last. *You cannot even assume that only the highest priority runnable thread is executing* because a multiple-CPU system may execute the N highest priority threads.

The only safe assumption is that all threads are executing simultaneously and that—in the absence of explicit interlocking or semaphore calls—each thread is always doing the "worst possible thing" in terms of simultaneously updating static data or structures. Writing to looser standards and then testing the program "to see if it's OK" is unacceptable. The very nature of such race conditions, as they are called, makes them extremely difficult to find during testing. Murphy's law says that such problems are rare during testing and become a plague only after the program is released.

5.1.3.1 Local Variables

The best way to avoid a collision of threads over static data is to write your program to minimize static data. Because each thread has its own stack, each thread has its own *stack frame* in which to store *local variables*. For example, if one thread opens and reads a file and no other thread ever manipulates that file, the memory location where that file's handle is stored should be in the thread's stack frame, not in static memory. Likewise, buffers and work areas that are private to a thread should be on that thread's stack frame. Stack variables that are local to the current procedure are easily referenced in high-level languages and in assembly language. Data items that are referenced by multiple procedures can still be located on the stack. Pascal programs can address such items directly via the data scope mechanism. C and assembly language programs will need to pass pointers to the items into the procedures that use them.

5.1.3.2 RAM Semaphores

Although using local variables on stack frames greatly reduces problems among threads, there will always be at least a few cases in which more than one thread needs to access a static data item or a static resource such as a file handle. In this situation, write the code that manipulates the static item as a *critical section* (a body of code that manipulates a data resource in a nonreentrant way) and then use RAM semaphores to reserve each critical section before it is executed. This procedure guarantees that only one thread at a time is in a critical section. See 16.2 Data Integrity for a more detailed discussion.

5.1.3.3   DosSuspendThread

In some situations it may be possible to enumerate all threads that might enter a critical section. In these cases, a process's thread can use **DosSuspendThread** to suspend the execution of the other thread(s) that might enter the critical section. The **DosSuspendThread** call can only be used to suspend threads that belong to the process making the call; it cannot be used to suspend a thread that belongs to another process. Multiple threads can be suspended by making multiple **DosSuspendThread** calls, one per thread. If a just-suspended thread is in the middle of a system call, work on that system call may or may not proceed. In either case, there will be no further execution of application (ring 3) code by a suspended thread.

It is usually better to protect critical sections with a RAM semaphore than to use **DosSuspendThread.** Using a semaphore to protect a critical section is analogous to using a traffic light to protect an intersection (an automotive "critical section" because conflicting uses must be prevented). Using **DosSuspendThread,** on the other hand, is analogous to your stopping the other cars each time you go through an intersection; you're interfering with the operation of the other cars *just in case* they might be driving through the same intersection as you, presumably an infrequent situation. Furthermore, you need a way to ensure that another vehicle isn't already in the middle of the intersection when you stop it. Getting back to software, you need to ensure that the thread you're suspending isn't already executing the critical section at the time that you suspend it. We recommend that you avoid **DosSuspendThread** when possible because of its adverse effects on process performance and because of the difficulty in guaranteeing that all the necessary threads have been suspended, especially when a program undergoes future maintenance and modification.

A **DosResumeThread** call restores the normal operation of a suspended thread.

5.1.3.4   DosEnterCritSec/DosExitCritSec

DosSuspendThread suspends the execution of a single thread within a process. **DosEnterCritSec** suspends all threads in a process except the one making the **DosEnterCritSec** call. Except for the scope of their operation, **DosEnterCritSec** and **DosExitCritSec** are similar to **DosSuspendThead** and **DosResumeThread,** and the same caveats and observations apply.

DosExitCritSec will not undo a **DosSuspendThread** that was already in effect. It releases only those threads that were suspended by **DosEnterCritSec.**

5.1.4   Thread 1

Each thread in a process has an associated *thread ID*. A thread's ID is a magic cookie. Its value has no intrinsic meaning to the application; it has meaning only as a name for a thread in an operating system call. The one exception to this is the process's first thread, whose thread ID is always 1.

Thread 1 is special: It is the thread that is interrupted when a process receives a signal. See Chapter 12, Signals, for further details.

5.1.5   Thread Death

A thread can die in two ways. First, it can terminate itself with the **DosExit** call. Second, when any thread in a process calls **DosExit** with the "exit entire process" argument, all threads belonging to that process are terminated "as soon as possible." If they were executing application code at the time **DosExit** was called, they terminate immediately. If they were in the middle of a system call, they terminate "very quickly." If the system call executes quickly enough, its function may complete (although the CPU will not return from the system call itself); but if the system call involves delays of more than 1 second, it will terminate without completing. Whether a thread's last system call completes is usually moot, but in a few cases, such as writes to some types of devices, it may be noticed that the last write was only partially completed.

When a process wants to terminate, it should use the "terminate entire process" form of **DosExit** rather than the "terminate this thread" form. Unbeknownst to the calling process, some dynlink packages, including some OS/2 system calls, may create threads. These threads are called *captive threads* because only the original calling thread returns from the dynlink call; the created thread remains "captive" inside the dynlink package. If a program attempts to terminate by causing all its known threads to use the **DosExit** "terminate this thread" form, the termination may not be successful because of such captive threads.

Of course, if the last remaining thread of a process calls **DosExit** "terminate this thread," OS/2 terminates the process.

5.1.6   **Performance Characteristics**

Threads are intended to be fast and cheap. In OS/2 version 1.0, each additional thread that is created consumes about 1200 bytes of memory inside the OS/2 kernel for its kernel mode stack. This is in addition to the 2048 bytes of user mode stack space that we recommend you provide from the process's data area. Terminating a thread does not release the kernel stack memory, but subsequently creating another thread reuses this memory. In other words, the system memory that a process's threads consume is the maximum number of threads simultaneously alive times 1200 bytes. This figure is exclusive of each thread's stack, which is provided by the process from its own memory.

The time needed to create a new thread depends on the process's previous thread behavior. Creating a thread that will reuse the internal memory area created for a previous thread that has terminated takes approximately 3 milliseconds.[2] A request to create a new thread that extends the process's "thread count high-water mark" requires an internal memory allocation operation. This operation may trigger a memory compaction or even a segment swapout, so its time cannot be accurately predicted.

It takes about 1 millisecond for the system to begin running an unblocked thread. In other words, if a lower-priority thread releases a RAM semaphore that is being waited on by a higher-priority thread, approximately 1 millisecond passes between the lower-priority thread's call to release the semaphore and the return of the higher-priority thread from its **DosSemRequest** call.

Threads are a key feature of OS/2; they will receive strong support in future versions of OS/2 and will play an increasingly important architectural role. You can, therefore, expect thread costs and performance to be the same or to improve in future releases.

5.2   **Scheduler/Priorities**

A typical running OS/2 system contains a lot of threads. Frequently, several threads are ready to execute at any one time. The OS/2 *scheduler* decides which thread to run next and how long to run it before

---

2. All timings in this book refer to a 6 mHz IBM AT with one wait-state memory. This represents a worst case performance level.

assigning the CPU to another thread. OS/2's scheduler is a *priority-based* scheduler; it assigns each thread a priority and then uses that priority to decide which thread to run. The OS/2 scheduler is also a *preemptive* scheduler. If a higher-priority thread is ready to execute, OS/2 does not wait for the lower-priority thread to finish with the CPU before reassigning the CPU; the lower-priority thread is *pre-empted*—the CPU is summarily yanked away. Naturally, the state of the preempted thread is recorded so that its execution can resume later without ill effect.

The scheduler's dispatch algorithm is very straightforward: It executes the highest-priority runnable thread for as long as the thread wants the CPU. When that thread gives up the CPU—perhaps by waiting for an I/O operation—that thread is no longer runnable, and the scheduler executes the thread with the highest priority that *is* runnable. If a blocked thread becomes runnable and it has a higher priority than the thread currently running, the CPU is immediately preempted and assigned to the higher-priority thread. In summary, the CPU is always running the highest-priority runnable thread.

The scheduler's dispatcher is simplicity itself: It's blindly priority based. Although the usual focus for OS/2 activities is the process—a process lives, dies, opens files, and so on—the scheduler components of OS/2 know little about processes. Because the *thread* is the dispatchable entity, the scheduler is primarily thread oriented. If you're not used to thinking in terms of threads, you can mentally substitute the word *process* for the word *thread* in the following discussion. In practice, all of a process's threads typically share the same priority, so it's not too inaccurate to view the system as being made up of processes that compete for CPU resources.

In OS/2 threads are classified and run in three categories: general priority, time-critical priority, and low priority. These categories are further divided into subcategories. Figure 5-1 shows the relationship of the three priority categories and their subcategories.

5.2.1 General Priority Category

The majority of threads in the system run in the *general priority* category and belong to one of three subcategories: background, foreground, or interactive. To a limited extent, OS/2 dynamically modifies the priorities of threads in the general priority category.

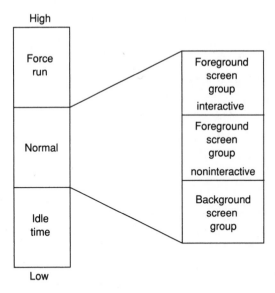

Figure 5-1.
Priority categories.

5.2.1.1 **Background Subcategory**

The purpose of the OS/2 priority design is to optimize response rather than throughput. In other words, the system is not concerned about ensuring that all runnable threads get at least some CPU time, and the system is not primarily concerned about trying to keep the disks busy when the highest-priority thread is compute bound. Instead, OS/2 is concerned about keeping less important work from delaying or slowing more important work. This is the reason for the background subcategory. The word *background* has been used in many different ways to describe how tasks are performed in many operating systems; we use the word to indicate processes that are associated with a screen group not currently being displayed.

For example, a user is working with a word-processing program but then switches from that program to a spreadsheet program. The word-processing program becomes background, and the spreadsheet program is promoted from background to foreground. When the user selects different screen groups, threads change from foreground to background or background to foreground. Background threads have the lowest priority in the general priority category. Background applications get the CPU (and, through it, the disks) only when all foreground threads are idle.

As soon as a foreground thread is runnable, the CPU is preempted from the background thread. Background threads can use leftover machine time, but they can never compete with foreground threads.

5.2.1.2 Foreground and Interactive Subcategories

All processes associated with the currently active screen group are made members of the foreground subcategory. The process that is currently interacting with the keyboard is promoted to the interactive subcategory. This ensures that the user will get the fastest possible response to a command. When the interactive process's threads release the CPU (via blocking on some OS/2 call), the noninteractive foreground threads get the next crack at it because those threads are usually doing work on behalf of the interactive process or work that is in some way related. If no foreground thread needs the CPU, background threads may run.

Although the scheduler concerns itself with threads rather than processes, it's *processes* that switch between categories—foreground, background, and interactive. When a process changes category—for example, when a process shows itself to be in the interactive subcategory by doing keyboard I/O—the priorities of all its threads are adjusted appropriately.

Because background threads are the "low men on the totem pole" that is composed of quite a few threads, it may seem that they'll never get to run. This isn't the case, though, over a long enough period of time. Yes, a background thread can be totally starved for CPU time during a 5-second interval, but it would be very rare if it received no service during a 1-minute interval. Interactive application commands that take more than a few seconds of CPU time are rare. Commands involving disk transfer may take longer, but the CPU is available for lower-priority threads while the interactive process is waiting for disk operations. Finally, a user rarely keeps an interactive application fully busy; the normal "type, look, and think" cycle has lots of spare time in it for background threads to run.

But how does this apply to the presentation manager? The presentation manager runs many independent interactive tasks within the same screen group, so are they all foreground threads? How does OS/2 know which is the interactive process? The answer is that the presentation manager advises the scheduler. When the presentation manager screen group is displayed, all threads within that screen group are placed in the foreground category. When the user selects a particular window to receive keyboard or mouse events, the presentation manager tells the scheduler that the process using that window is now the interactive process. As a result, the system's interactive performance is preserved in the presentation manager's screen group.

5.2.1.3   Throughput Balancing

We mentioned that some operating systems try to optimize system throughput by trying to run CPU-bound and I/O-bound applications at the same time. The theory is that the I/O-bound application ties up the disk but needs little CPU time, so the disk work can be gotten out of the way while the CPU is running the CPU-bound task. If the disk thread has the higher priority, the tasks run in tandem. Each time the disk operation is completed, the I/O-bound thread regains the CPU and issues another disk operation. Leftover CPU time goes to the CPU-bound task that, in this case, has a lower priority.

This won't work, however, if the CPU-bound thread has a higher priority than the I/O-bound thread. The CPU-bound thread will tend to hold the CPU, and the I/O-bound thread won't get even the small amount of CPU time that it needs to issue another I/O request. Traditionally, schedulers have been designed to deal with this problem by boosting the priority of I/O-bound tasks and lowering the priority of CPU-bound tasks so that, eventually, the I/O-bound thread gets enough service to make its I/O requests.

The OS/2 scheduler incorporates this design to a limited extent. Each time a thread issues a system call that blocks, the scheduler looks at the period between the time the CPU was assigned to the thread and the time the thread blocked itself with a system call.[3] If that period of time is short, the thread is considered I/O bound, and its priority receives a small increment. If a thread is truly I/O bound, it soon receives several such increments and, thus, a modest priority promotion. On the other hand, if the thread held the CPU for a longer period of time, it is considered CPU bound, and its priority receives a small decrement.

---

3. We use "blocking" rather than "requesting an I/O operation" as a test of I/O boundedness because nearly all blocking operations wait for I/O. If a thread's data were all in the buffer cache, the thread could issue many I/O requests and still be compute bound. In other words, when we speak of I/O-bound threads, we really mean device bound—not I/O request bound.

The I/O boundedness priority adjustment is small. No background thread, no matter how I/O bound, can have its priority raised to the point where it has a higher priority than any foreground thread, no matter how CPU bound. This throughput enhancing optimization applies only to "peer" threads—threads with similar priorities. For example, the threads of a single process generally have the same base priority, so this adjustment helps optimize the throughput of that process.

5.2.2 Time-Critical Priority Category

Foreground threads, particularly interactive foreground threads, receive CPU service whenever they want it. Noninteractive foreground threads and, particularly, background threads may not receive any CPU time for periods of arbitrary length. This approach improves system response, but it's not always a good thing. For example, you may be running a network or a telecommunications application that drops its connection if it can't respond to incoming packets in a timely fashion. Also, you may want to make an exception to the principle of "response, not throughput" when it comes to printers. Most printers are much slower than their users would like, and most printer spooler programs require little in the way of CPU time; so the OS/2 print spooler (the program that prints queued output on the printer) would like to run at a high priority to keep the printer busy.

Time-critical applications are so called because the ability to run in a timely fashion is critical to their well-being. Time-critical applications may or may not be interactive, and they may be in the foreground or in a background screen group, but this should not affect their high priority. The OS/2 scheduler contains a time-critical priority category to deal with time-critical applications. A thread running in this priority category has a higher priority than any non–time-critical thread in the system, including interactive threads. Unlike priorities in the general category, a time-critical priority is never adjusted; once given a time-critical priority, a thread's priority remains fixed until a system call changes it.

Naturally, time-critical threads should consume only modest amounts of CPU time. If an application has a time-critical thread that consumes considerable CPU time—say, more than 20 percent—the foreground interactive application will be noticeably slowed or even momentarily stopped. System usability is severely affected when the interactive application can't get service. The screen output stutters and stumbles, characters are dropped when commands are typed, and, in general, the computer becomes unusable.

Not all threads in a process have to be of the same priority. An application may need time-critical response for only some of its work; the other work can run at a normal priority. For example, in a telecommunications program a "receive incoming data" thread might run at a time-critical priority but queue messages in memory for processing by a normal-priority thread. If the time-critical thread finds that the normal-priority thread has fallen behind, it can send a "wait for me" message to the sending program.

We strongly recommend that processes that use monitors run the monitor thread, and only the monitor thread, at a time-critical priority. This prevents delayed device response because of delays in processing the monitor data stream. See 16.1 Device Monitors for more information.

5.2.3 Low Priority Category

If you picture the general priority category as a range of priorities, with the force run priority category as a higher range, there is a third range, called the *low priority* category, that is lower in priority than the general priority category. As a result, threads in this category get CPU service only when no other thread in the other categories needs it. This category is a mirror image of the time-critical priority category in that the system call that sets the thread fixes the priority; OS/2 never changes a low priority.

I don't expect the low priority category to be particularly popular. It's in the system primarily because it falls out for free, as a mirror image of the time-critical category. Turnkey systems may want to run some housekeeping processes at this priority. Some users enjoy computing PI, doing cryptographic analysis, or displaying fractal images; these recreations are good candidates for soaking up leftover CPU time. On a more practical level, you could run a program that counts seconds of CPU time and yields a histogram of CPU utilization during the course of a day.

5.2.4 **Setting Process/Thread Priorities**

We've discussed at some length the effect of the various priorities, but we haven't discussed how to set these priorities. Because inheritance is an important OS/2 concept, how does a parent's priority affect that of the child? Finally, although we said that priority is a thread issue rather than a process one, we kept bringing up processes anyway. How does all this work?

Currently, whenever a thread is created, it inherits the priority of its creator thread. In the case of **DosCreateThread,** the thread making the call is the creator thread. In the case of thread 1, the thread in the parent process that is making the **DosExecPgm** call is the creator thread. When a process makes a **DosSetPrty** call to change the priority of one of its own threads, the new priority always takes effect. When a process uses **DosSetPrty** to change the priority of another process, only the threads in that other process which have not had their priorities explicitly set from within their own process are changed. This prevents a parent process from inadvertently lowering the priority of, say, a time-critical thread by changing the base priority of a child process.

In a future release, we expect to improve this algorithm so that each process has a base priority. A new thread will inherit its creator's base priority. A process's thread priorities that are in the general priority category will all be relative to the process's base priority so that a change in the base priority will raise or lower the priority of all the process's general threads while retaining their relative priority relationships. Threads in the time-critical and low priority categories will continue to be unaffected by their process's base priority.

6

The User
Interface

OS/2 contains several important subsystems: the file system, the memory management subsystem, the multitasking subsystem, and the user interface subsystem—the *presentation manager*. MS-DOS does not define or support a user interface subsystem; each application must provide its own. MS-DOS utilities use a primitive line-oriented interface, essentially unchanged from the interface provided by systems designed to interface with TTYs.

OS/2 is intended to be a graphics-oriented operating system, and as such it needs to provide a standard graphical user interface (GUI) subsystem—for several reasons. First, because such systems are complex to create, to expect that each application provide its own is unreasonable. Second, a major benefit of a graphical user interface is that applications can be intermingled. For example, their output windows can share the screen, and the user can transfer data between applications using visual metaphors. If each application had its own GUI package, such sharing would be impossible. Third, a graphical user interface is supposed to make the machine *easier* to use, but this will be so only if the user can learn one interface that will work with all applications.

6.1 VIO User Interface

The full graphical user interface subsystem will not ship with OS/2 version 1.0, so the initial release will contain the character-oriented

VIO/KBD/MOU subsystem (see Chapter 13, The Presentation Manager and VIO, for more details). Although VIO doesn't provide any graphical services, it does allow applications to sidestep VIO and construct their own. The VIO screen group interface is straightforward. When the machine is booted up, the screen displays the screen group list. The user can select an existing screen group or create a new one. From within a screen group, the user can type a magic key sequence to return the screen to the screen group list. Another magic key sequence allows the user to toggle through all existing screen groups. One screen group is identified in the screen group list as the real mode screen group.

6.2 The Presentation Manager User Interface

The OS/2 presentation manager is a powerful and flexible graphical user interface. It supports such features as windowing, drop-down and pop-up menus, and scroll bars. It works best with a graphical pointing device such as a mouse, but it can be controlled exclusively from the keyboard.

The presentation manager employs screen windows to allow multiple applications to use the screen and keyboard simultaneously. Each application uses one or more windows to display its information; the user can size and position each window, overlapping some and perhaps shrinking others to icons. Mouse and keyboard commands change the input focus between windows; this allows the presentation manager to route keystrokes and mouse events to the proper application.

Because of its windowing capability, the presentation manager doesn't need to use the underlying OS/2 screen group mechanism to allow the user to switch between running applications. The user starts an application by pointing to its name on a menu display; for most applications the presentation manager creates a new window and assigns it to the new process. Some applications may decline to use the presentation manager's graphical user interface and prefer to take direct control of the display. When such an application is initiated, the presentation manager creates a private screen group for it and switches to that screen group. The user can switch away by entering a special key sequence that brings up a menu which allows the user to select any running program. If the selected program is using the standard presentation manager GUI, the screen is switched to the screen group shared by those programs. Otherwise, the screen is switched to the private screen group that the specified application is using.

To summarize, only the real mode application and applications that take direct control of the display hardware need to run in their own screen groups. The presentation manager runs all other processes in a single screen group and uses its windowing facilities to share the screen among them. The user can switch between applications via a special menu; if both the previous and the new application are using the standard interface, the user can switch the focus directly without going though the menu.

6.3 Presentation Manager and VIO Compatibility

In OS/2 version 1.1 and in all subsequent releases, the presentation manager will replace and superset the VIO interface. Applications that use the character mode VIO interface will continue to work properly as windowable presentation manager applications, as will applications that use the STDIN and STDOUT file handles for interactive I/O. Applications that use the VIO interface to obtain direct access to the graphical display hardware will also be supported; as described above, the presentation manager will run such applications in their own screen group.

7

Dynamic Linking

A central component of OS/2 is dynamic linking. Dynamic links play several critical architectural roles. Before we can discuss them at such an abstract level, however, we need to understand the nuts and bolts of their workings.

7.1 Static Linking

A good preliminary to the study of dynamic links (called *dynlinks*, for short) is a review of their relative, static links. Every programmer who has gone beyond interpreter-based languages such as BASIC is familiar with static links. You code a subroutine or a procedure call to a routine that is not present in that compiland (or source file), which we'll call **Foo.** The missing routine is declared *external* so that the assembler or compiler doesn't flag it as an undefined symbol. At linktime, you present the linker with the .OBJ file that you created from your compiland, and you also provide a .OBJ file[1] that contains the missing routine **Foo.** The linker combines the compilands into a final executable image—the .EXE file—that contains the routine **Foo** as well as the routines that call it. During the combination process, the linker adjusts the calls to **Foo,** which had been undefined external references, to point to the place in the .EXE file where the linker relocated the **Foo** routine. This process is diagramed in Figure 7-1 on the following page.

In other words, with static linking you can write a program in pieces. You can compile one piece at a time by having it refer to the other pieces as externals. A program called a linker or a link editor

---

1. Or a .LIB library file that contains the .OBJ file as a part of it.

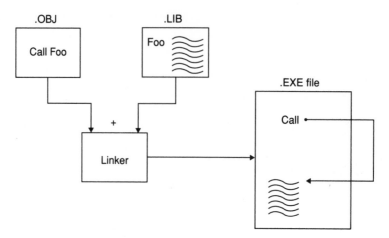

Figure 7-1.
Static linking.

combines these pieces into one final .EXE image, fixing up the external references (that is, references between one piece and another) that those pieces contain.

Writing and compiling your program piecemeal is useful, but the primary advantage of static linking is that you can use it to reference a standard set of subroutines—a *subroutine library*—without compiling or even possessing the source code for those subroutines. Nearly all high-level language packages come with one or more standard *runtime libraries* that contain various useful subroutines that the compiler can call implicitly and that the programmer can call explicitly. Source for these runtime libraries is rarely provided; the language supplier provides only the .OBJ object files, typically in library format.

To summarize, in traditional static linking the target code (that is, the external subroutine) must be present at linktime and is built into the final .EXE module. This makes the .EXE file larger, naturally, but more important, the target code can't be changed or upgraded without relinking to the main program's .OBJ files. Because the personal computer field is built on commercial software whose authors don't release source or .OBJ files, this relinking is out of the question for the typical end user. Finally, the target code can't be shared among several (different) applications that use the same library routines. This is true for two reasons. First, the target code was relocated differently by the linker for each client; so although the code remains logically the same for each application, the address components of the binary instructions are different in each .EXE file. Second, the operating system has no way of knowing that these applications are using the same library, and it has no way of knowing where that library is in each .EXE file. Therefore, it can't avoid having duplicate copies of the library in memory.

7.2 Loadtime Dynamic Linking

The mechanical process of loadtime dynamic linking is the same as that of static linking. The programmer makes an external reference to a subroutine and at linktime specifies a library file (or a .OBJ file) that defines the reference. The linker produces a .EXE file that OS/2 then loads and executes. Behind the scenes, however, things are very much different.

Step 1 is the same for both kinds of linking. The external reference is compiled or assembled, resulting in a .OBJ file that contains an external reference fixup record. The assembler or compiler doesn't know about dynamic links; the .OBJ file that an assembler or a compiler produces may be used for static links, dynamic links, or, more frequently, a combination of both (some externals become dynamic links, others become static links).

In static linking, the linker finds the actual externally referenced subroutine in the library file. In dynamic linking, the linker finds a special record that defines a module name string and an entry point name string. For example, in our hypothetical routine **Foo,** the library file contains only these two name strings, not the code for **Foo** itself. (The entry point name string doesn't have to be the name by which programs called the routine.) The resultant .EXE file doesn't contain the code for **Foo;** it contains a special dynamic link record that specifies these module and entry point names for **Foo.** This is illustrated in Figure 7-2 on the following page.

When this .EXE file is run, OS/2 loads the code in the .EXE file into memory and discovers the dynamic link record(s). For each dynamic link module that is named, OS/2 locates the code in the system's dynamic link library directory and loads it into memory (unless the module is already in use; see below). The system then links the external references in the application to the addresses of the called entry points. This process is diagrammed in Figure 7-3 on the following page.

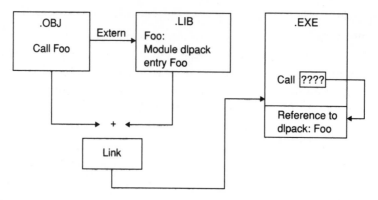

Figure 7-2.
Dynamic linking.

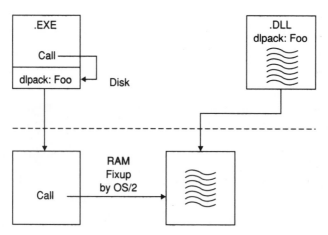

Figure 7-3.
Loadtime dynlink fixups.

To summarize, instead of linking in the target code at linktime, the linker places a module name and an entry point name into the .EXE file. When the program is loaded (that is, executed), OS/2 locates the target code, loads it, and does the necessary linking. Although all we're doing is postponing the linkage until loadtime, this technique has several important ramifications. First, the target code is not in the .EXE file but in a separate dynamic link library (.DLL) file. Thus, the .EXE file is smaller because it contains only the name of the target code, not the code itself. You can change or upgrade the target code at any time simply by replacing this .DLL file. The next time a referencing application is loaded,[2] it is linked to the new version of the target code. Finally, having the target code in a .DLL file paves the way for automatic code sharing. OS/2 can easily understand that two applications are using the same dynlink code because it loaded and linked that code, and it can use this knowledge to share the pure segments of that dynlink package rather than loading duplicate copies.

A final advantage of dynamic linking is that it's totally invisible to the user, and it can even be invisible to the programmer. You need to understand dynamic linking to create a dynamic link module, but you can use one without even knowing that it's not an ordinary static link. The one disadvantage of dynamic linking is that programs sometimes take longer to load into memory than do those linked with static linking. The good news about dynamic linking is that the target code(s) are separate from the main .EXE file; this is also the bad news. Because the target code(s) are separate from the main .EXE file, a few more disk operations may be necessary to load them.

The actual performance ramifications depend on the kind of dynlink module that is referenced and whether this .EXE file is the first to reference the module. This is discussed in more detail in 7.11 Implementation Details.

Although this discussion has concentrated on processes calling dynlink routines, dynlink routines can in fact be called by other dynlink routines. When OS/2 loads a dynlink routine in response to a process's request, it examines that routine to see if it has any dynlink references of its own. Any such referenced dynlink routines are also loaded and so on until no unsatisfied dynlink references remain.

7.3   Runtime Dynamic Linking

The dynamic linking that we have been describing is called loadtime dynamic linking because it occurs when the .EXE file is loaded. All dynamic link names need not appear in the .EXE file at loadtime; a process can link itself to a dynlink package at runtime as well. Runtime dynamic linking works exactly like loadtime dynamic linking

---

2. With some restrictions. See 7.11.2 Dynlink Life, Death, and Sharing.

except that the process creates the dynlink module and entry point names at runtime and then passes them to OS/2 so that OS/2 can locate and load the specified dynlink code.

Runtime linking takes place in four steps.

1. The process issues a **DosLoadModule** call to tell OS/2 to locate and load the dynlink code into memory.

2. The **DosGetProcAddr** call is used to obtain the addresses of the routines that the process wants to call.

3. The process calls the dynlink library entry points by means of an indirect call through the address returned by **DosGetProcAddr.**

4. When the process has no more use for the dynlink code, it can call **DosFreeModule** to release the dynlink code. After this call, the process will still have the addresses returned by **DosGet-ProcAddr,** but they will be illegal addresses; referencing them will cause a GP fault.

Runtime dynamic links are useful when a program knows that it will want to call some dynlink routines but doesn't know which ones. For example, a charting program may support four plotters, and it may want to use dynlink plotter driver packages. It doesn't make sense for the application to contain loadtime dynamic links to all four plotters because only one will be used and the others will take up memory and swap space. Instead, the charting program can wait until it learns which plotter is installed and then use the runtime dynlink facility to load the appropriate package. The application need not even call **DosLoadModule** when it initializes; it can wait until the user issues a plot command before it calls **DosLoadModule,** thereby reducing memory demands on the system.

The application need not even be able to enumerate all the modules or entry points that may be called. The application can learn the names of the dynlink modules from another process or by looking in a configuration file. This allows the user of our charting program, for example, to install additional plotter drivers that didn't even exist at the time that the application was written. Of course, in this example the calling sequences of the dynlink plotter driver must be standardized, or the programmer must devise a way for the application to figure out the proper way to call these newly found routines.

Naturally, a process is not limited to one runtime dynlink module; multiple calls to **DosLoadModule** can be used to link to several dynlink modules simultaneously. Regardless of the number of modules in use, **DosFreeModule** should be used if the dynlink module will no longer be used and the process intends to continue executing. Issuing **DosFreeModule**s is unnecessary if the process is about to terminate; OS/2 releases all dynlink modules at process termination time.

7.4 Dynlinks, Processes, and Threads

Simply put, OS/2 views dynlinks as a fancy subroutine package. Dynlinks aren't processes, and they don't own any resources. A dynlink executes only because a thread belonging to a client process called the dynlink code. The dynlink code is executing *as the client thread and process* because, in the eyes of the system, the dynlink is merely a subroutine that process has called. Before the client process can call a dynlink package, OS/2 ensures that the dynlink's segments are in the *address space* of the client. No ring transition or context switching overhead occurs when a client calls a dynlink routine; the far call to a dynlink entry point is just that—an ordinary far call to a subroutine in the process's address space.

One side effect is that dynlink calls are very fast; little CPU time is spent getting to the dynlink package. Another side effect is no separation between a client's segments and a dynlink package's segments[3] because segments belong to processes and only one process is running both the client and the dynlink code. The same goes for file handles, semaphores, and so on.

7.5 Data

The careful reader will have noticed something missing in this discussion of dynamic linking: We've said nothing about how to handle a dynlink routine's data. Subroutines linked with static links have no problem with having their own static data; when the linker binds the external code with the main code, it sees how much static data the external code needs and allocates the necessary space in the proper data

---

3. Subsystem dynlink packages may be sensitive to this. For detailed information, see 7.11.1 Dynlink Data Security.

segment(s). References that the external code makes to its data are then fixed up to point to the proper location. Because the linker is combining all the .OBJ files into a .EXE file, it can easily divide the static data segment(s) among the various compilands.

This technique doesn't work for dynamic link routines because their code and therefore their data requirements aren't present at linktime. It's possible to extend the special dynlink .OBJ file to describe the amount of static data that the dynlink package will need, but it won't work.[4] Because the main code in each application uses different amounts of static data, the data area reserved for the dynlink package would end up at a different offset in each .EXE file that was built. When these .EXE files were executed, the one set of shared dynlink code segments would need to reference the data that resides at different addresses for each different client. Relocating the static references in all dynlink code modules at each occurrence of a context switch is clearly out of the question.

An alternative to letting dynamic link routines have their own static data is to require that their callers allocate the necessary data areas and pass pointers to them upon every call. We easily rejected this scheme: It's cumbersome; *call* statements must be written differently if they're for a dynlink routine; and, finally, this hack wouldn't support sub-systems, which are discussed below.

Instead, OS/2 takes advantage of the segmented architecture of the 80286. Each dynamic link routine can use one or more data segments to hold its static data. Each client process has a separate set of these segments. Because these segments hold only the dynlink routine's data and none of the calling process's data, the offsets of the data items within that segment will be the same no matter which client process is calling the dynlink code. All we need do to solve our static data addressability problem is ensure that the segment selectors of the dynlink routine's static data segments are the same for each client process.

OS/2 ensures that the dynlink library's segment selectors are the same for each client process by means of a technique called the *disjoint LDT space*. I won't attempt a general introduction to the segmented architecture of the 80286, but a brief summary is in order. Each process in 80286 protect mode can have a maximum of 16,383 segments. These

---

4.   And even if it did work, it would be a poor design because it would restrict our ability to up-grade the dynlink code in the field.

segments are described in two tables: the LDT (Local Descriptor Table) and the GDT (Global Descriptor Table). An application can't read from or write to these tables. OS/2 manages them, and the 80286 microprocessor uses their contents when a process loads selectors into its segment registers.

In practice, the GDT is not used for application segments, which leaves the LDT 8192 segments—or, more precisely, 8192 *segment selectors*, which OS/2 can set up to point to memory segments. The 80286 does not support efficient position-independent code, so 80286 programs contain within them, as part of the instruction stream, the particular segment selector needed to access a particular memory location, as well as an offset within that segment. This applies to both code and data references.

When OS/2 loads a program into memory, the .EXE file describes the number, type, and size of the program's segments. OS/2 creates these segments and allocates a selector for each from the 8192 possible LDT selectors. There isn't any conflict with other processes in the system, at this point, because each process has its own LDT and its own private set of 8192 LDT selectors. After OS/2 chooses a selector for each segment, both code and data, it uses a table of addresses provided in the .EXE file to *relocate* each segment reference in the program, changing the place holder value put there by the linker into the proper segment selector value. OS/2 never combines or splits segments, so it never has to relocate the offset part of addresses, only the segment parts. Address offsets are more common than segment references. Because the segment references are relatively few, this relocation process is not very time-consuming.

If OS/2 discovers that the process that it's loading references a dynlink routine—say, our old friend **Foo**—the situation is more complex. For example, suppose that the process isn't the first caller of **Foo**; **Foo** is already in memory and already relocated to some particular LDT slots *in the LDT of the earlier client of Foo.* OS/2 has to fill in those same slots in the new process's LDT with pointers to **Foo**; it can't assign different LDT slots because **Foo**'s code and data have already been relocated to the earlier process's slots. If the new process is already using **Foo**'s slot numbers for something else, then we are in trouble. This is a problem with all of **Foo**'s segments, both data segments and code segments.

This is where the disjoint LDT space comes in. OS/2 reserves many of each process's LDT slots[5] for the disjoint space. The same slot numbers are reserved in every process's LDT. When OS/2 allocates an LDT selector for a memory segment that *may* be shared between processes, it allocates an entry from the disjoint LDT space. After a selector is allocated, that same slot in all other LDTs in the system is reserved. The slot either remains empty (that is, invalid) or points to this shared segment; it can have no other use. This guarantees that a process that has been running for hours and that has created dozens of segments can still call **DosLoadModule** to get access to a dynlink routine; OS/2 will find that the proper slots in this process's LDT are ready and waiting. The disjoint LDT space is used for *all* shared memory objects, not just dynlink routines. Shared memory data segments are also allocated from the disjoint LDT space. A process's code segments are not allocated in the disjoint LDT space, yet they can still be shared.[6] Figure 7-4 illustrates the disjoint LDT concept. Bullets in the shaded selectors denote reserved but invalid disjoint selectors. These are reserved in case that process later requests access to the shared memory segments that were assigned those disjoint slots. Only process A is using the dynlink package DLX, so its assigned disjoint LDT slots are reserved for it in Process B's LDT as well as in the LDT of all other processes in the system. Both processes are using the dynlink package DLY.

7.5.1 Instance Data

OS/2 supports two types of data segments for dynlink routines — *instance* and *global*. Instance data segments hold data specific to each instance of the dynlink routine. In other words, a dynlink routine has a separate set of instance data segments for each process using it. The dynlink code has no difficulty addressing its data; the code can reference the data segment selectors as immediate values. The linker and OS/2's loader conspire so that the proper selector value is in place when the code executes.

---

5. In version 1.0, more than half the LDT slots are reserved for this disjoint area.
6. The sharing of pure segments between multiple copies of the same program is established when the duplicate copies are loaded. OS/2 will use the same selector to do segment mapping as it did when it loaded the first copy, so these segments can be shared even though their selectors are not in the disjoint space.

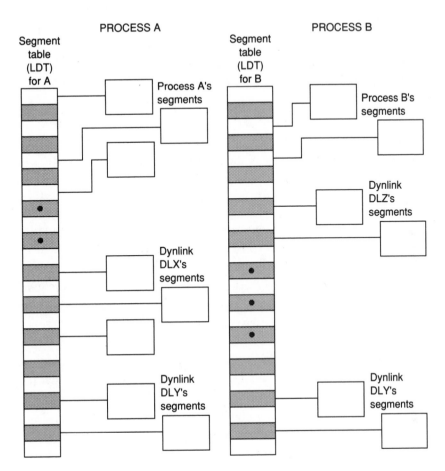

Figure 7-4.
The disjoint LDT space.

The use of instance data segments is nearly invisible both to the client process and to the dynlink code. The client process simply calls the dynlink routine, totally unaffected by the presence or absence of the routine's instance data segment(s). A dynlink routine can even return addresses of items in its data segments to the client process. The client cannot distinguish between a dynlink routine and a statically linked one. Likewise, the code that makes up the dynlink routine doesn't need to do anything special to use its instance data segments. The dynlink code was assembled or compiled with its static data in one or more segments; the code itself references those segments normally. The linker and OS/2 handle all details of allocating the disjoint LDT selectors, loading the segments, fixing up the references, and so on.

A dynlink routine that uses only instance data segments (or no data segments at all) can be written as a single client package, as would be a statically linked subroutine. Although such a dynlink routine may have multiple clients, the presence of multiple clients is invisible to the routine itself. Each client has a separate copy of the instance data segment(s). When a new client is created, OS/2 loads virgin copies of the instance data segments from the .DLL file. The fact that OS/2 is sharing the pure code segments of the routine has no effect on the operation of the routine itself.

7.5.2   Global Data

The second form of data segment available to a dynlink routine is a *global* data segment. A global data segment, as the name implies, is not duplicated for each client process. There is only one copy of each dynlink module's global data segment(s); each client process is given shared access to that segment. The segment is loaded only once—when the dynlink package is first brought into memory to be linked with its first client process. Global data segments allow a dynlink routine to be explicitly aware of its multiple clients because changes to a global segment made by calls from one client process are visible to the dynlink code when called from another client process. Global data segments are provided to support *subsystems*, which are discussed later. Figure 7-5 illustrates a dynlink routine with both instance and global data segments.

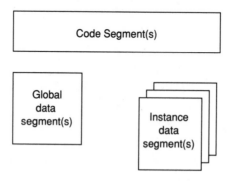

Figure 7-5.
Dynlink segments.

7.6 **Dynamic Link Packages As Subroutines**

Dynamic link subroutines (or packages) generally fall into two categories—*subroutines* and *subsystems*. As we discussed earlier, a dynamic link subroutine is written and executes in much the same way as a statically linked subroutine. The only difference is in the preparation of the dynamic link library file, which contains the actual subroutines, and in the preparation of the special .OBJ file, to which client programs can link. During execution, both the dynlink routines and the client routines can use their own static data freely, and they can pass pointers to their data areas back and forth to each other. The only difference between static linking and dynamic linking, in this model, is that the dynlink routine cannot reference any external symbols that the client code defines, nor can the client externally reference any dynlink package symbols other than the module entry points. Figure 7-6 illustrates a dynamic link routine being used as a subroutine. The execution environment is nearly identical to that of a traditional statically linked subroutine; the client and the subroutine each reference their own static data areas, all of which are contained in the process's address space. Note that a dynlink package can reference the application's data and the application can reference the dynlink package's data, but only if the application or the dynlink package passes a pointer to its data to the other.

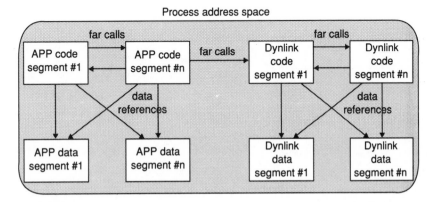

Figure 7-6.
Dynamic link routines as subroutines.

7.7 Subsystems

The term *dynlink subsystems* refers to the design and intended function of a particular style of dynlink package and is somewhat artificial. Although OS/2 provides special features to help support subsystems, OS/2 does not actually classify dynlink modules as subroutines or subsystems; *subsystem* is merely a descriptive term.

The term *subsystem* refers to a dynlink module that provides a set of services built around a resource.[7] For example, OS/2's VIO dynlink entry points are considered a dynlink subsystem because they provide a set of services to manage the display screen. A subsystem usually has to manage a limited resource for an effectively unlimited number of clients; VIO does this, managing a single physical display controller and a small number of screen groups for an indefinite number of clients.

Because subsystems generally manage a limited resource, they have one or more global data segments that they use to keep information about the state of the resource they're controlling; they also have buffers, flags, semaphores, and so on. Per-client work areas are generally kept in instance data segments; it's best to reserve the global data segment(s) for global information. Figure 7-7 illustrates a dynamic link routine being used as a subsystem. A dynlink subsystem differs from a dynlink being used as a subroutine only by the addition of a static data segment.

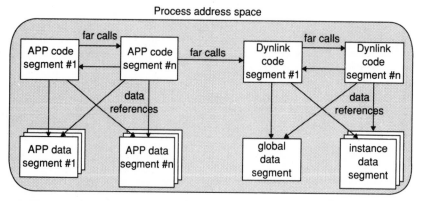

Figure 7-7.
Dynamic link routines as subsystems.

---

7. In the most general sense of the word. I don't mean a "presentation manager resource object."

7.7.1 **Special Subsystem Support**

Two OS/2 features are particularly valuable to subsystems: global data segments (which we've already discussed) and special client initialization and termination support. Clearly, if a subsystem is going to manage a resource, keeping track of its clients in a global data segment, it needs to know when new clients arrive and when old clients terminate. The simple dynlink subroutine model doesn't provide this information in a reliable fashion. A subsystem undoubtedly has initialize and terminate entry points, but client programs may terminate without having called a subsystem's terminate entry point. Such a failure may be an error on the part of the client, but the system architecture decrees that errors should be localized; it's not acceptable for a bug in a client process to be able to hang up a subsystem and thus all its clients as well.

The two forms of subsystem initialization are global and instance. A subsystem can specify either service but not both. If global initialization is specified, the initialization entry point is called only once per activation of the subsystem. When the subsystem dynlink package is first referenced, OS/2 allocates the subsystem's global data segment(s), taking their initial values from the .DLL file. OS/2 then calls the subsystem's global initialization entry point so that the module can do its one-time initialization. The thread that is used to call the initialization entry point belongs to that first client process,[8] so the first client's instance data segments are also set up and may be used by the global initialization process. This means that although the dynlink subsystem is free to open files, read and write their contents, and close them again, it may not open a handle to a file, store the handle number in a global data segment, and expect to use that handle in the future.

Remember, subsystems don't own resources; processes own resources. When a dynlink package opens a file, that file is open only for that one client process. That handle has meaning only when that particular client is calling the subsystem code. If a dynlink package were to store process A's handle number in a global data segment and then attempt to do a read from that handle when running as process B,

---

8. The client process doesn't explicitly call a dynlink package's initialization entry points. OS/2 uses its godlike powers to borrow a thread for the purpose. The mechanism is invisible to the client program. It goes without saying, we hope, that it would be extremely rude to the client process, not to say damaging, were the dynlink package to refuse to return that initialization thread or if it were to damage it in some way, such as lowering its priority or calling **DosExit** with it!

at best the read would fail with ''invalid handle''; at worst some unrelated file of B's would be molested. And, of course, when client process A eventually terminates, the handle becomes invalid for all clients.

The second form of initialization is instance initialization. The instance initialization entry point is called in the same way as the global initialization entry point except that it is called for every new client when that client first attaches to the dynlink package. Any instance data segments that exist will already be allocated and will have been given their initial values from the .DLL file. The initialization entry point for a loadtime dynlink is called before the client's code begins executing. The initialization entry point for a runtime dynlink is called when the client calls the **DosLoadModule** function. A dynlink package may not specify both global and instance initialization; if it desires both, it should specify instance initialization and use a counter in one of its global data segments to detect the first instance initialization.

Even more important than initialization control is termination control. In its global data area, a subsystem may have records, buffers, or semaphores on behalf of a client process. It may have queued-up requests from that client that it needs to purge when the client terminates. The dynlink package need not release instance data segments; because these belong to the client process, they are destroyed when the client terminates. The global data segments themselves are released if this is the dynlink module's last client, so the module may want to take this last chance to update a log file, release a system semaphore, and so on.

Because a dynlink routine runs as the calling client process, it could use **DosSetSigHandler** to intercept the termination signal. This should never be done, however, because the termination signal is not activated for all causes of process termination. For example, if the process calls **DosExit,** the termination signal is not sent. Furthermore, there can be only one handler per signal type per process. Because client processes don't and shouldn't know what goes on inside a dynlink routine, the client process and a dynlink routine may conflict in the use of the signal. Such a conflict may also occur between two dynlink packages.

Using **DosExitList** service prevents such a collision. **DosExitList** allows a process to specify one or more subroutine addresses that will be called when the process terminates. Addresses can be added to and removed from the list. **DosExitList** is ideally suited for termination control. There can be many such addresses, and the addresses are called under all termination conditions. Both the client process and the subsystem dynlinks that it calls can have their own termination routine or routines. **DosExitList** is discussed in more detail in 16.2 Data Integrity.

7.8   Dynamic Links As Interfaces to Other Processes

Earlier, I mentioned that dynlink subsystems have difficulty dealing with resources—other than global memory—because resource ownership and access are on a per-process basis. Life as a dynlink subsystem can be schizophrenic. Which files are open, which semaphores are owned and so on depends on which client is running your code at the moment. Global memory is different; it's the one resource that all clients own jointly. The memory remains as long as the client count doesn't go to zero.

One way to deal with resource issues is for a dynlink package to act as a front end for a server process. During module initialization, the dynlink module can check a system semaphore to see whether the server process is already running and, if not, start it up. It needs to do this with the "detach" form of **DosExecPgm** so that the server process doesn't appear to the system as a child of the subsystem's first client. Such a mistake could mean that the client's parent thinks that the command subtree it founded by running the client never terminates because the server process appears to be part of the command subtree (see Figure 7-8 on the following page).

When the server process is running, the dynlink subsystem can forward some or all requests to it by one of the many IPC facilities. For example, a database subsystem might want to use a dedicated server process to hold open the database file and do reads and writes to it. It might keep buffers and ISAM directories in a shared memory segment to which the dynlink subsystem requests access for each of its clients; then requests that can be satisfied by data from these buffers won't require the IPC to the server process.

The only function of some dynlink packages is to act as a procedural interface to another process. For example, a spreadsheet program might provide an interface through which other applications can retrieve data

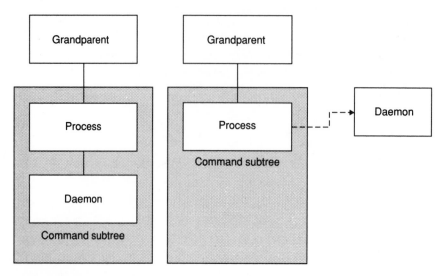

Figure 7-8.
Dynlink daemon initiation.

values from a spreadsheet. The best way to do this is for the spreadsheet package to contain a dynamic link library that provides clients a procedural interface to the spreadsheet process. The library routine itself will invoke a noninteractive copy (perhaps a special subset .EXE) of the spreadsheet to recover the information, passing it back to the client via IPC. Alternatively, the retrieval code that understands the spreadsheet data formats could be in the dynlink package itself because that package ships with the spreadsheet and will be upgraded when the spreadsheet is. In this case, the spreadsheet itself could use the package instead of duplicating the functionality in its own .EXE file. In any case, the implementation details are hidden from the client process; the client process simply makes a procedure call that returns the desired data.

Viewed from the highest level, this arrangement is simple: A client process uses IPC to get service from a server process via a subroutine library. From the programmer's point of view, though, the entire mechanism is encapsulated in the dynlink subsystem's interface. A future upgrade to the dynlink package may use an improved server process and different forms of IPC to talk to it but retain full binary compatibility with the existing client base. Figure 7-9 illustrates a

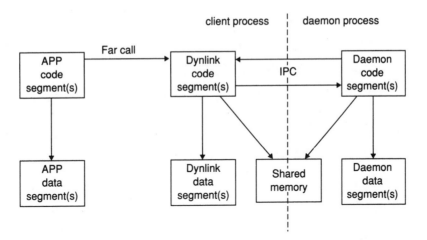

Figure 7-9.
Dynamic link routines as daemon interfaces.

dynlink package being used as an interface to a daemon process. The figure shows the dynlink package interfacing with the daemon process by means of a shared memory segment and some other form of IPC, perhaps a named pipe.

7.9 Dynamic Links As Interfaces to the Kernel

We've seen how dynlink libraries can serve as simple subroutine libraries, how they can serve as subsystems, and how they can serve as interfaces to other processes. OS/2 has one more trick up its sleeve: Dynlink libraries can also serve as interfaces to OS/2 itself.

Some OS/2 calls are actually implemented as simple library routines. For example, **DosErrClass** is implemented in OS/2 version 1.0 as a simple library routine. It takes an error code and locates, in a table, an explanatory text string, an error classification, and a recommended action. Services such as these were traditionally part of the kernel of operating systems, not because they needed to use privileged instructions, but because their error tables needed to be changed each time an upgrade to the operating system was released. If the service has been provided as a statically linked subroutine, older applications running on newer releases would receive new error codes that would not be in the library code's tables.

Although OS/2 implements **DosErrClass** as a library routine, it's a dynlink library routine, and the .DLL file is bundled with the operating system itself. Any later release of the system will contain an upgraded version of the **DosErrClass** routine, one that knows about new error codes. Consequently, the dynlink facility provides OS/2 with a great deal of flexibility in packaging its functionality.

Some functions, such as "open file" or "allocate memory," can't be implemented as ordinary subroutines. They need access to key internal data structures, and these structures are of course protected so that they can't be changed by unprivileged code. To get these services, the processor must make a system call, entering the kernel code in a very controlled fashion and there running with sufficient privilege to do its work. This privilege transition is via a *call gate*—a feature of the 80286/80386 hardware. A program calls a call gate exactly as it performs an ordinary far call; special flags in the GDT and LDT tell the processor that this is a call gate rather than a regular call.

In OS/2, system calls are indistinguishable from ordinary dynlink calls. All OS/2 system calls are defined in a dynlink module called **DosCalls.** When OS/2 fixes up dynlink references to this module, it consults a special table, built into OS/2, of *resident functions*. If the function is not listed in this table, then an ordinary dynlink is set up. If the function is in the table, OS/2 sets up a call gate call in place of the ordinary dynlink call. The transparency between library and call gate functions explains why passing an invalid address to an OS/2 system call causes the calling process to GP fault. Because the OS/2 kernel code controls and manages the GP fault mechanism, OS/2 calls that are call gates could easily return an error code if an invalid address causes a GP fault. If this were done, however, the behavior of OS/2 calls would differ depending on their implementation: Dynlink entry points would GP fault for invalid addresses;[9] call gate entries would return an error code. OS/2 prevents this dichotomy and preserves its freedom to, in future releases, move function between dynlink and call gate entries by providing a uniform reaction to invalid addresses. Because non-call-gate dynlink routines must generate GP faults, call gate routines produce them as well.

---

9. The LAR and LSL instructions are not sufficient to prevent this because another thread in that process may free a segment after the LAR but before the reference.

7.10   **The Architectural Role of Dynamic Links**

Dynamic links play three major roles in OS/2: They provide the system interface; they provide a high-bandwidth device interface; and they support open architecture nonkernel service packages.

The role of dynamic links as the system interface is clear. They provide a uniform, high-efficiency interface to the system kernel as well as a variety of nonkernel services. The interface is directly compatible with high-level languages, and it takes advantage of special speed-enhancing features of the 80286 and 80386 microprocessors.[10] It provides a wide and convenient name space, and it allows the distribution of function between library code and kernel code. Finally, it provides an essentially unlimited expansion capability.

But dynamic links do much more than act as system calls. You'll recall that in the opening chapters I expressed a need for a device interface that was as device independent as device drivers but without their attendant overhead. Dynamic links provide this interface because they allow applications to make a high-speed call to a subroutine package that can directly manipulate the device (see Chapter 18, I/O Privilege Mechanism and Debugging/Ptrace). The call itself is fast, and the package can specify an arbitrarily wide set of parameters. No privilege or ring transition is needed, and the dynlink package can directly access its client's data areas. Finally, the dynlink package can use subsystem support features to virtualize the device or to referee its use among multiple clients. Device independence is provided because a new version of the dynlink interface can be installed whenever new hardware is installed. VIO and the presentation manager are examples of this kind of dynlink use. Dynlink packages have an important drawback when they are being used as device driver replacements: They cannot receive hardware interrupts. Some devices, such as video displays, do not generate interrupts. Interrupt-driven devices, though, require a true device driver. That driver can contain all of the device interface function, or the work can be split between a device driver and a dynlink package that acts as a front end for that device driver. See Chapters 17 and 18 for further discussion of this.

Dynlink routines can also act as nonkernel service packages—as an *open system* architecture for software. Most operating systems are like

---

10. Specifically, automatic argument passing on calls to the ring 0 kernel code.

the early versions of the Apple Macintosh computer: They are *closed systems*; only their creators can add features to them. Because of OS/2's open system architecture, third parties and end users can add system services simply by plugging in dynlink modules, just as hardware cards plug into an open hardware system. The analogy extends further: Some hardware cards become so popular that their interface defines a standard. Examples are the Hayes modem and the Hercules Graphics Card. Third-party dynlink packages will, over time, establish similar standards. Vendors will offer, for example, improved database dynlink routines that are advertised as plug compatible with the standard database dynlink interface, but better, cheaper, and faster.

Dynlinks allow third parties to add interfaces to OS/2; they also allow OS/2's developers to add future interfaces. The dynlink interface model allows additional functionality to be implemented as subroutines or processes or even to be distributed across a network environment.

7.11 Implementation Details

Although dynlink routines often act very much like traditional static subroutines, a programmer must be aware of some special considerations involved. This section discusses some issues that must be dealt with to produce a good dynlink package.

7.11.1 Dynlink Data Security

We have discussed how a dynlink package runs as a subroutine of the client process and that the client process has access to the dynlink package's instance and global data segments.[11] This use of the dynlink interface is efficient and thus advantageous, but it's also disadvantageous because aberrant client processes can damage the dynlink package's global data segments.

In most circumstances, accidental damage to a dynlink package's data segments is rare. Unless the dynlink package returns pointers into its data segments to the client process, the client doesn't "know" the dynlink package's data segment selectors. The only way such a process could access the dynlink's segments would be to accidentally create a random selector value that matched one belonging to a dynlink

---

11. A client process has memory access (addressability) to all of the package's global segments but only to those instance data segments associated with that process.

package. Because the majority of selector values are illegal, a process would have to be very "lucky" to generate a valid dynlink package data selector before it generated an unused or code segment selector.[12] Naturally, dynlink packages shouldn't use global data segments to hold sensitive data because a malicious application can figure out the proper selector values.

The measures a programmer takes to deal with the security issue depend on the nature and sensitivity of the dynlink package. Dynlink packages that don't have global data segments are at no risk; an aberrant program can damage its instance data segments and thereby fail to run correctly, but that's the expected outcome of a program bug. A dynlink package with global data segments can minimize the risk by never giving its callers pointers into its (the dynlink package's) global data segment. If the amount of global data is small and merely detecting damage is sufficient, the global data segments could be checksummed.

Finally, if accidental damage would be grave, a dynlink package can work in conjunction with a special dedicated process, as described above. The dedicated process can keep the sensitive data and provide it on a per-client basis to the dynlink package in response to an IPC request. Because the dedicated process *is* a separate process, its segments are fully protected from the client process as well as from all others.

7.11.2   Dynlink Life, Death, and Sharing

Throughout this discussion, I have referred to *sharing* pure segments. The ability to share pure segments is an optimization that OS/2 makes for all memory segments whether they are dynlink segments or an application's .EXE file segments. A *pure* segment is one that is never modified during its lifetime. All code segments (except for those created by **DosCreateCSAlias**) are pure; read-only data segments are also pure. When OS/2 notices that it's going to load two copies of the same pure segment, it performs a behind-the-scenes optimization and gives the second client access to the earlier copy of the segment instead of wasting memory with a duplicate version.

For example, if two copies of a program are run, all code segments are pure; at most, only one copy of each code segment will be in

---

12. Because if a process generates and writes with a selector that is invalid or points to a code segment, the process will be terminated immediately with a GP fault.

memory. OS/2 flags these segments as "internally shared" and doesn't release them until the last user has finished with the segment. This is not the same as "shared memory" as it is generally defined in OS/2. Because pure segments can only be read, never written, no process can tell that pure segments are being shared or be affected by that sharing. Although threads from two or more processes may execute the same shared code segment at the same time, this is not the same as a multithreaded process. Each copy of a program has its own data areas, its own stack, its own file handles, and so on. They are totally independent of one another even if OS/2 is quietly sharing their pure code segments among them. Unlike multiple threads within a single process, threads from different processes cannot affect one another; the programmer can safely ignore their possible existence in shared code segments.

Because the pure segments of a dynlink package are shared, the second and subsequent clients of a dynlink package can load much more quickly (because these pure segments don't have to be loaded from the .DLL disk file). This doesn't mean that OS/2 doesn't have to "hit the disk" at all: Many dynlink packages use instance data segments, and OS/2 loads a fresh copy of the initial values for these segments from the .DLL file.

A dynlink package's second client is its second *simultaneous* client. Under OS/2, only processes have a life of their own. Objects such as dynlink packages and shared memory segments exist only as possessions of processes. When the last client process of such an object dies or otherwise releases the object, OS/2 destroys it and frees up the memory. For example, when the first client (since bootup) of a dynlink package references it, OS/2 loads the package's code and data segments. Then OS/2 calls the package's initialization routine—if the package has one. OS/2 records in an internal data structure that this dynlink package has one client. If additional clients come along while the first is still using the dynlink package, OS/2 increments the package's user count appropriately. Each time a client disconnects or dies, the user count is decremented. As long as the user count remains nonzero, the package remains in existence, each client sharing the original global data segments. When the client count goes to zero, OS/2 discards the dynlink package's code and global data segments and in effect forgets all about the package. When another client comes along, OS/2 reloads the package and reloads its global data segment as if the earlier use had never occurred.

This mechanism affects a dynlink package only in the management of the package's global data segment. The package's code segments are pure, so it doesn't matter if they are reloaded from the .DLL file. The instance data segments are always reinitialized for each new client, but the data in a package's global data segment remains in existence only as long as the package has at least one client process. When the last client releases the package, the global data segment is discarded. If this is a problem for a dynlink package, an associated "dummy" process (which the dynlink package could start during its loadtime initialization) can reference the dynlink package. As long as this process stays alive, the dynlink package and its global data segments stay alive.[13]

An alternative is for the dynlink package to keep track of the count of its clients and save the contents of its global data segments to a disk file when the last client terminates, but this is tricky. Because a process may fail to call a dynlink package's "I'm finished" entry point (presumably part of the dynlink package's interface) before it terminates, the dynlink package must get control to write its segment via **DosExitList.** If the client process is connected to the dynlink package via **DosLoadModule** (that is, via runtime dynamic linking), it cannot disconnect from the package via **DosFreeModule** as long as a **DosExitList** address points into the dynlink package. An attempt to do so returns an error code. Typically, one would expect the application to ignore this error code; but because the dynlink package is still attached to the client process, it will receive **DosExitList** service when the client eventually terminates. It's important that dynlink packages which maintain client state information and therefore need **DosExitList** also offer an "I'm finished" function. When a client calls this function, the package should close it out and then remove its processing address from **DosExitList** so that **DosFreeModule** can take effect if the client wishes.

Note that OS/2's habit of sharing in-use dynlink libraries has implications for the replacement of dynlink packages. Specifically, OS/2 holds the dynlink .DLL file open for as long as that library has any

---

13. If you use this technique, be sure to use the detached form of **DosExec**; see the warning in 7.8 Dynamic Links As Interfaces to Other Processes.

clients. To replace a dynlink library with an upgraded version, you must first ensure that all clients of the old package have been terminated.

While we're on the subject, I'll point out that dynlink segments, like .EXE file segments, can be marked (by the linker) as "preload" or "load on demand." When a dynlink module or a .EXE file is loaded, OS/2 immediately loads all segments marked "preload" but usually[14] does not load any segments marked "load on demand." These segments are loaded only when (and if) they are referenced. This mechanism speeds process and library loading and reduces swapping by leaving infrequently used segments out of memory until they are needed. Once a segment is loaded, its "preload" or "load on demand" status has no further bearing; the segment will be swapped or discarded without consideration for these bits.

Finally, special OS/2 code keeps track of dynamic link "circular references." Because dynlink packages can call other dynlink packages, package A can call package B, and package B can call package A. Even if the client process C terminates, packages A and B might appear to be in use by each other, and they would both stay in memory. OS/2 keeps a graph of dynlink clients, both processes and other dynlink packages. When a process can no longer reach a dynlink package over this graph—in other words, when a package doesn't have a process for a client and when none of its client packages have processes for clients and so on—the dynlink package is released. Figure 7-10 illustrates a dynamic link circular reference. PA and PB are two processes, and LA through LG are dynlink library routines.

7.11.3 Dynlink Side Effects

A well-written dynlink library needs to adhere to the OS/2 religious tenet of zero side effects. A dynlink library should export to the client process only its functional interface and not accidentally export side effects that may interfere with the consistent execution of the client.

Some possible side effects are obvious: A dynlink routine shouldn't close any file handles that it didn't itself open. The same applies to other system resources that the client process may be accessing, and it applies in the inverse, as well: A dynlink routine that obtains resources

---

14. Segments that are loaded from removable media will be fully loaded, regardless of the "load on demand" bit.

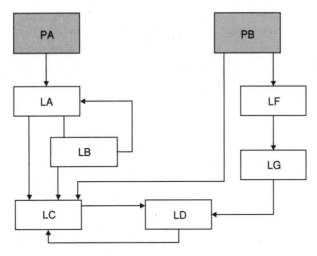

Figure 7-10.
Dynamic link circular references.

for itself, in the guise of the client process, should do so in a way that doesn't affect the client code. For example, consuming many of the available file handles would be a side effect because the client would then unexpectedly be short of available file handles. A dynlink package with a healthy file handle appetite should be sure to call OS/2 to raise the maximum number of file handles so that the client process isn't constrained. Finally, the amount of available stack space is a resource that a dynlink package must not exhaust. A dynlink routine should try to minimize its stack needs, and an upgrade to an existing dynlink package must not consume much more stack space than did the earlier version, lest the upgrade cause existing clients to fail in the field.

Dynlink routines can also cause side effects by issuing some kinds of system calls. Because a dynlink routine runs as a subroutine of the client process, it must be sure that calls that it makes to OS/2 on behalf of the client process don't affect the client application. For example, each signal event can have only one handler address; if a dynlink routine establishes a signal handler, then that signal handler preempts any handler set up by the client application. Likewise, if a dynlink routine changes the priority of the thread with which it was called, the dynlink routine must be sure to restore that priority before it returns to its caller. Several other system functions such as **DosError** and **DosSetVerify** also cause side effects that can affect the client process.

Enumerating all forms of side effects is not possible; it's up to the programmer to take the care needed to ensure that a dynlink module is properly house-trained. A dynlink module should avoid the side effects mentioned as well as similar ones, and, most important, it should behave consistently so that if a client application passes its acceptance tests in the lab it won't mysteriously fail in the field. This applies doubly to upgrades for existing dynlink routines. Upgrades must be written so that if a client application works with the earlier release of the dynlink package it will work with the new release; obviously the author of the application will not have an opportunity to retest existing copies of the application against the new release of the dynlink module.

7.12 Dynlink Names

Each dynlink entry point has three names associated with it: an external name, a module name, and an entry point name. The name the client program calls as an external reference is the *external name*. The programmer works with this name, and its syntax and form must be compatible with the assembler or compiler being used. The name should be simple and explanatory yet unlikely to collide with another external name in the client code or in another library. A name such as READ or RESET is a poor choice because of the collision possibilities; a name such as XR23P11 is obviously hard to work with.

The linker replaces the external name with a *module name* and an *entry point name*, which are embedded in the resultant .EXE file. OS/2 uses the module name to locate the dynlink .DLL file; the code for module **modname** is in file MODNAME.DLL. The entry point name specifies the entry point in the module; the entry point name need not be the same as the external name. For modules with a lot of entry points, the client .EXE file size can be minimized and the loading speed maximized by using entry *ordinals* in place of entry point names. See the OS/2 technical reference literature for details.

Runtime dynamic links are established by using the module name and the entry point name; the external name is not used.

8

File System Name Space

File system name space is a fancy term for how names of objects are defined in OS/2. The words *file system* are a hint that OS/2 uses one naming scheme both for files and for everything else with a name in ASCII format—system semaphores, named shared memory, and so forth. First, we'll discuss the syntax of names and how to manipulate them; we'll wind up with a discussion of how and why we use one naming scheme for all named objects.

8.1 Filenames

Before we discuss OS/2 filenames, let's review the format of filenames under MS-DOS. In MS-DOS, filenames are required to fit the 8.3 format: a name field (which can contain a maximum of 8 characters) and an extension field (which can contain a maximum of 3 characters).[1] The period character (.) between the name and the extension is not part of the filename; it's a separator character. The filename can consist of uppercase characters only. If a user or an application creates a filename that contains lowercase characters or a mixture of uppercase and

---

1. As an aside, these sizes date from a tradition established many years ago by Digital Equipment Corporation. Digital's very early computers used a technique called RAD50 to store 3 uppercase letters in one 16-bit word, so their file systems allowed a 6-character filename and a 3-character extension. CP/M later picked up this filename structure. CP/M didn't use RAD50, so, in a moment of generosity, it allowed 8-character filenames; but the 3-character extension was kept.

lowercase, MS-DOS converts the filename to all uppercase. If an application presents a filename whose name or extension field exceeds the allotted length, MS-DOS silently truncates the name to the 8.3 format before using it. MS-DOS establishes and enforces these rules and maintains the file system structure on the disks. The file system that MS-DOS version 3.x supports is called the FAT (File Allocation Table) file system. The following are typical MS-DOS and OS/2 filenames:

\FOOTBALL\SRC\KERNEL\SCHED.ASM

Football is a development project, so this name describes the source for the kernel scheduler for the football project.

\MEMOS\286\MODESWIT.DOC

is a memo discussing 80286 mode switching.

\\HAGAR\SCRATCH\GORDONL\FOR_MARK

is a file in my scratch directory on the network server HAGAR, placed there for use by Mark.

The OS/2 architecture views file systems quite differently. As microcomputers become more powerful and are used in more and more ways, file system characteristics will be needed that might not be met by a built-in OS/2 file system. Exotic peripherals, such as WORM[2] drives, definitely require special file systems to meet their special characteristics. For this reason, the file system is not built into OS/2 but is a closely allied component—an installable file system (IFS). An IFS is similar to a device driver; it's a body of code that OS/2 loads at boot time. The code talks to OS/2 via a standard interface and provides the software to manage a file system on a storage device, including the ability to create and maintain directories, to allocate disk space, and so on.

If you are familiar with OS/2 version 1.0, this information may be surprising because you have seen no mention of an IFS in the reference manuals. That's because the implementation hasn't yet caught up with the architecture. We designed OS/2, from the beginning, to support installable file systems, one of which would of course be the familiar FAT file system. We designed the file system calls, such as **DosOpen**

---

2. Write Once, Read Many disks. These are generally laser disks of very high capacity, but once a track is written, it cannot be erased. These disks can appear to be erasable by writing new copies of files and directories each time a change is made, abandoning the old ones.

and **DosClose,** with this in mind. Although scheduling pressures forced us to ship OS/2 version 1.0 with only the FAT file system—still built in—a future release will include the full IFS package. Although at this writing the IFS release of OS/2 has not been announced, this information is included here so that you can understand the basis for the system name architecture. Also, this information will help you write programs that work well under the new releases of OS/2 that contain the IFS.

Because the IFS will interpret filenames and pathnames and because installable file systems can vary considerably, OS/2[3] doesn't contain much specific information about the format and meaning of filenames and pathnames. In general, the form and meaning of filenames and pathnames are private matters between the user and the IFS; both the application and OS/2 are simply go-betweens. Neither should attempt to parse or understand filenames and pathnames. Applications shouldn't parse names because some IFSs will support names in formats other than the 8.3 format. Applications shouldn't even assume a specific length for a filename or a pathname. All OS/2 filename and pathname interfaces, such as **DosOpen, DosFindNext,** and so on, are designed to take name strings of arbitrary length. Applications should use name buffers of at least 256 characters to ensure that a long name is not truncated.

8.2 Network Access

Two hundred and fifty-six characters may seem a bit extreme for the length of a filename, and perhaps it is. But OS/2 filenames are often pathnames, and pathnames can be quite lengthy. To provide transparent access to files on a LAN (local area network), OS/2 makes the network part of the file system name space. In other words, a file's pathname can specify a machine name as well as a directory path. An application can issue an open to a name string such as \WORK\BOOK.DAT or \\VOGON\TEMP\RECALC.ASM. The first name specifies the file BOOK.DAT in the directory WORK on the current drive of the local machine; the second name specifies the file RECALC.ASM in the directory TEMP on the machine VOGON.[4] Future releases of the

---

3. Excluding the IFS part.
4. Network naming is a bit more complex than this; the name TEMP on the machine VOGON actually refers to an offered network resource and might appear in any actual disk directory.

Microsoft LAN Manager will make further use of the file system name space, so filenames, especially program-generated filenames, can easily become very long.

8.3 Name Generation and Compatibility

Earlier, I said that applications should pass on filenames entered by the user, ignoring their form. This is, of course, a bit unrealistic. Programs often need to generate filenames—to hold scratch files, to hold derivative filenames (for example, FOO.OBJ derived from FOO.ASM), and so forth. How can an application generate or permute such filenames and yet ensure compatibility with all installable file systems? The answer is, of course: Use the least common denominator approach. In other words, you can safely assume that a new IFS must accept the FAT file system's names (the 8.3 format) because otherwise it would be incompatible with too many programs. So if an application sticks to the 8.3 rules when it creates names, it can be sure that it is compatible with future file systems. Unlike MS-DOS, OS/2[5] will not truncate name or extension fields that are too long; instead, an error will be returned. The case of a filename will continue to be insignificant. Some operating systems, such as UNIX, are case sensitive; for example, in UNIX the names "foo" and "Foo" refer to different files. This works fine for a system used primarily by programmers, who know that a lowercase f is ASCII 66_{16} and that an uppercase F is ASCII 46_{16}. Nonprogrammers, on the other hand, tend to see f and F as the same character. Because most OS/2 users are nonprogrammers, OS/2 installable file systems will continue to be case insensitive.

I said that it was safe if program-generated names adhered to the 8.3 rule. Program-permuted names are likewise safe if they only substitute alphanumeric characters for other alphanumeric characters, for example, FOO.OBJ for FOO.ASM. Lengthening filenames is also safe (for example, changing FOO.C to FOO.OBJ) if your program checks for "invalid name" error codes for the new name and has some way to deal with that possibility. In any case, write your program so that it isn't confused by enhanced pathnames; in the above substitution cases, the algorithm should work from the end of the path string and ignore what comes before.

---

5. More properly, the FAT installable file system installed in OS/2.

8.4 **Permissions**

Future releases of OS/2 will use the file system name space for more than locating a file; it will also contain the permissions for the file. A uniform mechanism will associate an access list with every entry in the file system name space. This list will prevent unauthorized access — accidental or deliberate — to the named file.

8.5 **Other Objects in the File System Name Space**

As we've seen, the file system name space is a valuable device in several aspects. First, it allows the generation of a variety of names. You can group names together (by putting them in the same directory), and you can generate entire families of unique names (by creating a new subdirectory). Second, the name space can encompass all files and devices on the local machine as well as files and devices on remote machines. Finally, file system names will eventually support a flexible access and protection mechanism.

Thus, it comes as no surprise that when the designers of OS/2 needed a naming mechanism to deal with nonfile objects, such as shared memory, system semaphores, and named pipes, we chose to use the file system name space. One small disadvantage to this decision is that a shared memory object cannot have a name identical to that of a system semaphore, a named pipe, or a disk file. This drawback is trivial, however, compared with the benefits of sharing the file system name space. And, of course, you can use separate subdirectory names for each type of object, thus preventing name collision.

Does this mean that system semaphores, shared memory, and pipes have actual file system entries on a disk somewhere? Not yet. The FAT file system does not support special object names in its directories. Although changing it to do so would be easy, the file system would no longer be downward compatible with MS-DOS. (MS-DOS 3.x could not read such disks written under OS/2.) Because only the FAT file system is available with OS/2 version 1.0, that release keeps special RAM-resident pseudo directories to hold the special object names. These names must start with \SEM\, \SHAREMEM\, \QUEUES\, and \DEV\ to minimize the chance of name collision with a real file when they do become special pseudo files in a future release of OS/2.

Although all file system name space features—networking and (in the future) permissions—apply to all file system name space objects from an architectural standpoint, not all permutations may be supported. Specifically, supporting named shared memory across the network is very costly[6] and won't be implemented.

---

6. The entire shared memory segment must be transferred across the network each time any byte within it is changed. Some clever optimizations can reduce this cost, but none works well enough to be feasible.

9

Memory Management

A primary function of any multitasking operating system is to allocate system resources to each process according to its need. The scheduler allocates CPU time among processes (actually, among threads); the *memory manager* allocates both physical memory and virtual memory.

9.1 Protection Model

Although MS-DOS provided a simple form of memory management, OS/2 provides memory protection. Under MS-DOS 3.x, for example, a program should ask the operating system to allocate a memory area before the program uses it. Under OS/2, a program *must* ask the operating system to allocate a memory area before the program uses it. As we discussed earlier, the 80286 microprocessor contains special memory protection hardware. Each memory reference that a program makes explicitly or implicitly references a segment selector. The segment selector, in turn, references an entry in the GDT or the LDT, depending on the form of the selector. Before any program, including OS/2 itself, can reference a memory location, that memory location must be described in an LDT or a GDT entry, and the selector for that entry must be loaded into one of the four segment registers.

This hardware design places some restrictions on how programs can use addresses.

- A program cannot address memory not set up for it in the LDT or GDT. The only way to address memory is via the LDT and GDT.

- Each segment descriptor in the LDT and GDT contains the physical address and the length of that segment. A program cannot reference an offset into a segment beyond that segment's length.

- A program can't put garbage (arbitrary values) into a segment register. Each time a segment register is loaded, the hardware examines the corresponding LDT and GDT to see if the entry is valid. If a program puts an arbitrary value—for example, the lower half of a floating point number—into a segment register, the arbitrary value will probably point to an invalid LDT or GDT entry, causing a GP fault.

- A program can't execute instructions from within a data segment. Attempting to load a data segment selector into the CS register (usually via a far call or a far jump) causes a GP fault.

- A program can't write into a code segment. Attempting to do so causes a GP fault.

- A program can't perform *segment arithmetic*. Segment arithmetic refers to activities made possible by the addressing mechanism of the 8086 and 8088 microprocessors. Although they are described as having a segment architecture, they are actually linear address space machines that use offset registers—the so-called segment registers. An 8086 can address 1 MB of memory, which requires a 20-bit address. The processor creates this address by multiplying the 16-bit segment value by 16 and adding it to the 16-bit offset value. The result is an address between 0 and 1,048,575 (that is, 1 MB).[1] The reason these are not true segments is that they don't have any associated length and their names (that is, their selectors) aren't names at all but physical addresses divided by 16. These segment values are actually scaled offsets. An address that has a segment value of 100 and an offset value of 100 (shown as $100_{10}{:}100_{10}$), and the address ($99_{10}{:}116_{10}$) both refer to the same memory location.

---

1. Actually, it's possible to produce addresses beyond 1 MB (2^{20}) by this method if a large enough segment and offset value are chosen. The 8086 ignores the carry into the nonexistent 21st address bit, effectively wrapping around such large addresses into the first 65 KB-16 bytes of physical memory.

Many real mode programs take advantage of this situation. Some programs that keep a great many pointers store them as 20-bit values, decomposing those values into the segment:offset form only when they need to de-reference the pointer. To ensure that certain objects have a specific offset value, other programs choose a matching segment value so that the resultant 20-bit address is correct. Neither technique works in OS/2 protect mode. Each segment selector describes its own segment, a segment with a length and an address that are independent of the numeric value of the segment selector. The memory described by segment N has nothing in common with the memory described by segment N+4 or by any other segment unless OS/2 explicitly sets it up that way.

The segmentation and protection hardware allows OS/2 to impose further restrictions on processes.

- Processes cannot edit or examine the contents of the LDT or the GDT. OS/2 simply declines to build an LDT or GDT selector that a process can use to access the contents of those tables. Certain LDT and GDT selectors describe the contents of those tables themselves, but OS/2 sets them up so that they can only be used by ring 0 (that is, privileged) code.

- Processes cannot hook interrupt vectors. MS-DOS version 3.x programs commonly hook interrupt vectors by replacing the address of the interrupt handler with an address from their own code. Thus, these programs can monitor or intercept system calls made via INT 21h, BIOS calls also made via interrupts, and hardware interrupts such as the keyboard and the system clock. OS/2 programs cannot do this. OS/2 declines to set up a segment selector that processes can use to address the interrupt vector table.

- Processes cannot call the ROM BIOS code because no selector addresses the ROM BIOS code. Even if such a selector were available, it would be of little use. The ROM BIOS is coded for real mode execution and performs segment arithmetic operations that are no longer legal. If OS/2 provided a ROM BIOS selector, calls to the ROM BIOS would usually generate GP faults.

■ Finally, processes cannot run in ring 0, that is, in privileged mode. Both OS/2 and the 80286 hardware are designed to prevent an application program from ever executing in ring 0. Code running in ring 0 can manipulate the LDT and GDT tables as well as other hardware protection features. If OS/2 allowed processes to run in ring 0, the system could never be stable or secure. OS/2 obtains its privileged (literally) state by being the first code loaded at boot time. The boot process takes place in ring 0 and grants ring 0 permission to OS/2 by transferring control to OS/2 while remaining in ring 0. OS/2 does not, naturally, extend this favor to the application programs it loads; it ensures that applications can only run in ring 3 user mode.[2]

9.2 Memory Management API

OS/2 provides an extensive memory management API. This book is not a reference manual, so I won't cover all the calls. Instead, I'll focus on areas that may not be completely self-explanatory.

9.2.1 Shared Memory

OS/2 supports two kinds of shared memory—named shared memory and giveaway shared memory. In both, the memory object shared is a segment. Only an entire segment can be shared; sharing part of a segment is not possible. Named shared memory is volatile because neither the name of the named shared memory nor the memory itself can exist on the FAT file system. When the number of processes using a shared memory segment goes to zero, the memory is released. Shared memory can't stay around in the absence of client processes; it must be reinitialized via **DosAllocShrSeg** after a period of nonuse.

Giveaway shared memory allows processes to share access to the same segment. Giveaway shared memory segments don't have names because processes can't ask to have access to them; a current user of the segment has to give access to the segment to a new client process. The term *giveaway* is a bit of a misnomer because the giving process retains access to the memory—the access is "given" but not especially "away." Giveaway shared memory is not as convenient as named shared memory. The owner[3] has to know the PID of the recipient and

---

2. Applications can also run in ring 2 (see 18.1 I/O Privilege Mechanism).
3. One of the owners. Anyone with access to a giveaway shared segment can give it away itself.

then communicate the recipient's segment selector (returned by **DosGiveSeg**) to that recipient process via some form of IPC.

Despite its limitations, giveaway shared memory has important virtues. It's a fast and efficient way for one process to transfer data to another; and because access is passed "hand to hand," the wrong process cannot accidentally or deliberately gain access to the segment. Most clients of giveaway shared memory don't retain access to the segment once they've passed it off; they typically call **DosFreeSeg** on their handle after they've called **DosGiveSeg.** For example, consider the design of a database dynlink subsystem that acts as a front end for a database serving process. As part of the dynlink initialization process, the package arranged for its client process to share a small named shared memory segment with the database process. It might be best to use a named pipe or named shared memory—created by the database process—to establish initial communication and then use this interface only to set up a private piece of giveaway shared memory for all further transactions between the client process (via the dynlink subsystem) and the database process. Doing it this way, rather than having one named shared segment hold service requests from all clients, provides greater security. Because each client has its own separate shared memory communications area, an amok client can't damage the communications of other clients.

When a client process asks the database process to read it a record, the database process must use a form of IPC to transfer the data to the client. Pipes are too slow for the volume of data that our example anticipates; shared memory is the best technique. If we were to use named shared memory, the database package would have to create a unique shared memory name for each record, allocate the memory, and then communicate the name to the client (actually, to the dynlink subsystem called by the client) so that it can request access. This process has some drawbacks:

- A new unique shared memory name must be created for each request. We could reuse a single shared memory segment, but this would force the client to copy the data out of the segment before it could make another request—too costly a process for an application that must handle a high volume of data.

■ Creating named shared memory segments is generally slower than creating giveaway shared memory segments, especially if a large number of named shared memory objects exist, as would be the case in this scenario. The client spends more time when it then requests access to the segment. Creating named shared memory segments is plenty fast enough when it's done once in a while, but in a high-frequency application such as our example, it could become a bottleneck.

Instead, the database process can create a giveaway shared memory segment, load the data into it, and then give it to the client process. The database process can easily learn the client's PID; the dynlink interface, which runs as the client process, can include it as part of the data request. Likewise, the database process can easily return the new client selector to the client. This process is fast and efficient and doesn't bog down the system by forcing it to deal with a great many name strings.

Note that you must specify, at the time of the **DosAllocSeg,** that the segment might be "given away." Doing so allows OS/2 to allocate the selector in the disjoint space, as we discussed earlier.

9.2.2   Huge Memory

The design of the 80286 microprocessor specifies the maximum size of a memory segment as 64 KB. For many programs, this number is far too small. For example, the internal representation of a large spreadsheet commonly takes up 256 KB or more. OS/2 can do nothing to set up a segment that is truly larger than 64 KB, but the OS/2 facility called *huge segments* provides a reasonable emulation of segments larger than 64 KB. The trick is that a huge segment of, for example, 200 KB is not a single segment but a group of four segments, three of which are 64 KB and a fourth of 8 KB. With minimal programming burden, OS/2 allows an application to treat the group of four segments as a single huge segment.

When a process calls **DosAllocHuge** to allocate a huge segment, OS/2 allocates several physical segments, the sum of whose size equals the size of the virtual huge segment. All component segments are 64 KB, except possibly the last one. Unlike an arbitrary collection of segment selectors, **DosAllocHuge** guarantees that the segment selectors it returns are spaced uniformly from each other. The selector of the

N+1th component segment is that of the Nth segment plus i, where i is a power of two. The value of i is constant for any given execution of OS/2, but it may vary between releases of OS/2 or as a result of internal configuration during bootup. In other words, a program must learn the factor i every time it executes; it must not hard code the value. There are three ways to learn this value. First, a program can call **DosGetHugeShift;** second, it can read this value from the global infoseg; and third, it can reference this value as the undefined absolute externals DOSHUGESHIFT ($\log_2(i)$) or DOSHUGEINCR (i). OS/2 will insert the proper value for these externals at loadtime. This last method is the most efficient and is recommended, but it is not compatible with the Family API mechanism. Family API programs should call **DosGetHugeShift.** Figure 9-1 illustrates the layout of a 200 KB

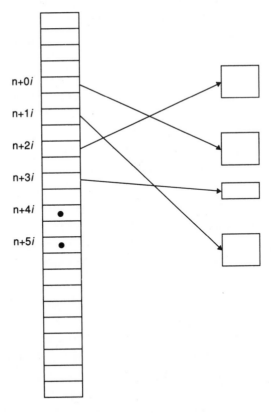

Figure 9-1.
Huge memory objects.

huge memory object. Selectors $n + 4i$ and $n + 5i$ are currently invalid but are reserved for future growth of the huge object.

Once an application has the first segment selector of the huge segment group, called the *base segment*, and the value $\log_2(i)$, computing the address of the Nth byte in the huge segment is easy. Take the high-order word of the value of N (that is, N/64 KB), shift it left by $\log_2(i)$ (that is, by the **DosGetHugeShift** value), and add the base segment selector returned by **DosAllocHuge.** The resultant value is the segment selector for the proper component segment; the low-order 16 bits of i are the offset into that segment. This computation is reasonably quick to perform since it involves only a shift and an addition.

Huge segments can be shrunk or grown via **DosReallocHuge.** If the huge segment is to be grown, creating more component physical segments may be necessary. Because the address generation rules dictate which selector this new segment may have, growing the huge segment may not be possible if that selector has already been allocated for another purpose. **DosAllocHuge** takes a maximum growth parameter; it uses this value to reserve sufficient selectors to allow the huge segment to grow that big. Applications should not provide an unrealistically large number for this argument because doing so will waste LDT selectors.

The astute reader will notice that the segment arithmetic of the 8086 environment is not dead; in a sense, it's been resurrected by the huge segment mechanism. Applications written for the 8086 frequently use this technique to address memory regions greater than 64 KB, using a shift value of 12. In other words, if you add 2^{12} to an 8086 segment register value, the segment register will point to an address $2^{12}*16$, or 64 KB, further in physical memory. The offset value between the component segment values was always 4096 because of the way the 8086 generated addresses. Although the steps involved in computing the segment value are the same in protect mode, what's actually happening is considerably different. When you do this computation in protect mode, the segment selector value has no inherent relationship to the other selectors that make up the huge object. The trick only works because OS/2 has arranged for equally spaced-out selectors to exist and for each to point to an area of physical memory of the appropriate size. Figure 9-2 illustrates the similarities and differences between huge model

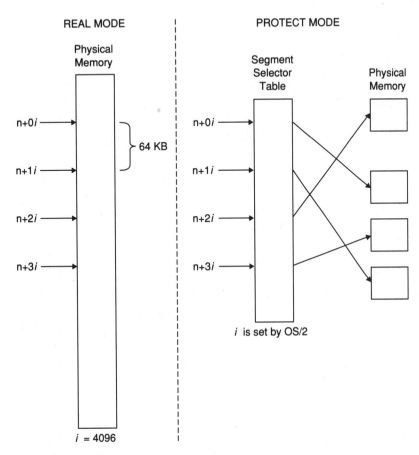

Figure 9-2.
Huge model addressing in real mode and in protect mode.

addressing in real and protect modes. The application code sequence is identical: A segment selector is computed by adding $N*i$ to the base selector. In real mode i is always 4096; in protect mode OS/2 provides i.

Although the similarity between 8086 segment arithmetic and OS/2 huge segments is only apparent, it does make it easy to write a program as a *dual mode* application. By using the shift value of 12 in real mode and using the OS/2 supplied value in protect mode, the same code functions correctly in either mode.

9.2.3   Executing from Data Segments

We saw that OS/2 provides the huge segment mechanism to get around the segment size restriction imposed by the hardware. OS/2 likewise circumvents another hardware restriction—the inability to execute code from data segments. Although the demand loading, the discarding, and the swapping of code segments make one use of running code from data segments—code overlays—obsolete, the capability is still needed. Some high-performance programs—the presentation manager, for example—compile "on the fly" special code to perform time-critical tasks, such as flipping bits in EGA display memory. The optimal sequence may differ depending on several factors, so a program may need to compile such code and execute it, gaining a significant increase in efficiency over some other approach. OS/2 supports this need by means of the **DosCreateCSAlias** call.

When **DosCreateCSAlias** is called with a selector for a data segment, it creates a totally different code segment selector (in the eyes of 80286 hardware) that by some strange coincidence points to exactly the same memory locations as does the data segment selector. As a result, code is not actually executing from a data segment but from a code segment. Because the code segment exactly overlaps that other data segment, the desired effect is achieved. The programmer need only be careful to use the data selector when writing the segment and to use the code selector when executing it.

9.2.4   Memory Suballocation

All memory objects discussed so far have been segments. OS/2 provides a facility called *memory suballocation* that allocates pieces of memory from within an application's segment. Pieces of memory can be suballocated from within a segment, grown, shrunk, and released. OS/2 uses a classic heap algorithm to do this. The **DosSubAlloc** call uses space made available from earlier **DosSubFree**s when possible, growing the segment as necessary when the free heap space is insufficient. We will call the pieces of memory returned by **DosSubAlloc** *heap objects*.

The memory suballocation package works within the domain of a process. The suballocation package doesn't allocate the memory from some "system pool" outside the process's address space, as does the segment allocator. The suballocation package doesn't even allocate segments; it manages only segments supplied by and owned by (or at least accessible to) the caller. This is a feature because memory protection is on a per-segment basis. If the suballocation package were to get its space from some system global segment, a process that overwrote its heap object could damage one belonging to another process. Figure 9-3 illustrates memory suballocation. It shows a segment j being suballocated. H is the suballocation header; the shaded areas are free space.

We said that the memory suballocator subdivides segments that are accessible to the client process. This means that you can use it to subdivide space in a shared memory segment. Such a technique can be handy when two or more processes are using a shared memory segment for intercommunication, but there is risk because an error in one process can easily corrupt the heap objects of another.

Earlier, in the discussion of dynamic link subsystems, we described facilities and techniques for writing a reliable subsystem. The OS/2 memory suballocation package is a good example of such a subsystem, so let's look at its workings more closely. The first try at the suballocation package produced a straightforward heap allocator, much like the one in a C or Pascal runtime library. It maintained a free chain of heap objects and allocated them at its client's request. If the closest-size free heap object was still bigger than the request, it was split into an allocated part and a free part. Freed heap objects were coalesced with any adjacent free objects. The suballocation package took a segment pointer and some other arguments and returned some values—an offset and the changed data in the segment itself where the heap headers were stored. If we stretch things a little and consider the changed state of the supplied data segment as a returned value, then the suballocation package at this stage is much like a function: It has no state of its own; it

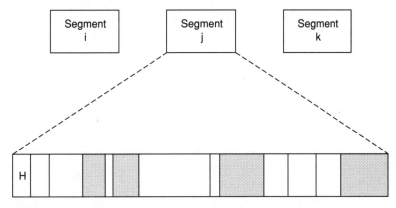

Figure 9-3.
Memory suballocation.

merely returns values computed only from the input arguments. This simple suballocation dynlink routine uses no global data segments and doesn't even need an instance data segment.

This simple implementation has an important drawback: More than one process can't safely use it to manage a shared memory segment; likewise, multiple threads within one process can't use it. The heap free list is a critical section; if multiple threads call the suballocator on the same segment, the heap free list can become corrupted. This problem necessitated upgrading the suballocation package to use a semaphore to protect the critical section. If we didn't want to support suballocation of shared memory and were only worried about multiple threads within a task, we could use RAM semaphores located in the managed segment itself to protect the critical section. The semaphore might be left set if the process died unexpectedly, but the managed segment isn't shared. It's going to be destroyed in any case, so we don't care.

But, even in this simple situation of managing only privately owned segments, we must concern ourselves with some special situations. One problem is signals: What if the suballocator is called with thread 1, and a signal (such as SIGINT, meaning that the user pressed Ctrl-C) comes in? Thread 1 is interrupted from the suballocation critical section to execute the signal handler. Often signal handlers return to the interrupted code, and all is well. But what if the signal handler does not return but jumps to the application's command loop? Or what if it does return, but before it does so calls the memory suballocator? In these two cases, we'd have a deadlock on the critical section. We can solve these problems by using the **DosHoldSignal** function. **DosHoldSignal** does for signals what the CLI instruction does for hardware interrupts: It holds them off for a short time. Actually, it holds them off forever unless the application releases them, but holding signals for more than a second or two is poor practice. If you precede the critical section's semaphore claim call with a signal hold and follow the critical section's semaphore release call with a signal release, you're protected from deadlocks caused by signal handling.

Note that unlike the CLI instruction, **DosHoldSignal** calls nest. OS/2 counts the number of **DosHoldSignal** ''hold'' calls made and holds signals off until an equal number of ''release'' calls are issued. This means that a routine can safely execute a hold/release pair without affecting the state of its calling code. If the caller had signals held at the time of the call, they will remain held. If signals were free at the time of the call, the callee's "release" call restores them to that state.

Whenever dynlink packages make any call that changes the state of the process or the thread, they must be sure to restore that state before they return to their caller. Functions that nest, such as **DosHoldSignal,** accomplish this automatically. For other functions, the dynlink package should explicitly discover and remember the previous state so that it can be restored.

Our problems aren't over though. A second problem is brought about by the **DosExitList** facility. If a client process's thread is in the suballocation package's critical section and the client terminates suddenly—it could be killed externally or have a GP fault—the process might not die immediately. If any **DosExitList** handlers are registered, they will be called. They might call the memory suballocator, and once again we face deadlock. We could solve this situation with the classic approach of making a bug into a feature: Document that the suballocator can't be called at exitlist time. This may make sense for some dynlink subsystems, but it's too restrictive for an important OS/2 facility. We've got to deal with this problem too.

The **DosHoldSignal** trick won't help us here. It would indeed prevent external kills, but it would not prevent GP faults and the like. We could say, "A program that GP faults is very sick, so all bets are off." This position is valid, except that if the program or one of its dynlink subsystems uses **DosExitList** and the **DosExitList** handler tries to allocate or release a heap object, the process will hang and never terminate correctly. This is unacceptable because the user would be forced to reboot to get rid of the moribund application. The answer is to use a system semaphore rather than a RAM semaphore to protect the memory segment. System semaphores are a bit slower than RAM semaphores, but they have some extra features. One is that they can be made exclusive; only the thread that owns the semaphore can release it. Coupled with this is an "owner death" notification facility that allows a process's **DosExitList** handler an opportunity to determine that one of its threads has orphaned a semaphore (see 16.2 Data Integrity for details). Our suballocation package can now protect itself by using exclusive system semaphores to protect its critical section and by registering a **DosExitList** handler to release that semaphore. The exitlist code can discover if a thread in its process has orphaned the semaphore and, if so, can release it. Of course, releasing the semaphore won't help if the heap headers are in an inconsistent state. You can write the suballocation package so that the heap is never in an inconsistent state, or you can write it to keep track of the modified state so that the exitlist handler can repair the heap structure.

In this later case, be sure the **DosExitList** handler you establish to clean up the heap is called first (see **DosExitList** documentation).

Finally, even if we decide that the client application won't be allowed to issue suballocation requests during its own exitlist processing, we want the memory suballocator to support allocating a shared segment among many different processes. Because of this, the actual OS/2 suballocation package makes use of **DosExitList** so that the suballocation structure and semaphores can be cleaned up should a client thread terminate while in the suballocation critical section.

The suballocation dynlink package does more than illustrate subsystem design; it also illustrates the value of a system architecture that uses dynlinks as a standard system interface, regardless of the type of code that provides the service. As you have seen, the memory suballocation package released with OS/2 version 1.0 doesn't reside in the kernel; it's effectively a subroutine package. OS/2 in an 80286 environment will undoubtedly preserve this approach in future releases, but a forthcoming 80386 version of OS/2 may not. The 80386 architecture supports paged virtual memory, so memory swapping (actually, paging) can take place on part of a segment. This future paging environment may precipitate some changes in the memory suballocator. Perhaps we'll want to rearrange the heap for better efficiency with paging, or perhaps the OS/2 kernel will want to become involved so that it can better anticipate paging demands. In any case, any future release of OS/2 has complete flexibility to upgrade the memory suballocation package in any externally compatible fashion, thanks to the standard interface provided by dynamic links.

9.3 Segment Swapping

One of the most important features of the 80286 memory management hardware is swapping support. Swapping is a technique by which some code or data segments in memory are written to a disk file, thus allowing the memory they were using to be reclaimed for another purpose.

Later, the swapped-out code or data is reloaded into memory. This technique lets you run more programs than can simultaneously fit in memory; all you need is enough memory to hold the programs that are running at that particular moment. Quiescent programs can be swapped to disk to make room for active ones. Later, when the swapped programs become active, OS/2 reads them in and resumes them. If necessary OS/2 first makes memory available by swapping out another quiescent program.

Although I used the word *program* above, swapping is actually done on a segment basis. Segments are swapped out individually and completely; the OS/2 swapping code doesn't pay attention to relationships between segments (they aren't swapped in groups), and the 80286 hardware does not allow only part of a segment to be swapped. I simplified the concept a bit in the above paragraph. You need not swap out an entire process; you can swap out some segments and leave others in memory. OS/2 can and commonly does run a process when some of its segments are swapped out. As long as a process does not try to use the swapped-out segments, it runs unhindered. If a process references a swapped-out segment, the 80286 hardware generates a special trap that OS/2 intercepts. The *segment fault* trap handler swaps in the missing segment, first swapping out some other if need be, and then the process resumes where it left off. Segment faulting is invisible to a process; the process executes normally, except that a segment load instruction takes on the order of 30 milliseconds instead of the usual 3 microseconds.

When memory is depleted and a segment must be swapped, OS/2 has to choose one to swap out. Making the right choice is important; for example, consider a process that alternates references between segment A and segment B. If A is swapped out, a poorly designed system might choose B to swap out to make room for A. After a few instructions are executed, B has to be swapped in. If A is in turn swapped out to make room for B, the system would soon spend all its time swapping A and B to and from the disk. This is called *thrashing*, and thrashing can destroy system performance. In other words, the effect of swapping is to make some segment loads take 10,000 times longer than they would if the segment were in memory. Although the number 10,000 seems very large, the actual time of about 30 milliseconds is not, *as long as we don't have to pay those 30 milliseconds very often.*

A lot hinges on choosing segments to swap out that won't be referenced in the near future. OS/2 uses the LRU (Least Recently Used) scheme to determine which segment it will swap out. The ideal choice is the segment—among those currently in memory—that will be referenced last because this postpones the swap-in of that segment as long as possible. Unfortunately, it's mathematically provable that no operating system can predict the behavior of arbitrary processes. Instead, operating systems try to make an educated guess as to which segment in memory is least likely to be referenced in the immediate future. The LRU scheme is precisely that—a good guess. OS/2 figures that if a segment hasn't been used in a long time then it probably won't be used for a long time yet, so it swaps out the segment that was last used the longest time ago—in other words, the least recently used segment.

Of course, it's easy to construct an example where the LRU decision is the wrong one or even the worst one. The classic example is a program that references, round robin, N segments when there is room in memory for only N−1. When you attempt to make room for segment *I*, the least recently used segment will be *I*+1, which in fact is the segment that will next be used. A discussion of *reference locality* and *working set* problems, as these are called, is beyond the scope of this book. Authors of programs that will make repetitive accesses to large bodies of data or code should study the available literature on virtual memory systems. Remember, on an 80286, OS/2 swaps only on a segment basis. A future 80386 release of OS/2 will swap, or page, on a 4 KB page basis.

The swapping algorithm is strictly LRU among all swap-eligible segments in the system. Thread/process priority is not considered; system segments that are marked swappable get no special treatment. Some system segments are marked nonswappable, however. For example, swapping out the OS/2 code that performs swap-ins would be embarrassing. Likewise, the disk driver code for the swapping disk must not be swapped out. Some kernel and device driver code is called at interrupt time; this is never swapped because of the swap-in delay and because of potential interference between the swapped-out interrupt handling code and the interrupt handling code of the disk driver that will do the swap-in. Finally, some kernel code is called in real mode in response to requests from the 3x box. No real mode code can be swapped because the processor does not support segment faults when running in real mode.

The technique of running more programs then there is RAM to hold them is called *memory overcommit*. OS/2 has to keep careful track of the degree of overcommit so that it doesn't find itself with too much of a good thing—not enough free RAM, even with swapping, to swap in a swapped-out process. Such a situation is doubly painful: Not only can the user not access or save the data that he or she has spent the last four hours working on, but OS/2 can't even tell the program what's wrong because it can't get the program into memory to run it. To prevent this, OS/2 keeps track of its commitments and overcommitments in two ways. First, before it starts a process, OS/2 ensures that there is enough swap space to run it. Second, it ensures that there is always enough available RAM to execute a swapped-out process.

At first glance, knowing if RAM is sufficient to run a process seems simple—either the process fits into memory or it doesn't. Life is a bit more complicated than that under OS/2 because the segments of a program or a dynlink library may be marked for demand loading. This means that they won't come in when the program starts executing but may be called in later. Obviously, once a program starts executing, it can make nearly unlimited demands for memory. When a program requests a memory allocation, however, OS/2 can return an error code if available memory is insufficient. The program can then deal with the problem: make do with less, refuse the user's command, and so forth.

OS/2 isn't concerned about a program's explicit memory requests because they can always be refused; the implicit memory requests are the problem—faulting in a demand load segment, for example. Not only is there no interface to give the program an error code,[4] but the program may be unable to proceed without the segment. As a result, when a program is first loaded (via a **DosExecPgm** call), OS/2 sums the size of all its impure segments even if they are marked for "load on demand." The same computation is done for all the loadtime dynlink libraries it references and for all the libraries *they* reference and so on. This final number, plus the internal system per-process overhead, is the maximum *implicit* memory demand of the program. If that much free swap space is available, the program can start execution.

You have undoubtedly noticed that I said we could run the program if there was enough swap space. But a program must be in RAM to

---

4. A demand load segment is faulted in via a "load segment register" instruction. These CPU instructions don't return error codes!

execute, so why don't we care about the amount of available RAM space? We do care. Not about the actual amount of free RAM when we start a program, but about the amount of RAM that can be made free— by swapping—if needed. If some RAM contains a swappable segment, then we *can* swap it because we set aside enough swap space for the task. Pure segments, by the way, are not normally swapped. In lieu of a swap-out, OS/2 simply discards them. When it's time to swap them in, OS/2 reloads them from their original .EXE or .DLL files.[5]

Because not all segments of a process need to be in memory for the process to execute, we don't have to ensure enough free RAM for the entire process, just enough so that we can simultaneously load six 64 KB segments—the maximum amount of memory needed to run any process. The numbers 6 and 64 KB are derived from the design of the 80286. To execute even a single instruction of a process, all the segments selected by the four segment registers must be in memory. The other two necessary segments come from the worst case scenario of a program trying to execute a far return instruction from a ring 2 segment (see 18.1 I/O Privilege Mechanism). The four segments named in the registers must be present for the instruction to start, and the two new segments—CS and SS—that the far return instruction will reference must be present for the instruction to complete. That makes six; the 64 KB comes from the maximum size a segment can reach. As a result, as long as OS/2 can free up those six 64 KB memory regions, by swapping and discarding if necessary, any swapped-out program can execute.

Naturally, if that were the only available memory and it had to be shared by all running processes, system response would be very poor. Normally, much more RAM space is available. The memory overcommit code is concerned only that all processes *can* run; it won't refuse to start a process because it might execute slowly. It could be that the applications that a particular user runs and their usage pattern are such that the user finds the performance acceptable and thus hasn't bought more memory. Or perhaps the slowness is a rare occurrence, and the user is willing to accept it just this once. In general, if the system

5. An exception to this is programs that were executed from removable media. OS/2 preloads all pure segments from such .EXE and .DLL files and swaps them as necessary. This prevents certain deadlock problems involving the hard error daemon and the volume management code.

thrashes—spends too much time swapping—it's a soft failure: The user knows what's wrong, the user knows what to do to make it get better (run fewer programs or buy more memory), and the user can meanwhile continue to work.

Clearly, because all segments of the applications are swappable and because we've ensured that the swap space is sufficient for all of them, initiating a new process doesn't consume any of our free or freeable RAM. It's the device drivers and their ability to allocate nonswappable segments that can drain the RAM pool. For this reason, OS/2 may refuse to load a device driver or to honor a device driver's memory allocation request if to do so would leave less than six 64 KB areas of RAM available.

9.3.1   Swapping Miscellany

The system swap space consists of a special file, called SWAP-PER.DAT, created at boot time. The location of the file is described in the CONFIG.SYS file. OS/2 may not allocate the entire maximum size of the swap file initially; instead, it may allocate a smaller size and grow the swap file to its maximum size if needed. The swap file may grow, but in OS/2 version 1.0 it never shrinks.

The available swap space in the system is more than the maximum size of the swap file; it also includes extra RAM. Clearly, a system with 8 MB of RAM and a 200 KB swap file should be able to run programs that consume more than 200 KB. After setting aside the memory consumed by nonswappable segments and our six 64 KB reserved areas, the remaining RAM is considered part of the swap file for memory overcommit accounting purposes.

We mentioned in passing that memory used in real mode can't be swapped. This means that the entire 3x box memory area is nonswappable. In fact, the casual attitude of MS-DOS applications toward memory allocation forces OS/2 to keep a strict boundary between real mode and protect mode memory. Memory below the RMSIZE value specified in CONFIG.SYS belongs exclusively to the real mode program, minus that consumed by the device drivers and the parts of the OS/2 kernel that run in real mode.

Early in the development of OS/2, attempts were made to put protect mode segments into any unused real mode memory, but we abandoned this approach. First, because the risk was great that the real mode program might overwrite part of the segment. Although this is technically a bug on the part of the real mode application, such bugs generally do not affect program execution in an MS-DOS environment because that memory is unused at the time. Thus, such bugs undoubtedly exist unnoticed in today's MS-DOS applications, waiting to wreak havoc in the OS/2 environment.

A second reason concerns existing real mode applications having been written for a single-tasking environment. Such an application commonly asks for 1 MB of memory, a request that must be refused. The refusal, however, also specifies the amount of memory available at the time of the call. Real mode applications then turn around and ask for *that* amount, but they don't check to see if an "insufficient memory" error code was returned from the second call. After all, how could such a code be returned? The operating system has just said that the memory was available. This coding sequence can cause disaster in a multitasking environment where the memory might have been allocated elsewhere between the first and second call from the application. This is another reason OS/2 sets aside a fixed region of memory for the 3x box and never uses it for other purposes, even if it appears to be idle.

We mentioned that OS/2's primary concern is that programs be able to execute at all; whether they execute *well* is the user's problem. This approach is acceptable because OS/2 is a single-user system. Multiuser systems need to deal with thrashing situations because the users that suffer from thrashing may not be the ones who created it and may be powerless to alleviate it. In a single-user environment, however, the user is responsible for the load that caused the thrashing, the user is the one who is suffering from it, and the user is the one who can fix the situation by buying more RAM or terminating a few applications. Nevertheless, applications with considerable memory needs should be written so as to minimize their impact on the system swapper.

Fundamentally, all swapping optimization techniques boil down to one issue: *locality of reference*. This means keeping the memory locations that are referenced near one another in time and in space. If your program supports five functions, put the code of each function in a separate segment, with another segment holding common code. The user can then work with one function, and the other segments can be swapped. If each function had some code in each of five segments, all segments would have to be in memory at all times.

A large body of literature deals with these issues because of the prevalence of virtual memory systems in the mainframe environment. Most of this work was done when RAM was very expensive. To precisely determine which segments or pages should be resident and which should be swapped was worth a great deal of effort. Memory was costly, and swapping devices were fast, so algorithms were designed to "crank the screws down tight" and free up as much memory as possible. After all, if they misjudged and swapped something that was needed soon, it could be brought back in quickly. The OS/2 environment is inverted: RAM is comparatively cheap, and the swapping disk, being the regular system hard disk, is comparatively slow. Consequently, OS/2's swapping strategy is to identify segments that are clearly idle and swap them (because cheap RAM doesn't mean *free* RAM) but not to judge things so closely that segments are frequently swapped when they should not be.

A key concept derived from this classic virtual memory work is that of the *working set*. A thread's working set is the set of segments it will reference "soon"—in the next several seconds or few minutes. Programmers should analyze their code to determine its working sets; obviously the set of segments in the working set will vary with the work the application is doing. Code and data should be arranged between segments so that the size of each common working set consists of a minimum amount of memory. For example, if a program contains extensive code and data to deal with uncommon error situations, these items should reside in separate segments so that they aren't resident except when needed. You don't want to burden the system with too many segments; two functions that are frequently used together should occupy the same segment, but large unrelated bodies of code and data should have their own segments or be grouped with other items that are in their working set. Consider segment size when packing items into segments. Too many small segments increase system overhead; large segments decrease the efficiency of the swap mechanism. Splitting a segment in two doesn't make sense if all code in the segment belongs to the same working set, but it does make sense to split large bodies of unrelated code and data.

As we said before, an exhaustive discussion of these issues is beyond the scope of this book. Programmers writing memory-intensive applications should study the literature and their programs to optimize their performance in an OS/2 environment. Minimizing an application's memory requirements is more than being a ''good citizen''; the smaller a program's working set, the better it will run when the system load picks up.

9.4   Status and Information

OS/2 takes advantage of the 80286 LDT and GDT architecture in providing two special segments, called *infosegs*, that contain system information. OS/2 updates these segments when changes take place, so their information is always current. One infoseg is global, and the other is local. The global infoseg contains information about the system as a whole; the local infoseg contains process specific data. Naturally, the global infoseg is read only and is shared among all processes. Local infosegs are also read only, but each process has its own.

The global infoseg contains time and date information. The ''seconds elapsed since 1970'' field is particularly useful for time-stamping events because calculating the interval between two times is easy. Simply subtract and then divide by the number of seconds in the unit of time in which you're interested. It's important that you remember that the date/time fields are 32-bit fields but the 80286 reads data 16 bits at a time. Thus, if an application reads the two time-stamp words at the same time as they are being updated, it may read a bad value—not a value off by 1, but a value that is off by 63335. The easiest way to deal with this is to read the value and then compare the just read value with the infoseg contents. If they are the same, your read value is correct. If they differ, continue reading and comparing until the read and infoseg values agree. The RAS[6] information is used for field system diagnosis and is not of general interest to programmers.

The local infoseg segment contains process and thread information. The information is accurate for the currently executing thread. The subscreen group value is used by the presentation manager subsystem and is not of value to applications. For more information on global and local infosegs, see the OS/2 reference manual.

---

6. Reliability, Availability, and Serviceability. A buzzword that refers to components intended to aid field diagnosis of system malfunctions.

10

Environment Strings

A major requirement of OS/2 is the ability to support logical device and directory names. For example, a program needs to write a temporary scratch file to the user's fastest disk. Which disk is that? Is it drive C, the hard disk? Some machines don't have a hard disk. Is it drive B, the floppy drive? Some machines don't have a drive B. And even if a hard disk on drive C exists, maybe drive D also exists and has more free space. Or perhaps drive E is preferred because it's a RAM disk. Perhaps it's not, though, because the user wants the scratch file preserved when the machine is powered down. This program needs the ability to specify a logical directory—the scratch file directory— rather than a physical drive and directory such as A:\ or C:\TEMP. The user could then specify the physical location (drive and directory) that corresponds to the logical directory.

Another example is a spell-checker program that stores two dictionaries on a disk. Presumably, the dictionary files were copied to a hard disk when the program was installed, but on which drive and directory? The checker's author could certainly hard code a directory such as C:\SPELLCHK\DICT1. But what if the user doesn't have a C drive, or what if drive C is full and the user wants to use drive D instead? How can this program offer the user the flexibility of putting the dictionary files where they best fit and yet still find them when it needs them?

The answer to these problems is a *logical device and directory name* facility. Such a facility should have three characteristics:

■ It should allow the user to map the logical directories onto the actual (physical) devices and directories at will. It should be possible to change these mappings without changing the programs that use them.

■ The set of possible logical devices and directories should be very large and arbitrarily expandable. Some new program, such as our spelling checker, will always need a new logical directory.

■ The *name set* should be large and collision free. Many programs will want to use logical directory names. If all names must come from a small set of possibilities, such as X1, X2, X3, and so on, two applications, written independently, may each choose the same name for conflicting uses.

The original version of MS-DOS did not provide for logical devices and directories. In those days a maximum PC configuration consisted of two floppy disks. Operating the machine entailed playing a lot of "disk jockey" as the user moved system, program, and data disks in and out of the drives. The user was the only one who could judge which drive should contain which floppy and its associated data, and data files moved from drive to drive dynamically. A logical device mechanism would have been of little use. Logical directories were not needed because MS-DOS version 1.0 didn't support directories. MS-DOS versions 2.x and 3.x propagated the "physical names only" architecture because of memory limitations and because of the catch-22 of new operating system features: Applications won't take advantage of the new feature because many machines are running older versions of MS-DOS without that new feature.

None of these reasons holds true for OS/2. All OS/2 protect mode applications will be rewritten. OS/2 has access to plenty of memory. Finally, OS/2 needs a logical drive/directory mechanism: All OS/2 machines have hard disks or similar facilities, and all OS/2 machines will run a variety of sophisticated applications that need access to private files and work areas. As a result, the environment string mechanism in MS-DOS has been expanded to serve as the logical name in OS/2.

Because of the memory allocation techniques employed by MS-DOS programs and because of the lack of segment motion and swapping in real mode, the MS-DOS environment list was very limited in size. The size of the environment segment was easily exceeded. OS/2 allows environment segments to be grown arbitrarily, at any time, subject only to the hardware's 64 KB length limitation. In keeping with the OS/2 architecture, each process has its own environment segment. By default, the child inherits a copy of the parent's segment, but the parent can substitute other environment values at **DosExecPgm** time.

Using the environment string facility to provide logical names is straightforward. If a convention for the logical name that you need doesn't already exist, you must choose a meaningful name. Your installation instructions or software should document how to use the environment string; the application should display an error message or use an appropriate default if the logical names do not appear in the environment string. Because each process has its own environment segment that it inherited from its parent, batch files, startup scripts, and initiator programs that load applications can conveniently set up the necessary strings. This also allows several applications or multiple copies of the same application to define the same logical name differently.

The existing conventions are:

PATH=
PATH defines a list of directories that CMD.EXE searches when it has been instructed to execute a program. The directories are searched from left to right and are separated by semicolons. For example,

    PATH=C:\BIN;D:\TOOLS;.

means search C:\BIN first, D:\TOOLS second, and the current working directory third.

DPATH=
DPATH defines a list of directories that programs may search to locate a data file. The directories are searched from left to right and are separated by semicolons. For example:

    DPATH=C:\DBM;D:\TEMP;.

Applications use DPATH as a convenience to the user: A user can work from one directory and reference data files in another directory, named in the DPATH string, without specifying the full path names of the data files. Obviously, applications and users must use this technique with care. Searching too widely for a filename is extremely dangerous; the wrong file may be found because filenames themselves are often duplicated in different directories. To use the DPATH string, an application must first use **DosScanEnv** to locate the DPATH string, and then it must use **DosSearchPath** to locate the data file.

INCLUDE=
The INCLUDE name defines the drive and directory where compiler and assembler standard include files are located.

INIT=
The INIT name defines the drive and directory that contains initialization and configuration information for the application. For example, some applications define files that contain the user's preferred defaults. These files might be stored in this directory.

LIB=
The LIB name defines the drive and directory where the standard language library modules are kept.

PROMPT=
The PROMPT name defines the CMD.EXE prompt string. Special character sequences are defined so that the CMD.EXE prompt can contain the working directory, the date and time, and so on. See CMD.EXE documentation for details.

TEMP=
The TEMP name defines the drive and directory for temporary files. This directory is on a device that is relatively fast and has sufficient room for scratch files. The TEMP directory should be considered volatile; its contents can be lost during a reboot operation.

The environment segment is a very flexible tool that you can use to customize the environment of an application or a group of applications. For example, you can use environment strings to specify default options for applications. Users can use the same systemwide default or change that value for a particular screen group or activation of the application.

11

Interprocess Communication

Interprocess Communication (IPC) is central to OS/2. As we discussed earlier, effective IPC is needed to support both the tool-based architecture and the dynlink interface for interprocess services. Because IPC is so important, OS/2 provides several forms to fulfill a variety of needs.

11.1 Shared Memory

Shared memory has already been discussed in some detail. To summarize, the two forms are named shared memory (access is requested by the client by name) and giveaway shared memory (a current owner gives access to another process). Shared memory is the most efficient form of IPC because no data copying or calls to the operating system kernel are involved once the shared memory has been set up. Shared memory does require more effort on the part of the client processes; a protocol must be established, semaphores and flags are usually needed, and exposure to amok programs and premature termination must be considered. Applications that expect to deal with a low volume of data may want to consider using named pipes.

11.2 Semaphores

A semaphore is a flag or a signal. In its basic form a semaphore has only two states—on and off or stop and go. A railroad semaphore, for example, is either red or green—stop or go. In computer software, a semaphore is a flag or a signal used by one thread of execution to flag or signal another. Often it's for purposes of mutual exclusion: "I'm in here, stay out." But sometimes it can be used to indicate other events: "Your data is ready."

OS/2 supports two kinds of semaphores, each of which can be used in two different ways. The two kinds of semaphores—RAM semaphores and system semaphores—have a lot in common, and the same system API is used to manipulate both. A RAM semaphore, as its name implies, uses a 4-byte data structure kept in a RAM location that must be accessible to all threads that use it. The system API that manipulates RAM semaphores is located in a dynlink subsystem. This code claims semaphores with an atomic test-and-set operation,[1] so it need not enter the kernel (ring 0) to protect itself against preemption. As a result, the most common tasks—claiming a free semaphore and freeing a semaphore that has no waiters—are very fast, on the order of 100 microseconds on a 6-MHz 1-wait-state IBM PC/AT.[2] If the semaphore is already claimed and the caller must block or if another thread is waiting on the semaphore, the semaphore dynlink package must enter kernel mode.

System semaphores, on the other hand, use a data structure that is kept in system memory outside the address space of any process. Therefore, system semaphore operations are slower than RAM semaphore operations, on the order of 350 microseconds for an uncontested semaphore claim. Some important advantages offset this operating speed however. System semaphores support mechanisms that prevent deadlock by crashing programs, and system semaphores support exclusivity and counting features. As a general rule, you should use RAM semaphores when the requirement is wholly contained within one process. When multiple processes may be involved, use system semaphores.

The first step, regardless of the type or use of the semaphore, is to create it. An application creates RAM semaphores simply by allocating a 4-byte area of memory initialized to zero. The far address of this area is the RAM semaphore handle. The **DosCreateSem** call creates system semaphores. (The **DosCreateSem** call takes an exclusivity argument, which we'll discuss later.) Although semaphores control thread execution, semaphore handles are owned by the process. Once a

---

1. An atomic operation is one that is indivisible and therefore cannot be interrupted in the middle.

2. This is the standard environment when quoting speeds; it's both the common case and the worst case. Machines that don't run at this speed run faster.

semaphore is created and its handle obtained, all threads in that process can use that handle. Other processes must open the semaphore via **DosOpenSem.** There is no explicit open for a RAM semaphore. To be useful for IPC, the RAM semaphore must be in a shared memory segment so that another process can access it; the other process simply learns the far address of the RAM semaphore. A RAM semaphore is initialized by zeroing out its 4-byte memory area.

Except for opening and closing, RAM and system semaphores use exactly the same OS/2 semaphore calls. Each semaphore call takes a *semaphore handle* as an argument. A RAM semaphore's handle is its address; a system semaphore's handle was returned by the create or open call. The OS/2 semaphore routines can distinguish between RAM and system semaphores by examining the handle they are passed. Because system semaphores and their names are kept in an internal OS/2 data area, they are a finite resource; the number of RAM semaphores is limited only by the amount of available RAM to hold them.

The most common use of semaphores is to protect critical sections. To reiterate, a critical section is a body of code that manipulates a data resource in a nonreentrant way. In other words, a critical section will screw up if two threads call it at the same time on the same data resource. A critical section can cover more than one section of code; if one subroutine adds entries to a table and another subroutine removes entries, both subroutines are in the table's critical section. A critical section is much like an airplane washroom, and the semaphore is like the sign that says "Occupied." The first user sets the semaphore and starts manipulating the resource; meanwhile others arrive, see that the semaphore is set, and block (that is, wait) outside. When the critical section becomes available and the semaphore is cleared, only one of the waiting threads gets to claim it; the others keep on waiting.

Using semaphores to protect critical sections is straightforward. At the top of a section of code that will manipulate the critical resource, insert a call to **DosSemRequest.** When this call returns, the semaphore is claimed, and the code can proceed. When the code is finished and the critical section is "clean," call **DosSemClear. DosSemClear** releases the semaphore and reactivates any thread waiting on it.

System semaphores are different from RAM semaphores in this application in one critical respect. If a system semaphore is created for exclusive use, it can be used as a counting semaphore. Exclusive use means that only the thread that set the semaphore can clear it;[3] this is expected when protecting critical sections. A counting semaphore can be set many times but must be released an equal number of times before it becomes free. For example, an application contains function A and function B, each of which manipulates the same critical section. Each claims the semaphore at its beginning and releases it at its end. However, under some circumstances, function A may need to call function B. Function A can't release the semaphore before it calls B because it's still in the critical section and the data is in an inconsistent state. But when B issues **DosSemRequest** on the semaphore, it blocks because the semaphore was already set by A.

A counting semaphore solves this problem. When function B makes the second, redundant **DosSemRequest** call, OS/2 recognizes it as the same thread that already owns the semaphore, and instead of blocking the thread, it increments a counter to show that the semaphore has been claimed twice. Later, when function B releases the semaphore, OS/2 decrements the counter. Because the counter is not at zero, the semaphore is not really clear and thus not released. The semaphore is truly released only after function B returns to function A, and A, finishing its work, releases the semaphore a second time.

A second major use of semaphores is signaling (unrelated to the *signal* facility of OS/2). Signaling is using semaphores to notify threads that certain events or activities have taken place. For example, consider a multithreaded application that uses one thread to communicate over a serial port and another thread to compute with the results of that communication. The computing thread tells the communication thread to send a message and get a reply, and then it goes about its own business. Later, the computing thread wants to block until the reply is received but only if the reply hasn't already been received—it may have already arrived, in which case the computing thread doesn't want to block.

You can handle this by using a semaphore as a flag. The computing thread sets the semaphore via **DosSemSet** before it gives the order to the communications thread. When the computing thread is ready to wait for the reply, it does a **DosSemWait** on the semaphore it set earlier. When the communications thread receives the reply, it clears the semaphore. When the computing thread calls **DosSemWait,** it will

---

3. This is a departure from the principle of resource ownership by process, not by thread. The thread, not the process, owns the privilege to clear a set "exclusive use" semaphore.

continue without delay if the semaphore is already clear. Otherwise, the computing thread blocks until the semaphore is cleared. In this example, we aren't protecting a critical section; we're using the semaphore transition from set to clear to flag an event between multiple threads. Our needs are the opposite of a critical section semaphore: We don't want the semaphore to be exclusively owned; if it were, the communications thread couldn't release it. We also don't want the semaphore to be counting. If it counts, the computing thread won't block when it does the **DosSemWait;** OS/2 would recognize that it did the **DosSemSet** earlier and would increment the semaphore counter.

OS/2 itself uses semaphore signaling in this fashion when asynchronous communication is needed. For example, asynchronous I/O uses semaphores in the signaling mode to indicate that an I/O operation has completed. The system timer services use semaphores in the signaling mode to indicate that the specified time has elapsed. OS/2 supports a special form of semaphore waiting, called **DosMuxSemWait,** which allows a thread to wait on more than one semaphore at one time. As soon as any specified semaphore becomes clear, **DosMuxSemWait** returns. **DosMuxSemWait,** like **DosSemWait,** only waits for a semaphore to become clear; it doesn't set or claim the semaphore as does **DosSemRequest. DosMuxSemWait** allows a thread to wait on a variety of events and to wake up whenever one of those events occurs.

11.2.1 Semaphore Recovery

We discussed earlier some difficulties that can arise if a semaphore is left set "orphaned" when its owner terminates unexpectedly. We'll review the topic because it's critical that applications handle the situation correctly and because that correctness generally has to be demonstrable by inspection. It's very difficult to demonstrate and fix timing-related bugs by just testing a program.

Semaphores can become orphaned in at least four ways:

1. An incoming signal can divert the CPU, and the signal handler can fail to return to the point of interruption.

2. A process can kill another process without warning.

3. A process can incur a GP fault, which is fatal.

4. A process can malfunction because of a coding error and fail to release a semaphore.

The action to take in such events depends on how semaphores are being used. In some situations, no action is needed. Our example of the computing and communications threads is such a situation. If the process dies, the semaphore and all its users die. Special treatment is necessary only if the application uses **DosExitList** to run code that needs to use the semaphore. This should rarely be necessary because semaphores are used within a process to coordinate multiple threads and only one thread remains when the exitlist is activated. Likewise, a process can receive signals only if it has asked for them, so an application that does not use signals need not worry about their interrupting its critical sections. An application that does use signals can use **DosHoldSignal,** always return from a signal handler, or prevent thread 1 (the signal-handling thread) from entering critical sections.

In other situations, the semaphore can protect a recoverable resource. For example, you can use a system semaphore to protect access to a printer that for some reason is being dealt with directly by applications rather than by the system spooler. If the owner of the ''I'm using the printer'' system semaphore dies unexpectedly, the next thread that tries to claim the semaphore will be able to do so but will receive a special error code that says, ''The owner of this semaphore died while holding it.'' In such a case, the application can simply write a form feed or two to the printer and continue. Other possible actions are to clean up the protected resource or to execute a process that will do so. Finally, an application can display a message to the user saying, ''Gee, this database is corrupt! You better do something,'' and then terminate. In this case, the application should *deliberately* terminate while holding the semaphore so that any other threads waiting on it will receive the ''owner died'' message. Once the ''owner died'' code is received, that state is cleared; so if the recipient of the code releases the semaphore without fixing the inconsistencies in the critical section, problems will result.

Additional matters must be considered if a process intends to clean up its own semaphores by means of a **DosExitList** handler. First, exclusive (that is, counting) semaphores must be used. Although an exitlist routine can tell that a RAM or nonexclusive system semaphore is reserved, it cannot tell whether *it* is the process that reserved it. You may be tempted simply to keep a flag byte that is set each time the semaphore is claimed and cleared each time the semaphore is released, but that solution contains a potentially deadly window of failure. If the thread sets the "I own it" flag before it calls **DosSemRequest,** the thread could terminate between setting the flag and receiving the semaphore. In that case, the exitlist routine would believe, wrongly, that it owns the semaphore and would therefore release it—a very unpleasant surprise for the true owner of the semaphore. Conversely, if the thread claims the semaphore and then sets the flag, a window exists in which the semaphore is claimed but the flag does not say so. This is also disastrous.

Using exclusive system semaphores solves these problems. As I mentioned earlier, when the thread that has set a system semaphore dies with the semaphore set, the semaphore is placed into a special "owner died" state so that the next thread to attempt to claim the semaphore is informed of its orphan status. There is an extra twist to this for exclusive-use system semaphores. Should the process die due to an external cause or due to a **DosExit** call *and* that process has a **DosExitList** handler, all orphaned system semaphores are placed in a special "owner died" state so that only that process's remaining thread—the one executing the **DosExitList** handlers—can claim the semaphore. When it does so, it still receives the special "owner died" code. The exitlist handler can use **DosSemWait** with a timeout value of 0 to see if the semaphore is set. If the "owner died" code is returned, then the **DosExitList** handler cleans up the resource and then issues **DosSemClear** to clear the semaphore. If a thread terminates by explicitly calling **DosExit** with the "terminate this thread" subcode, any exclusive-use system semaphores that it has set will *not* enter this special "owner died" state but will instead assume the general "owner died" state that allows any thread in the system to claim the semaphore and receive the "owner died" code. Likewise, any semaphores in the special "owner died" state that are not cleared by the **DosExitList** handlers become normal "owner died" semaphores when the process completely terminates.

11.2.2   Semaphore Scheduling

Although multiple threads can wait for a semaphore, only one thread gets the semaphore when it becomes available. OS/2 schedules semaphore grants based on CPU priority: The highest-priority waiting thread claims the semaphore. If several waiting threads are at the highest priority, OS/2 distributes the grants among them evenly.

11.3 Named Pipes

We've already discussed anonymous pipes—stream oriented IPC mechanisms that work via the **DosRead** and **DosWrite** calls. Two processes can communicate via anonymous pipes only if one is a descendant of the other and if the descendant has inherited the parent's handle to the pipe. Anonymous pipes are used almost exclusively to transfer input and output data to and from a child process or to and from a subtree of child processes.

OS/2 supports another form of pipes called *named pipes*. Named pipes are *not* available in OS/2 version 1.0; they will be available in a later release. I discuss them here because of their importance in the system architecture. Also, because of the extensible nature of OS/2, it's possible that named pipe functionality will be added to the system by including the function in some other Microsoft system software package that, when it runs under OS/2, installs the capability. In such a case, application programs will be unable to distinguish the ''add-on'' named pipe facility from the ''built-in'' version that will eventually be included in OS/2.

Named pipes are much like anonymous pipes in that they're a serial communications channel between two processes and they use the **DosRead** and **DosWrite** interface. They are different, however, in several important ways.

■ Named pipes have names in the file system name space. Users of a named pipe need not be related; they need only know the name of a pipe to access it.

■ Because named pipes use the file system name space and because that name space can describe machines on a network, named pipes work both locally (within a single machine) and remotely (across a network).

■ An anonymous pipe is a byte-stream mechanism. The system considers the data sent through an anonymous pipe as an undifferentiated stream of bytes. The writer can write a 100-byte block of data, and the reader can read the data with two 30-byte reads and one 40-byte read. If the byte stream contains individual messages, the recipient must determine where they start and stop. Named pipes can be used in this byte-stream mode, but named pipes also support *message mode,* in which processes read and write streams of messages. When the named pipe is in message mode, OS/2 (figuratively!) separates the messages from each other with pieces of waxed paper so that the reader can ask for "the next message" rather than for "the next 100 bytes."

■ Named pipes are full duplex, whereas anonymous pipes are actually a pair of pipes, each half duplex. When an anonymous pipe is created, two handles are returned—a read handle and a write handle. An open of a named pipe returns a single handle, which may (depending on the mode of the **DosOpen**) be both read and written. Although a full duplex named pipe is accessed via a single handle, the data moving in each direction is kept totally separate. A named pipe should be viewed as two separate pipes between the reader and the writer—one holds data going in, the other holds data coming back. For example, if a thread writes to a named pipe handle and then reads from that handle, the thread will not read back the data it just wrote. The data the thread just wrote in is in the outgoing side; the read reads from the incoming side.

■ Named pipes are frequently used to communicate with processes that provide a service to one or more clients, usually simultaneously. The named pipe API contains special functions to facilitate such use: pipe reusability, multiple pipes with identical names, and so on. These are discussed below.

■ Named pipes support transaction I/O calls that provide an efficient way to implement local and remote procedure call dialogs between processes.

■ Programs running on MS-DOS version 3.x workstations can access named pipes on an OS/2 server to conduct dialogs with server applications because, to a client, a named pipe looks exactly like a file.

You'll recall that the creator of an anonymous pipe uses a special interface (**DosMakePipe**) to create the pipe but that the client process can use the **DosRead** and **DosWrite** functions, remaining ignorant of the nature of the handle. The same holds true for named pipes when they are used in stream mode. The creator of a named pipe uses a special

API to set it up, but its clients can use the pipe while remaining ignorant of its nature as long as that use is serial.[4] Named pipes are created by the **DosMakeNmPipe** call. Once the pipe is created, one of the
serving process's threads must wait via the **DosConnectNmPipe** call
for the client to open the pipe. The client cannot successfully open the
pipe until a **DosConnectNmPipe** has been issued to it by the server
process.

Although the serving process understands that it's using a named
pipe and can therefore call a special named pipe API, the client process
need not be aware that it's using a named pipe because the normal
DosOpen call is used to open the pipe. Because named pipes appear in
the file system name space, the client can, for example, open a file
called \PIPE\STATUS, unaware that it's a named pipe being managed
by another process. The **DosMakeNmPipe** call returns a handle to the
serving end of the pipe; the **DosOpen** call returns a handle to the client
end. As soon as the client opens a pipe, the **DosConnectNmPipe** call
returns to the serving process.

Communication over a named pipe is similar to that over an anonymous pipe: The client and server each issue reads and writes to the handle, as appropriate for the mode of the open. When a process at one end
of the pipe closes it, the process at the other end gets an error code in
response to write operations and an EOF indication in response to read
operations.

The scenario just described is simple enough, but that's the problem:
It's too simple. In real life, a serving process probably stays around so
that it can serve the next client. This is the purpose behind the **DosConnectNmPipe** call. After the first client closes its end of the named pipe
and the server end sees the EOF on the pipe, the server end issues a
DosDisconnectNmPipe call to acknowledge that the client has closed
the pipe (either explicitly or via termination). It can then issue another
DosConnectNmPipe call to reenable that pipe for reopening by
another client or by the same client. In other words, the connect and
disconnect operations allow a server to let clients, one by one, connect
to it via a single named pipe. The **DosDisconnectNmPipe** call can be
used to forcibly disconnect a client. This action is appropriate if a client
makes an invalid request or otherwise shows signs of ill health.

---

4. Random access, using **DosSeek**, is not supported for pipes and will cause an error code to
be returned.

We can serve multiple clients, one at a time, but what about serving them in parallel? As we've described it so far, our serving process handles only one client. A client's **DosOpen** call fails if the named pipe already has a client user or if the server process hasn't issued the **DosConnectNmPipe** call. This is where the instancing parameter, supplied to **DosMakeNmPipe,** comes in.

When a named pipe is first opened,[5] the instance count parameter is specified in the pipe flag's word. If this count is greater than 1, the pipe can be opened by a server process more than once. Additional opens are done via **DosMakeNmPipe,** which returns another handle to access the new instance of the pipe. Obviously the pipe isn't being "made" for the second and subsequent calls to **DosMakeNmPipe,** but the **DosOpen** call can't be used instead because it opens the client end of the named pipe, not the server end. The instance count argument is ignored for the second and subsequent **DosMakeNmPipe** calls. Extra instances of a named pipe can be created by the same process that created the first instance, or they can be created by other processes. Figure 11-1 on the following page illustrates multiple instances of a named pipe.

When a client process does a **DosOpen** on a named pipe that has multiple instances, OS/2 connects it to any server instance of the pipe that has issued a **DosConnectNmPipe** call. If no instances are available and enabled, the client receives an error code. OS/2 makes no guarantees about distributing the incoming work evenly across all server instances; it assumes that all server threads that issued a **DosConnectNmPipe** call are equal.

The multiple instance capability allows a single server process or perhaps multiple server processes to handle many clients simultaneously. One process using four threads can serve four clients as rapidly as four processes, each with one thread, can do the job. As long as threads don't interfere with one another by blocking on critical sections, a multiprocess server has no inherent efficiency advantage over a multithread server.

The OS/2 named pipe package includes some composite operations for client processes: **DosTransactNmPipe** and **DosCallNmPipe.** **DosTransactNmPipe** is much like a **DosWrite** followed by a

---

5. Like other non–file-system resident named objects, a named pipe remains known to the system only as long as a process has it open. When all handles to a named pipe are closed, OS/2 forgets all information concerning the named pipe. The next **DosMakeNmPipe** call recreates the named pipe from ground zero.

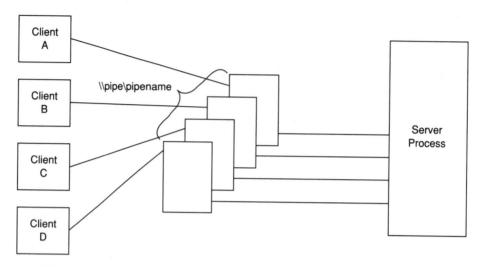

Figure 11-1.
Multiple instances of a named pipe.

DosRead: It sends a message to the server end of the named pipe and then reads a reply. **DosCallNmPipe** does the same on an unopened named pipe: It has the combined effect of a **DosOpen,** a **DosTransactNmPipe,** and a **DosClose.** These calls are of little value if the client and server processes are on the same machine; the client could easily build such subroutines itself by appropriately combining **DosOpen, DosClose, DosRead,** and **DosWrite.** These calls are in the named pipe package because they provide significant performance savings in a networked environment. If the server process is on a different machine from the client process, OS/2 and the network transport can use a datagramlike mechanism to implement these calls in a network-efficient fashion. Because named pipes work invisibly across the network, any client process that performs these types of operations should use these composite calls, even if the author of the program didn't anticipate the program being used in a networked environment. Using the composite calls will ensure the performance gains if a user decides to use a server process located across the network. Readers familiar with network architecture will recognize the **DosCallNmPipe** function as a form of *remote procedure call.* In effect, it allows a process to make a procedure call to another process, even a process on another machine.

The OS/2 named pipe facility contains a great many features, as befits its importance in realizing the OS/2 tool-based architecture. This book is not intended to provide an exhaustive coverage of features, but a few other miscellaneous items merit mention.

Our above discussion concentrated on stream-based communications, which can be convenient because they allow a client process to use a named pipe while ignorant of its nature. For example, you can write a spooler package for a device not supported by the system spoolers—say, for a plotter device. Input to the spooler can be via a named pipe, perhaps \PIPE\PLOTOUT. An application could then be told to write its plotter output to a file named \PIPE\PLOTOUT or even \\PLOTMACH\PIPE\PLOTOUT (across a network). The application will then use the spooler at the other end of the named pipe.

Sometimes, though, the client process does understand that it's talking to a named pipe, and the information exchanged is a series of messages rather than a long stream of plotter data. In this case, the named pipe can be configured as a message stream in which each message is indivisible and atomic at the interface. In other words, when a process reads from a named pipe, it gets only one message per read, and it gets the entire message. Messages can queue up in the pipe, but OS/2 remembers the message boundaries so that it can split them apart as they are read. Message streams can be used effectively in a networking environment because the network transport can better judge how to assemble packets.

Although our examples have shown the client and server processes issuing calls and blocking until they are done, named pipes can be configured to operate in a nonblocking fashion. This allows a server or a client to test a pipe to see if it's ready for a particular operation, thereby guaranteeing that the process won't be held up for some period waiting for a request to complete. Processes can also use **DosPeekNmPipe,** a related facility that returns a peek at any data (without consuming the data) currently waiting to be read in the pipe interface. Servers can use this to scan a client's request to see if they're interested in handling it at that time.

Finally, we mentioned that a process that attempts a **DosOpen** to a named pipe without any available instances is returned an error code. Typically, a client in this situation wants to wait for service to become available, and it doesn't want to sit in a polling loop periodically testing for server availability. The **DosWaitNmPipe** call is provided for this situation; it allows a client to block until an instance of the named pipe becomes available. When **DosWaitNmPipe** returns, the client must still do a **DosOpen.** The **DosOpen** can fail, however, if another process has taken the pipe instance in the time between the "wait" and the "open" calls. But because multiple waiters for a named pipe are serviced in priority order, such a "race" condition is uncommon.

11.4   Queues

Queues are another form of IPC. In many ways they are similar to named pipes, but they are also significantly different. Like named pipes, they use the file system name space, and they pass messages rather than byte streams. Unlike named pipes, queues allow multiple writes to a single queue because the messages bring with them information about their sending process that enables the queue reader to distinguish between messages from different senders. Named pipes are strictly FIFO, whereas queue messages can be read in a variety of orders. Finally, queues use shared memory as a transfer mechanism; so although they're faster than named pipes for higher volume data transfers on a single machine, they don't work across the network.

The interface to the queue package is similar but not identical to that of the named pipe interface. Like named pipes, each queue has a single owner that creates it. Clients open and close the queue while the owner, typically, lives on. Unlike named pipes, the client process must use a special queue API (**DosReadQueue, DosWriteQueue,** and so on) and thus must be written especially to use the queue package. Although each queue has a single owner, each queue can have multiple clients; so the queue mechanism doesn't need a facility to have multiple queues of the same name, nor does it need a **DosWaitNmPipe** equivalent.

Queue messages are somewhat different from named pipe messages. In addition to carrying the body of the message, each queue message carries two additional pieces of information. One is the PID of the sender; OS/2 provides this information, and the sender cannot affect it. The other is a word value that the sender supplied and that OS/2 and the queue package do not interpret. Queue servers and clients can use this information as they wish to facilitate communication.

The queue package also contains a peek facility, similar to that of named pipes but with an interesting twist. If a process peeks the named pipe and then later reads from it, it can be sure that the message it reads is the same one that it peeked because named pipes are always FIFO. Queues, however, allow records to be read in different orders of priority. If a queue is being read in priority order, a process might well peek a message, but by the time the process issues the queue read, some other message of higher priority may have arrived and thus be at the front of the list. To get around this problem, when the queue package peeks a message, it returns a magic cookie to the caller along with the message. The caller can supply this cookie to a subsequent **DosReadQueue** call to ensure that the peeked message is the one read, overriding the normal message-ranking process. This magic cookie can also be supplied to the **DosPeekQueue** call to peek the second and subsequent records in the queue.

Finally, one extremely important difference between queues and named pipes is that named pipes transfer (that is, copy) the *data* from the client to the server process. Queues transfer only the *address* of the data; the queue package does not touch the data itself. Thus, the data body of the queue message must be addressable to both the client and the serving process. This is straightforward if both the client and serving threads belong to the same process. If the client and serving threads are from different processes, however, the data body of the queue message must be in a shared memory segment that is addressable to both the client and the server.

A related issue is buffer reusability. An application can reuse a memory area immediately after its thread returns from the named pipe call that wrote the data from that area; but when using a queue, the sender must not overwrite the message area until it's sure the reading process is finished with the message.

One way to kill both these birds—the shared memory and the memory reuse problems—with one stone is to use the memory suballocation package. Both the client and the queue server need to have shared access to a memory segment that is then managed by the memory sub-allocation package. The client allocates a memory object to hold the queue message and write it to the queue. The queue server can address that queue message because it's in the shared memory segment. When the queue manager is finished with the message, it calls the memory suballocator to release the memory object. The client need not worry about when the server is finished with the message because the client allocates a new message buffer for each new message, relying on the server to return the messages fast enough so that the memory suballocator doesn't run out of available space.

A similar technique on a segment level is to use giveaway shared memory. The client allocates a giveaway segment for each message content, creates the message, gives away a shared addressability to the segment to the server process, and then writes the message (actually, the message's address) to the queue. Note that the sender uses the *recipient's* selector as the data address in this case, not its own selector. When the thread returns from that **DosWriteQueue** call, the client releases its access to the segment via **DosFreeSeg.** When the server process is finished with the message, it also releases the memory segment. Because the queue server is the last process with access to that segment, the segment is then returned to the free pool.

Software designers need to consider carefully the tradeoffs between queues, named pipes, and other forms of IPC. Queues are potentially very fast because only addresses are copied, not the data itself; but the work involved in managing and reusing the shared memory may consume the time savings if the messages are small. In general, small messages that are always read FIFO should go by named pipes, as should applications that communicate with clients and servers across a network. Very large or high data rate messages may be better suited to queues.

11.5 Dynamic Data Exchange (DDE)

DDE is a form of IPC available to processes that use the presentation manager API. The presentation manager's interface is message oriented; that is, the primary means of communication between a process and the presentation manager is the passing of messages. The presentation manager message interface allows applications to define private messages that have a unique meaning throughout the PC. DDE is, strictly speaking, a *protocol* that defines new messages for communication between applications that use it.

DDE messages can be directed at a particular recipient or broadcast to all presentation manager applications on a particular PC. Typically, a client process broadcasts a message that says, "Does anyone out there have this information?" or "Does anyone out there provide this service?" If no response is received, the answer is taken to be no. If a response *is* received, it contains an identifying code[6] that allows the two processes to communicate privately.

DDE's broadcast mechanism and message orientation gives it a lot of flexibility in a multiprocessing environment. For example, a specialized application might be scanning stock quotes that are arriving via a special link. A spreadsheet program could use DDE to tell this scanner application to notify it whenever the quotes change for certain stocks that are mentioned in its spreadsheet. Another application, perhaps called Market Alert, might ask the scanner to notify it of trades in a different set of stocks so that the alert program can flash a banner if those stocks trade outside a prescribed range. DDEs can be used only by presentation manager applications to communicate with the same.

11.6   Signaling

Signals are asynchronous notification mechanisms that operate in a fashion analogous to hardware interrupts. Like hardware interrupts, when a signal arrives at a process, that process's thread 1 stops after the instruction it is executing and begins executing at a specified handler address. The many special considerations to take into account when using signals are discussed in Chapter 12. This section discusses their use as a form of IPC.

Processes typically receive signals in response to external events that must be serviced immediately. Examples of such events are the user pressing Ctrl-C or a process being killed. Three signals (flag A, flag B, and flag C), however, are caused by another process[7] issuing an explicit **DosFlagProcess** API. **DosFlagProcess** is a unique form of IPC

---

6. A window handle.
7. This is the typical case; but like all other system calls that affect processes, a thread can make such a call to affect its own process.

because it's asynchronous. The recipient doesn't have to block or poll waiting for the event; it finds out about it (by discovering itself to be executing the signal handler) as soon as the scheduler gives it CPU time.

DosFlagProcess, however, has some unique drawbacks. First, a signal carries little information with it: only the number of the signal and a single argument word. Second, signals can interrupt and interfere with some system calls. Third, OS/2 views signals more as events than as messages; so if signals are sent faster than the recipient can process them, OS/2 discards some of the overrun. These disadvantages (discussed in Chapter 12) restrict signals to a rather specialized role as an IPC mechanism.

11.7 Combining IPC Forms

We've discussed each form of IPC, listing its strengths and weaknesses. If you use forms in conjunction, however, you benefit from their combined strengths. For example, a process can use named pipes or DDE to establish contact with another process and then agree with it to send a high volume of data via shared memory. An application that provides an IPC interface should also provide a dynlink package to hide the details of the IPC. This gives designers the flexibility to improve the IPC component of their package in future releases while still maintaining interface compatibility with their clients.

12

Signals

The OS/2 *signal* mechanism is similar, but not identical, to the UNIX signal mechanism. A signal is much like a hardware interrupt except that it is initiated and implemented in software. Just as a hardware interrupt causes the CS, IP, and Flags registers to be saved on the stack and execution to begin at a handler address, a signal causes the application's CS, IP, and Flags registers to be saved on the stack and execution to begin at a signal-handler address. An IRET instruction returns control to the interrupted address in both cases. Signals are different from hardware interrupts in that they are a software construct and don't involve privilege transitions, stack switches, or ring 0 code.

OS/2 supports six signals—three common signals (Ctrl-C, Ctrl-Break, and program termination) and three general-purpose signals. The Ctrl-C and Ctrl-Break signals occur in response to keyboard activity; the program termination signal occurs when a process is killed via the **DosKill** call.[1] The three general-purpose signals are generated by an explicit call from a thread, typically a thread from another process. A signal handler is in the form of a far subroutine, that is, a subroutine that returns with a far return instruction. When a signal arrives, the process's thread 1 is interrupted from its current location and made to call the signal-handler procedure with an argument provided by the signal generator. The signal-handler code can return,[2] in which

---

1. The process termination signal handler is not called under all conditions of process termination, only in response to **DosKill**. Normal exits, GP faults, and so on do not activate the process termination signal handler.

2. OS/2 interposes a code thunk, so the signal handler need not concern itself with executing an IRET instruction, which language compilers usually won't generate. When the signal handler is entered, its return address points to a piece of OS/2 code that contains the IRET instruction.

case the CPU returns from where it was interrupted, or the signal handler can clean its stack and jump into the process's code at some other spot, as in the C language's **long jmp** facility.

The analogy between signals and hardware interrupts holds still further. As it does in a hardware interrupt, the system blocks further interrupts from the same source so that the signal handler won't be arbitrarily reentered. The signal handler must issue a special form of **DosSetSigHandler** to dismiss the signal and allow further signals to occur. Typically this is done at the end of the signal-handling routine unless the signal handler is reentrant. Also, like hardware interrupts, the equivalent of the CLI instruction—the **DosHoldSignal** call—is used to protect critical sections from being interrupted via a signal.

Unlike hardware interrupts, signals have no interrupt priority. As each enabled signal occurs, the signal handler is entered, even if another signal handler must be interrupted. New signal events that come in while that signal is still being processed from an earlier event—before the signal has been dismissed by the handler—are held until the previous signal event has been dismissed. Like hardware interrupts, this is a pending-signal flag, not a counter. If three signals of the same kind are held off, only one signal event occurs when that signal becomes reenabled.

A signal event occurs in the context of a process whose thread of execution is interrupted for the signal handler; a signal doesn't cause the CPU to stop executing another process in order to execute the first process's signal handler. When OS/2 "posts" a signal to a process, it simply makes a mark that says, "The next time we run this guy, store his CS, IP, and Flags values on the stack and start executing here instead." The system uses its regular priority rules to assign the CPU to threads; when the scheduler next runs the signaled thread, the dispatcher code that sends the CPU into the application's code reads the "posted signal" mark and does the required work.

Because a signal "pseudo interrupt" is merely a trick of the dispatcher, signal handlers don't run in ring 0 as do hardware interrupt handlers; they run in ring 3 as do all application threads. In general, as far as OS/2 is concerned, the process isn't in any sort of special state when it's executing a signal handler, and no special rules govern what a thread can and cannot do in a signal handler.

Receiving a signal when thread 1 is executing an application or dyn-link code is straightforward: The system saves CS, IP, and Flags, and the signal handler saves the rest. The full register complement can be restored after the signal has been processed, and thread 1's normal execution resumes without incident. If thread 1 is executing a system call that takes the CPU inside the kernel, the situation is more complex. OS/2 can't emulate an interrupt from the system ring 0 code to the application's ring 3 code, nor can OS/2 take the chance that the signal handler never returns from the signal[3] and therefore leaves OS/2's internals in an intermediate state. Instead, when a signal is posted and thread 1 is executing ring 0 OS/2 code, the system either completes its operations before recognizing the signal or aborts the operation and then recognizes the signal. If the operation is expected to take place ''quickly,'' the system completes the operation, and the signal is recognized at the point where the CPU resumes executing the application's ring 3 code.

All non-I/O operations are deemed to complete ''quickly,'' with the exception of the explicit blocking operations such as **DosSleep, DosSemWait,** and so on. I/O operations depend on the specific device. Disk I/O completes quickly, but keyboard and serial I/O generally do not. Clearly, if we wait for the user to finish typing a line before we recognize a signal, we might never recognize it—especially if the signal is Ctrl-C! In the case of ''slow devices,'' OS/2 or the device driver terminates the operation and returns to the application with an error code. The signal is recognized when the CPU is about to resume executing the ring 3 application code that follows the system call that was interrupted.

Although the application is given an error code to explain that the system call was interrupted, the application may be unable to reissue the system call to complete the work. In the case of device I/O, the application typically can't tell how much, if any, of the requested output or input took place before the signal interrupted the operation. If an output operation is not reissued, some data at the end of the write may be missing. If an output operation is restarted, then some data at the

---

3. It's acceptable for a signal handler to clean up thread 1's stack, dismiss the signal, jump to another part of the application, and never return from the signal. For example, an application can jump into its ''prompt and command loop'' in response to the press of Ctrl-C.

beginning of the write may be written twice. In the case of **DosSleep,** the application cannot tell how much of the requested sleep has elapsed. These issues are not usually a problem; it's typically keyboard input that is interrupted. In the case of the common signals (Ctrl-C, Ctrl-Break, and process killed) the application typically flushes partial keyboard input anyway. Applications that use other "slow" devices or the IPC flag signals need to deal with this, however.

Although a process can have multiple threads, only thread 1 is used to execute the signal handler.[4] This leads to an obvious solution to the interrupted system call problem: Applications that will be inconvenienced by interrupted system calls due to signals should dedicate thread 1 to work that doesn't make interruptible system calls and use other thread(s) for that work. In the worst case, thread 1 can be totally dedicated to waiting for signals: It can block on a RAM semaphore that is never released, or it can execute a **DosSleep** loop.

A couple of practical details about signals are worth noting. First, the user of a high-level language such as C need not worry about saving the registers inside the signal-handler routine. The language runtimes typically provide code to handle all these details; as far as the application program is concerned, the signal handler is asynchronously far called, and it can return from the signal by the **return**() statement. Also, no application can receive a signal without first requesting it, so you need not worry about setting up signal handlers if your application doesn't explicitly ask to use them. A process can have only one signal-handling address for each signal, so general-purpose dynlink routines (ones that might be called by applications that aren't bundled with the dynlink package) should never set a signal handler; doing so might override a handler established by the client program code.

Signals interact with critical sections in much the same way as interrupts do. If a signal arrives while thread 1 is executing a critical section that is protected by a semaphore and if that signal handler never returns to the interrupted location, the critical section's semaphore will be left jammed on. Even if the signal handler eventually returns, deadlock occurs if it attempts to enter the critical section during processing of the signal (perhaps it called a dynlink package, unaware that the package

---

4. For this reason, a process should not terminate thread 1 and continue executing with others; then it cannot receive signals.

contained a critical section). Dynlink packages must deal with this problem by means of the **DosHoldSignal** call, which is analogous to the CLI/STI instructions for hardware interrupts: The **DosHoldSignal** holds off arriving signals until they are released. Held-off signals should be released within a second or two so that the user won't be pounding Ctrl-C and thinking that the application has crashed. Applications can use **DosHoldSignal,** or they can simply ensure that thread 1 never enters critical sections, perhaps by reserving it for signal handling, as discussed above.

Ctrl-C and Ctrl-Break are special, device-specific operations. Setting a signal handler for these signals is a form of I/O to the keyboard device; applications must never do this until they have verified that they have been assigned the keyboard device. See Chapter 14, Interactive Programs.

13

The Presentation Manager and VIO

In the early chapters of this book, I emphasized the importance of a high-powered, high-bandwidth graphical user interface. It's a lot of work for an application to manage graphical rendition, windowing, menus, and so on, and it's hard for the user to learn a completely different interface for each application. Therefore, OS/2 contains a subsystem called the *presentation manager* (PM) that provides these services and more. The presentation manager is implemented as a dynlink subsystem and daemon process combination, and it provides:

- High-performance graphical windowing.

- A powerful user interface model, including drop-down menus, scroll bars, icons, and mouse and keyboard interfaces. Most of these facilities are optional to the application; it can choose the standard services or "roll its own."

- Device independence. The presentation manager contains a sophisticated multilevel device interface so that as much work as possible is pushed down to "smart" graphics cards to optimize performance.

Interfacing an application with the presentation manager involves a degree of effort that not all programmers may want to put forth. The interface to the application may be so simple that the presentation manager's features are of little value, or the programmer may want to port an MS-DOS application to OS/2 with the minimum degree of change. For these reasons, OS/2 provides a second interface package called VIO,[1] which is primarily character oriented and looks much like the MS-DOS ROM BIOS video interface. The initial release of OS/2 contains only VIO, implemented as a separate package. The next release will contain the presentation manager, and VIO will then become an alternate interface to the presentation manager.

Fundamentally, the presentation manager and VIO are the equivalent of device drivers. They are implemented as dynlink packages because they are device dependent and need to be replaced if different devices are used. Dynlinks are used instead of true device drivers because they can provide high throughput for the screen device: A simple call is made directly to the code that paints the pixels on the screen. Also, the dynlink interface allows the presentation manager to be implemented partially as a dynlink subsystem and partially as a daemon process accessed by that subsystem.

These packages are complex; explaining them in detail is beyond the scope of this book. Instead, I will discuss from a general perspective the special issues for users of this package.

VIO is essentially character oriented. It supports graphics-based applications, but only to the extent of allowing them to manipulate the display controller directly so that they can "go around" VIO and provide special interfaces related to screen switching of graphics applications (see below). The base VIO package plays a role similar to that of the ROM BIOS INT 10/INT 16 interface used in MS-DOS. It contains some useful enhancements but in general is a superset of the ROM BIOS functions, so INT 10-based real mode applications can be quickly adjusted to use VIO instead. VIO is replaceable, in whole or in part, to allow applications being run with VIO to be managed later by the presentation manager package.

The presentation manager is entirely different from VIO. It offers an extremely rich and powerful set of functions that support windowing,

1. VIO is a convenience term that encompasses three dynlink subsystems: KBD (keyboard), VIO (Video I/O; the display adapter), and MOU (mouse).

and it offers a full, device-independent graphics facility. Its message-oriented architecture is well suited to interactive applications. Once the presentation manager programming model is learned and the key elements of its complex interface are understood, a programmer can take advantage of a very sexy user interface with comparatively little effort. The presentation manager also replaces the existing VIO/KBD/MOU calls in order to support older programs that use these interfaces.

13.1 Choosing Between PM and VIO

The roles of VIO and the presentation manager sometimes cause confusion: Which should you use for your application? The default interface for a new application should be the presentation manager. It's not in OS/2 version 1.0 because of scheduling restrictions; owners of version 1.0 will receive the presentation manager as soon as it is available, and all future releases will be bundled with the presentation manager. The presentation manager will be present on essentially all personal computer OS/2 installations, so you are not restricting the potential market for an application if you write it for the presentation manager.

The presentation manager interface allows an application to utilize a powerful, graphical user interface. In general form it's standardized for ease of use, but it can be customized in a specific implementation so that an application can provide important value-added features. On the other hand, if you are porting an application from the real mode environment, you will find it easier to use the VIO interface. Naturally, such programs run well under the presentation manager, but they forgo the ability to use graphics and to interact with the presentation manager. The user can still "window" the VIO application's screen image, but without the application's knowledge or cooperation. To summarize, you have three choices when writing an application:

1. Only use the VIO interface in character mode. This works well in a presentation manager environment and is a good choice for ported real mode applications. The VIO interface is also supported by the Family API mechanism. This mode is compatible with the Family API facility.

2. Use the special VIO interface facilities to sidestep VIO and directly manipulate the display screen in either character or

graphics mode. This also works in a presentation manager environment, but the application will not be able to run in a window. This approach can be compatible with the Family API if it is carefully implemented.

3. Use the presentation manager interface—the most sophisticated interface for the least effort. The presentation manager interface provides a way to "operate" applications that will become a widely known user standard because of the capabilities of the interface, because of the support it receives from key software vendors, and because it's bundled with OS/2. The user is obviously at an advantage if he or she does not have to spend time learning a new interface and operational metaphors to use your application. Finally, Microsoft is a strong believer in the power of a graphical user interface; future releases of OS/2 will contain "more-faster-better" presentation manager features. Many of these improvements will apply to existing presentation manager applications; others will expand the interface API. The standard of performance for application interfaces, as well as for application performance, continues to evolve. The rudimentary interfaces and function of the first-generation PC software are no longer considered competitive. Although OS/2 can do nothing to alleviate the developer's burden of keeping an application's function competitive, the presentation manager is a great help in keeping the application's interface state of the art.

Clearly, using the presentation manager interface is the best strategy for new or extensively reworked applications. The presentation manager API will be expanded and improved; the INT 10-like VIO functions and the VIO direct screen access capabilities will be supported for the foreseeable future, but they're an evolutionary dead end. Given that, you may want to use the VIO mechanism or the Family API facilities to quickly port an application from a real mode version and then use the presentation manager in a product upgrade release.

13.2 Background I/O

A process is in the background when it is no longer interacting directly with the user. In a presentation manager environment, this means that none of the process's windows are the keyboard focus. The windows themselves may still be visible, or they may be obscured or iconic. In a VIO environment, a process is in the background when the user has selected another screen group. In this case, the application's screen display is not visible.

A presentation manager application can easily continue to update its window displays when it is in the background; the application can continue to call the presentation manager to change its window contents in any way it wishes. A presentation manager application can arrange to be informed when it enters and leaves the background (actually, receives and loses the keyboard focus), or it can simply carry on with its work, oblivious to the issue. Background I/O can continue regardless of whether I/O form is character or graphics based.

VIO applications can continue to do I/O in background mode as well. The VIO package maintains a logical video buffer for each screen group; when VIO calls are made to update the display of a screen group that is in the background, VIO makes the requested changes to the logical video buffer. When the screen group is restored to the foreground, the updated contents of the logical video buffer are copied to the display's physical video buffer.

13.3 Graphics Under VIO

VIO is a character-oriented package and provides character mode applications with a variety of services. As we have just seen, when a screen switch takes place, VIO automatically handles saving the old screen image and restoring the new. VIO does provide a mechanism to allow an application to sidestep VIO and directly manipulate the physical video buffer, where it is then free to use any graphical capability of the hardware. There are two major disadvantages to sidestepping VIO for graphics rather than using the presentation manager services:

1. The application is device dependent because it must manipulate the video display hardware directly.

2. VIO can no longer save or restore the state of the physical video buffer during screen switch operations. The application must use a special VIO interface to provide these functions itself.

The following discussion applies only to applications that want to sidestep the presentation manager and VIO interfaces and interact directly with the display hardware.

Gaining access to the video hardware is easy; the VIO call **VioGetBuf** provides a selector to the video buffer and also gives the application's ring 2 code segments, if any, permission to program the video controller's registers. The complication arises from the screen-switching capabilities of OS/2. When the user switches the application into a background screen group, the contents of the video memory belong to someone else; the application's video memory is stored somewhere in RAM. It is disastrous when an application doesn't pay attention to this process and accidentally updates the video RAM or the video controller while they are assigned to another screen group.

Two important issues are connected with screen switching: (1) How does an application find out that it's in background mode? (2) Who saves and restores its screen image and where? The **VioScrLock** call handles screen access. Before *every* access to the display memory or the display controller, an application must *first* issue the **VioScrLock** call. While the call is in effect, OS/2 cannot perform any screen switches. Naturally, the application must do its work and quickly release the screen switch lockout. Failure to release the lock in a timely fashion has the effect of hanging the system, not only for a user's explicit screen switch commands, but also for other facilities that use the screen switch mechanism, such as the hard error handler. Hard errors can't be presented to the user while the screen lock is in effect. If OS/2 needs to switch screens, and an aberrant application has the screen lock set, OS/2 will cancel the lock and perform the screen switch after a period (currently 30 seconds). This is still a disaster scenario, although a mollified one, because the application that was summarily "delocked" will probably end up with a trashed screen image. The screen lock and unlock calls execute relatively rapidly, so they can be called frequently to protect only the actual write-to-screen operation, leaving the screen unlocked during computation. Basically, an application should use **VioScrLock** to protect a block of I/O that can be written, in its entirety, without significant recomputation. Examples of such blocks are a screen scroll, a screen erase, and a write to a cell in a spreadsheet program.

VioScrLock must be used to protect code sequences that program the display hardware as well as code sequences that write to video memory. Some peripheral programming sequences are noninterruptible. For example, a two-step programming sequence in which the first I/O write selects a multiplexed register and the second write modifies that register is uninterruptible because the first write placed the peripheral device into a special state. Such sequences must be protected within one lock/unlock pair.

Sometimes when an application calls **VioScrLock,** it receives a special error code that says, "The screen is unavailable." This means that the screen has been switched into the background and that the application may not—and must not—manipulate the display hardware. Typically, the program issues a blocking form of **VioScrLock** that suspends the thread until the screen is again in the foreground and the video display buffers contain that process's image.

An application that directly manipulates the video hardware must do more than simply lay low when it is in the background. It must also save and restore the entire video state—the contents of the display buffer and the modes, palates, cursors, and so on of the display controller. VIO does not provide this service to direct-screen manipulation processes for two reasons. First, the process is very likely using the display in a graphics mode. Some display cards contain a vast amount of video memory, and VIO would be forced to save it all just in case the application was using it all. Second, many popular display controllers such as the EGA and compatibles contain many write-only control registers. This means that VIO cannot read the controller state back from the card in order to save it for a later restoration. The only entity that understands the state of the card, and therefore the only entity that can restore that state, is the code that programmed it—the application itself.

But how does the system notify the process when it's time to save or restore? Processes can call the system in many ways, but the system can't call processes. OS/2 deals with this situation by inverting the usual meaning of *call* and *return.* When a process first decides to refresh its own screen, it creates an extra thread and uses that thread to call the **VioSavRedrawWait** function. The thread doesn't return from this call right away; instead, VIO holds the thread "captive" until it's time for a screen switch. To notify the process that it must now save its screen image, VIO allows the captive thread to return from the **VioSavRedrawWait** call. The process then saves the display state and screen contents, typically using the returned thread. When the save operation is complete, **VioSavRedrawWait** is called again. This notifies VIO that the save is complete and that the screen can now be switched; it also resets the cycle so that the process can again be notified when it's time to restore its saved screen image. In effect, this mechanism makes the return from **VioSavRedrawWait** analogous to a system-to-process call, and it makes the later call to **VioSavRedrawWait** analogous to a return from process to system.

The design of OS/2 generally avoids features in which the system calls a process to help a system activity such as screen switching. This is because a tenet of the OS/2 design religion is that an aberrant process should not be able to crash the system. Clearly, we're vulnerable to that in this case. VIO postpones the screen switch until the process saves its screen image, but what if the process somehow hangs up and doesn't complete the save? The screen is in an indeterminate state, and no process can use the screen and keyboard. As far as the user is concerned, the system has crashed. True, other processes in the system are alive and well, but if the user can't get to them, even to save his or her work, their continued health is of little comfort.

The designers of OS/2 were stuck here, between a rock and a hard place: Applications had to be able to save their screen image if they were to have direct video access, but such a facility violated the "no crashing" tenet of the design religion. Because the video access had to be supported and the system had to be crash resistant, we found a two-part workaround.

The first part concerns the most common cause of a process hanging up in its screen-save operation: hard errors. When a hard error occurs, the hard error daemon uses the screen switch mechanism to take control of the screen and the keyboard. The hard error daemon saves the existing screen image and keeps the application that was in the foreground at the time of the hard error from fighting with the daemon over control of the screen and the keyboard. However, if the hard error daemon uses the screen-switching mechanism and if the screen-switching mechanism allows the foreground process to save its own screen image, that process might, while saving its screen image, try to use the device that has the hard error and thus deadlock the system. The device in error won't service more requests until the hard error is cleared, but the hard error can't be cleared until the daemon takes control. The daemon can't take control until the foreground process is through saving, and the foreground process can't complete saving until the device services its request. Note that this deadlock doesn't require an explicit I/O operation on the part of the foreground process; simply allocating memory or referencing a segment might cause swapping or loading activity on the device that is experiencing the hard error.

A two-part approach is used to solve this problem. First, deadlocks involving the hard error daemon are managed by having the hard error screen switch do a partial screen save. When I said earlier that VIO would not save the video memory of direct access screen groups, I was lying a bit. When the system is doing a hard error screen switch, VIO will save the first part (typically 4 KB) of the video memory—enough to display a page of text. We don't have to worry about how much video RAM the application was using because the video display will be switched to character mode and the hard error daemon will overwrite only a small part of video memory. Naturally, this means that the hard error daemon must always restore the original screen group; it can't switch to a third screen group because the first one's video memory wasn't fully saved.

VIO and the hard error daemon keep enough free RAM around to save this piece of the video memory so that a hard error screen switch can always take place without the need for memory swapping. When the hard error daemon is finished with the screen, the overwritten video memory is restored from the buffer. As we discussed above, however, VIO can't restore the state of the video controller itself; only the application can do that. The **VioModeWait** function is used to notify the application that it must restore the screen state.

In summary, any application that directly accesses the video hardware must provide captive threads to **VioSavRedrawWait** and to **VioModeWait. VioSavRedrawWait** will return when the application is to save or to restore the video memory. **VioModeWait** will return when the application is to restore the state of the video controller from the application's own record of the controller's state.

The second part of the "application hangs while saving screen and hangs system" solution is unfortunately ad hoc: If the application does not complete its screen save operation within approximately 30 seconds, the system considers it hung and switches the screen anyway. The hung process is suspended while it's in background so that it won't suddenly "come alive" and manipulate the screen. When the process is again in the foreground, the system unsuspends it and hopes that it will straighten itself out. In such a case, the application's screen image may be trashed. At best, the user can enter a "repaint screen" command to the application and all will be well; at worst, the application is hung up, but the system itself is alive and well. Building a system that can detect and correct errors on the part of an application is impossible; the best that we can hope to do is to keep an aberrant application from damaging the rest of the system.

I hope that this long and involved discussion of rules, regulations, doom, and disaster has not frightened you into contemplating programs that communicate by Morse code. You need be concerned with these issues only if you write applications that manipulate the display device directly, circumventing either VIO or the presentation manager interfaces. These concerns are not an issue when you are writing ordinary text applications that use VIO or the presentation manager or graphics applications that use the presentation manager. VIO and the presentation manager handle screen saving and support background display writing. Finally, I'll point out, as a curiosity, that even processes that use handle operations only to write to STDOUT use VIO or the presentation manager. When STDOUT points to the screen device, the operating system routes STDOUT writes to the VIO/presentation manager packages. This is, of course, invisible to the application; it need not concern itself with foreground/background, EGA screen modes, hard error screen restorations, and the like.

14

Interactive Programs

A great many applications interact with the user via the screen and the keyboard. Because the primary function of most desktop computers is to run interactive applications, OS/2 contains a variety of services that make interaction powerful and efficient.

As we've seen in earlier chapters, interactive programs can use the presentation manager to manage their interface, or they can do it themselves, using VIO or direct video access for their I/O. The presentation manager provides a great deal of function and automatically solves a great many problems. For example, a presentation manager application doesn't have to concern itself with the sharing of the single keyboard among all processes in its screen group. The presentation manager takes care of that by handling the keyboard and by simply sending keyboard events to each process, as appropriate.

If you're writing an application that uses the presentation manager, then you can skip this chapter. If you're writing an application that does not use the presentation manager but that may be used in an interactive fashion, it's very important that you understand the issues discussed in this chapter. They apply to all programs that use VIO or the STDIN/STDOUT handles to do interactive I/O, even if such programs are being run via the presentation manager.

14.1   I/O Architecture

Simply put, the system I/O architecture says that all programs read their main input from the STDIN handle and write their main output to the STDOUT handle. This applies to all non-presentation manager applications, but especially to interactive applications. The reason is that OS/2 and program-execution utilities such as CMD.EXE (shell programs) cooperate to use the STDIN/STDOUT mechanism to control access to the screen and keyboard. For example, if two processes read from the keyboard at the same time, some keys go to one process, and the rest go to the other in an unpredictable fashion. Likewise, it is a bad idea for more than one process to write to the screen at the same time.[1] Clearly, you don't want too many processes doing keyboard/screen I/O within a single screen group, but you also don't want too few. It would be embarrassing if a user terminated one interactive application in a screen group, such as a program run from CMD.EXE, and CMD.EXE failed to resume use of the keyboard/screen to print a prompt.

So how will we handle this? We might be running a great many processes in a screen group. For example, you could use CMD.EXE to execute a spreadsheet program, which was told to execute a subshell—another copy of CMD.EXE. The user could then execute a program to interpret a special batch script, which in turn executes an editor. And this editor was told to run a copy of a C compiler to scan the source being edited for errors. Oh, yes, and we forgot to mention that the top level CMD.EXE was told to run a copy of the assembler in parallel with all these other operations (similar to the UNIX "&" operation).

Many processes are running in this screen group; some of them are interactive, and some are not, and at any time only one is using the keyboard and the screen. Although it would be handy to declare that the most recently executed process will use the keyboard and the screen, you can't: The most recently executed program was the C compiler, and it's not even interactive. OS/2 cannot decide which process should be using the screen and keyboard because OS/2 lacks any knowledge of the function of each process. OS/2 knows only their child-parent relationships, and the situation can be far too complex for that information to be sufficient.

---

1. Within the same screen group and/or window, of course. Applications that use different virtual screens can each write to their own screen without regard for other virtual screens.

Because OS/2 can't determine which process should be using the screen and the keyboard, it doesn't try. The processes themselves make the determination. The rule is simple: The process that is currently using the screen and the keyboard can grant access to a child process, or it can keep access for itself. If a process grants access to a child process, then it must keep off the screen and the keyboard until that child terminates. Once the child process is granted use of the screen and the keyboard, the child process is free to do as it wishes, perhaps granting access to its own children. Until that child process terminates, the parent must avoid device conflict by staying quiet.

Let's look at how this works in real life. For example, CMD.EXE, the first process in the screen group, starts up with STDIN open on the keyboard and STDOUT open on the screen. (The system did this by magic.) When this copy of CMD.EXE is told to execute the spreadsheet program, CMD.EXE doesn't know if the spreadsheet program is interactive or not, so it lets the child process—the spreadsheet program—inherit its STDIN and STDOUT handles, which point to the keyboard and to the screen. Because CMD.EXE granted access to the screen and the keyboard to the child, CMD.EXE can't use STDIN or STDOUT until that child process terminates. Typically, at this point CMD.EXE would **DosCWait** on its child process.

Now the spreadsheet program comes alive. It writes to STDOUT, which is the screen, and it reads from STDIN, which is the keyboard. When the spreadsheet program is instructed to run CMD.EXE, it does so, presuming, as did its parent, that CMD.EXE is interactive and therefore letting CMD.EXE inherit its STDIN and STDOUT handles. Now the spreadsheet must avoid any STDIN/STDOUT I/O until its child—CMD.EXE—terminates. As long as these processes continue to run interactive children, things are going to work out OK. When the children start to die and execution starts popping back up the tree, applications restart, using the screen and the keyboard in the proper order.

But what about the detached assembly that CMD.EXE started before it ran the spreadsheet? In this case, the user has explicitly told CMD.EXE that it wants the application run "detached" from the keyboard. If the user specified a STDIN for the assembler—perhaps a file—then CMD.EXE sets that up for the child's STDIN. If the user didn't specify an alternate STDIN, CMD.EXE opens STDIN on the

NULL device so that an application that reads it will receive EOF. In this way, CMD.EXE (which knew that the application wasn't to use the keyboard because the user gave explicit instructions) did not let the child process inherit STDIN, so CMD.EXE continues to use it, printing a new prompt and reading a new command. Figure 14-1 shows a typical process tree. The shaded processes have inherited a STDIN, which points to the keyboard, and a STDOUT, which points to the screen. All such processes must lie on a single path if the rules are followed because each process has the option of allowing a maximum of one child to inherit its STDIN and STDOUT handles unchanged.

You are undoubtedly becoming a bit concerned at this point: "Does this mean I'm forced to use the limited, serial STDIN/STDOUT interface for my high-resolution graphics output?" I'm glad you asked. What we've been discussing is the *architectural model* that must be followed because it's used systemwide to avoid screen and keyboard conflicts. However, applications can and should use special services to optimize their interactive I/O as long as they do so according to the

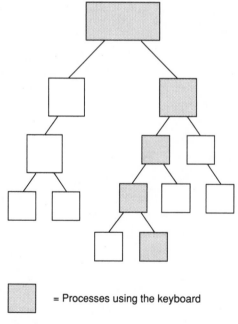

☐ = Processes using the keyboard

Figure 14-1.
Processes using the keyboard.

architectural model. Specifically, OS/2 provides the KBD, VIO, and MOU dynlink packages. These high-performance programs interface directly with the hardware, avoiding the STDIN/STDOUT limited interfaces. The key is "directly with the hardware": *A process is welcome to use hardware-specific interfaces to optimize performance, but only after it has ensured that the architectural model grants it access to that device.*

In practice, this is straightforward. Any interactive program that wants to use KBD first ensures (via **DosQHandType**) that its STDIN handle is open on the keyboard. If STDIN is not open on the keyboard, the keyboard belongs to another program, and the interactive program *must not* burst in on the rightful owner by using KBD. All dynlink device interfaces are trusting souls and won't check your bona fides before they do their stuff, so the application must look before it leaps. The same applies to STDOUT, to the keyboard device, and to the VIO package. All applications must verify that STDIN and STDOUT point to the keyboard and the screen before they use any device-direct interface, which includes VIO, KBD, MOU, and direct device access.

What's an interactive program to do if it finds that STDIN or STDOUT *doesn't* point to the keyboard and screen devices? I don't know, but the author of the application does. Some applications might not be truly interactive and therefore would work fine. For example, Microsoft Macro Assembler (MASM) can prompt the user for the names of source, object, and listing files. Although MASM is technically interacting with the user, MASM is not an interactive application because it doesn't depend on the ability to interact to do its work. If STDIN points to a file, MASM is perfectly happy reading the filenames from that file. MASM doesn't need to see if STDIN points to the keyboard because MASM doesn't need to use the KBD package. Instead, MASM reads its names from STDIN and takes what it gets.

Other programs may not require an interactive interface, but when they *are* interacting, they may want to use KBD or VIO to improve performance. Such applications should test STDIN and STDOUT to see if they point to the appropriate devices. If they do, applications can circumvent the STDIN/STDOUT limitations and use KBD and VIO. If they don't, the applications are stuck with STDIN and STDOUT. Finally, many interactive applications make no sense at all in a noninteractive environment. These applications need to check STDIN and

STDOUT, and, if they don't point to the devices, the applications should write an error message to STDERR and terminate. Admittedly, the user is in error if he or she attempts to run an interactive application, such as a WYSIWYG editor, detached, but printing an error message is far better than trashing the display screen and fighting with CMD.EXE over the keyboard. The screen group would then be totally unusable, and the user might not even be able to terminate the editor if he or she can't get the terminate command through the keyboard contention.

It's technically possible, although highly unusual, for an application to inherit access to the keyboard yet not have access to the screen. More commonly, an application has access to the screen but not to the keyboard. Although most users would find it confusing, power users can detach programs such as compilers so that any output summary or error messages they produce appear on the screen. Although the user may end up with intermingled output, he or she may like the instant notification. Each application that wants to use VIO, KBD, or the environment manager needs to check STDIN and STDOUT individually for access to the appropriate device.

Earlier in this section, we talked about how applications work when they create children that inherit the screen and the keyboard, and it probably sounded complicated. In practice, it can be simple. For example, the technique used to **DosExecPgm** a child that will inherit the keyboard can be used when the parent itself doesn't have the keyboard and thus can't bequeath it. Therefore, the parent doesn't need to check its STDIN status during the **DosExecPgm.** To summarize, here are the rules:

Executing Programs

- If the child process is to inherit the STDIN handle, the parent process must not access that handle any further until the child process terminates.

- If the child process is not to inherit the STDIN handle (so that your program can continue to interact), then the child process STDIN must be opened on a file or on the NULL device. Don't rely on the child not to use the handle; the child might **DosExecPgm** a grandchild that is not so well mannered.

- A process can let only one child at a time inherit its STDIN. If a process is going to run multiple child processes in parallel, only one can inherit STDIN; the others must use alternative STDIN sources.

- All these rules apply to STDINs open on pipes and files as well as to KBD, so your application needn't check the source of STDIN.

All Processes

- Verify that the STDIN handle points to the keyboard before using KBD, SIGBRK, or SIGCTLC (see below). You must not use these direct device facilities if STDIN is not open on the keyboard.

- Verify that the STDOUT handle points to the screen before using VIO. You must not use direct device facilities if STDOUT is not open on the screen.

- If the process executes any child that inherits its STDIN, it must not terminate itself until that child process terminates. This is because the parent will assume that the termination of the direct child means that the STDIN handle is now available.

14.2   Ctrl-C and Ctrl-Break Handling

Just when you think that it's safe to go back into the operating system, one more device and process tree issue needs to be discussed: the handling of Ctrl-C and Ctrl-Break. (Once again, this discussion applies only to programs that don't explicitly use the presentation manager facility. Those applications that do use the presentation manager have all these issues handled for them automatically.) These two events are tied to the keyboard hardware, so their routing has a great deal in common with the above discussion. The fundamental problem is simple: When the user presses Ctrl-C or Ctrl-Break, what's the operating system to do? Clearly, a process or processes or perhaps an entire subtree of processes must be killed or signaled. But do we kill or signal? And which one(s)?

OS/2 defines a convention that allows the processes themselves to decide. Consider a type of application—a "command application"— that runs in command mode. In command mode, a command application reads a command, executes the command, and then typically returns to command mode. Furthermore, when the user presses Ctrl-Break, the command application doesn't want to terminate but to stop what it's doing and return to command mode. This is the style of most interactive applications but not that of most noninteractive applications. For example, if the user types MASM to CMD.EXE, the CMD.EXE program runs MASM as a child process. CMD.EXE is a command application, but MASM is not. The distinction between "command application" and "noncommand application" is not made by OS/2 but is merely descriptive terminology that is useful in this discussion.

The system convention is that Ctrl-C and Ctrl-Break mean "Stop what you're doing." OS/2 generates signals in response to Ctrl-C and Ctrl-Break; it never directly kills a process. OS/2 can easily decide which process to signal when Ctrl-C or Ctrl-Break is pressed: It signals the lowest command process in the process tree in that screen group. At first glance, this may not seem easy. How can OS/2 distinguish command processes, and how can it determine the "lowest"? The total process tree in a screen group may be very complex; some processes in it may have died, creating multiple now-independent "treelets."

The process tree may be complex, but the tree of processes using the keyboard is simpler because a process can't let multiple children simultaneously inherit its STDIN. A process can only inherit the keyboard,[2] not open it explicitly; so a single path down the tree must intersect (or contain) all command processes. This single path can't be fragmented because of missing processes due to child death because a process that has let a child inherit its STDIN must not terminate until the child does. So, all OS/2 needs is to find any command process in the command subtree and then look at its descendants for another command process and so on. The bottommost process receives the signal.[3]

Figure 14-2 illustrates a possible process tree. The shaded processes have inherited handles to the keyboard and screen; those marked with C are command processes.

This now begs the final question: How can OS/2 tell if an application is a command process or not? It can tell because all command

---

2. Actually, a process *should* only inherit the keyboard. The keyboard device can be opened explicitly, but doing so when a process's inherited STDIN doesn't point to the keyboard device would be a serious error.

3. Actually, OS/2 uses a more efficient algorithm than this; I'm merely illustrating that finding the lowest command process is not difficult.

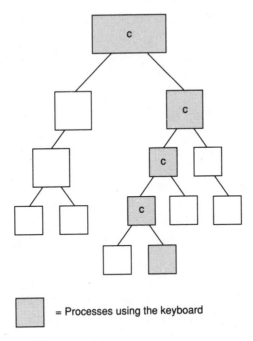

= Processes using the keyboard

Figure 14-2.
Ctrl-C routing in a process tree.

processes/command applications do something that other processes
never do. By definition, a command process doesn't want to be summarily killed when the user presses Ctrl-C or Ctrl-Break, so all command processes establish signal handlers for Ctrl-C and Ctrl-Break.
Because all command processes intercept Ctrl-C and Ctrl-Break, all we
need now is to establish the convention that *only* command processes
intercept Ctrl-C and Ctrl-Break. This hearkens back to our earlier
discussion of checking STDIN before directly using the keyboard
device. Telling the keyboard device that you want the Ctrl-C or Ctrl-
Break signals routed to your process is a form of I/O with the keyboard
device, and it must only be done if your program has verified that
STDIN points to the keyboard device. Furthermore, intercepting Ctrl-C
or Ctrl-Break just so that your program can clean up during unexpected
termination is unnecessary and insufficient. The SIGTERM signal or,
better, the exitlist mechanism provides this capability and covers
causes of death other than the keyboard. So all processes that intercept

Ctrl-C and Ctrl-Break have access to the keyboard, and they want to do something other than die when the user presses Ctrl-C or Ctrl-Break. They fit the command process definition.

Now that we've exhaustively shown how OS/2 finds which process to send a Ctrl-C signal, what should the process do when it gets the signal? Obey the system convention and stop what it's doing as quickly as is wise. If the application isn't working on a command, the application typically flushes the keyboard type-ahead buffer and reprompts. If the application is working on a command that is implemented in code within the application, the application jumps from the signal handler to its command loop or, more commonly, sets a flag to terminate the current command prematurely.[4]

Finally, if the application is running a child process, it typically stops what it's doing by issuing a **DosKill** on that child command subtree. This, then, is how Ctrl-C can kill a program such as MASM. Ctrl-C is sent to MASM's closest ancestor that is a command process,[5] which in turn issues a **DosKill** on MASM's subtree. MASM does any exitlist cleanup that it wishes (probably deleting scratch files) and then terminates. When the command process that ran MASM, typically CMD.EXE, sees that MASM has terminated, it prints ^C on the screen, followed by a new prompt.

---

4. Occasionally, terminating a command halfway through could leave the user's work trashed. In such a case, finishing the command is prudent.

5. Often, CMD.EXE is MASM's direct ancestor, but other programs, such as a build utility, could have come between CMD.EXE and MASM.

15

The File System

The file system in OS/2 version 1.0 is little changed from that of MS-DOS, partially in an effort to preserve compatibility with MS-DOS programs and partially due to limitations imposed by the project's schedule. When the schedule for an "all singing, all dancing" OS/2 was shown to be too long, planned file system improvements were moved to a future release. To explain the rationale for postponing something so useful, I'll digress a little.

The microcomputer industry developed around the dual concepts of mass market software and standards. Because software is mass marketed, you can buy some very sophisticated and useful programs for a modest sum of money—at least modest in comparison to the development cost, which is often measured in millions of dollars. Mass marketing encourages standards because users don't want to buy machines, peripherals, and systems that don't run these programs. Likewise, the acceptance of the standards encourages the development of mass market software because standards make it possible for a single binary program to execute correctly on a great many machines and thus provide a market big enough to repay the development costs of a major application.

This synergy, or positive feedback, between standards and mass market software affected the process of developing operating systems. At first glance, adding new features to an operating system seems straightforward. The developers create new features in a new release, and then applications are written to use those new features. However, with mass market software, it doesn't work that way. Microsoft could indeed release a new version of OS/2 with new features (and, in fact, we certainly will do so), but initially few new applications will use said new features. This is because of the initial limited market penetration of the new release. For example, let's assume that at a certain time after the availability of a new release, 10 percent of OS/2 users have upgraded. An ISV (Independent Software Vendor) is planning its next new product—one it hopes will be a bestseller. The ISV must decide whether to use the new feature and automatically lock itself out of 90 percent of the potential market or to use the common subset of features contained in the earlier OS/2 release and be able to run on all machines, including the 10 percent running the OS/2 upgrade. In general, ISVs won't use a nonvital feature until the great majority of existing systems support that feature.

The key to introducing new features in an operating system isn't that they be available and useful; it's that the release which contains those new features sees widespread use as quickly as possible. If this doesn't happen, then the new feature pretty much dies stillborn. This is why each MS-DOS release that contained major new functionality coincided with a release that was required to use new hardware. MS-DOS version 2.0 was required for the IBM XT product line; MS-DOS version 3.0 was required for the IBM AT product line. And OS/2 is no exception: It wasn't required for a new "box," but it was required to bring out the protect mode machine lying fallow inside 80286-based machines. If a new release of a system doesn't provide a new feature that makes people want it or need it badly, then market penetration will be slow. People will pay the cost and endure the hassle of upgrading only if their applications require it, and those applications dare require it only if most people have already upgraded.

Because of this, the initial release of OS/2 is "magical" in the eyes of its developers. It provides a window of opportunity in which to introduce new features into the PC operating system standard, a window that won't be open quite as wide again for a long time. And this postponed major file system enhancements: The file system can be enhanced in a later release and benefit existing applications without any change on their part, whereas many other OS/2 features needed to be in the first release or they might never be available.

15.1   The OS/2 File System

Although OS/2 version 1.0 contains little in the way of file system improvements, it does contain two that are significant. The first is *asynchronous I/O*. Asynchronous I/O consists of two functions, **DosReadAsync** and **DosWriteAsync.** These functions are identical to **DosRead** and **DosWrite** except that they return to the caller immediately, usually before the I/O operation has completed. Each takes the handle of a semaphore that is cleared when the I/O operation completes. The threads of the calling process can use this semaphore to poll for operation complete, or they can wait for the operation to complete. The **DosMuxSemWait** call is particularly useful in this regard because it allows a process to wait for several semaphore events, which can be asynchronous I/O events, IPC events, and timer events, intermingled as the programmer wishes.

The second file system feature is *extended partitioning;* it supports dividing large physical disks into multiple sections, several of which may contain FAT file systems. In effect, it causes OS/2 to treat a large hard disk as two or more smaller ones, each of which meets the file system's size limits. It's widely believed that MS-DOS is limited to disks less than 32 MB in size. This isn't strictly true. The limitation is that a disk can have no more than 65,535 *sectors*; the standard sector size is 512 bytes, which gives the 32 MB value. Furthermore, each disk is limited to 32,768 clusters. A sector is the unit of disk storage; disks can read and write only integral sectors. A sector's size is established when the disk is formatted. A cluster is the unit of disk space allocation for files and directories. It may be as small as one sector, or it may be four sectors, eight sectors, or some other size. Because the MS-DOS file system supports a maximum of 65 KB sectors but only 32 KB clusters, a 32 MB disk must be allocated in two-sector (or bigger) clusters. It's possible to write a device driver that uses a sector size that is a multiple of 512 bytes, which gets around the 65 KB sector restriction and allows the use of a disk greater than 32 MB. This trick works for MS-DOS and for OS/2, but it's not optimal because it doesn't do anything to increase the maximum number of allocation clusters from the existing 32 KB value,[1] which means that because many disk files are small a lot of space is wasted due to internal fragmentation.

The OS/2 version 1.0 extended partitioning feature provides an interim solution that is not quite as convenient as large sectors but that reduces the wastage from internal fragmentation: It allows more than one disk partition to contain a FAT file system. Multipartitioned disks are possible under MS-DOS, but only one partition can be an MS-DOS (that is, FAT) file system. This restriction has been relaxed in OS/2 so that, for example, a 60 MB disk can be partitioned into two separate logical disks (for example, C and D), each 30 MB.

15.2   Media Volume Management

The multitasking capability of OS/2 necessitated major file system enhancements in the area of volume management. A disk *volume* is the name given to the file system and files on a particular disk medium. A disk drive that contains a fixed medium always contains the same volume, but a disk drive from which the media (such as floppy disks) can be removed will contain whatever disk—whatever volume—the user has in it at the time. That volumes can change becomes a problem in a multitasking environment. For example, suppose a user is using a word processor to edit a file on a floppy disk in drive A. The editor has opened the file and is keeping it open for the duration of the edit. Without closing the file or terminating the editor, the user can switch to a screen group in which a spreadsheet program is running. The user might then need to insert a different disk into drive A—one that contains data needed by the spreadsheet. If the user then switches back to the word processor without remembering to change the floppy disk, disaster will strike. Pressing the Page Down key will cause the editor to try to read another sector from its already open disk file. The operating system knows—because of FAT information stored in RAM buffers—that the next sector in the text file is sector N, and it will issue a read to sector N on the wrong medium—the spreadsheet floppy disk—and return that to the word processor program as the next sector of the text

---

1. The FAT file system can deal with a maximum of 32 KB allocation units, or clusters. No matter what the size of the disk, all files must consume disk space in increments of no smaller than $\frac{1}{32}$Kth of the total disk size. This means that a 60 MB disk, using 1024 byte sectors, allocates space in 2048-byte increments.

file. And, at that, the user is getting off lightly; he or she might just as easily have given the word processor a command that caused it to write a sector to the disk, which would do double damage. A file on the spreadsheet floppy would be destroyed by the "random" write, and the text file would be corrupted as well because it's missing a sector write that it should have received.

We can't solve this problem by admonishing the user to be careful; many programs read from and write to disk without direct user intervention. For example, the word processor might save work in progress to disk every two minutes. If this time interval elapses while the user is still working with the spreadsheet program on the spreadsheet floppy disk, our hypothetical "flawless" user is still S.O.L.[2]

OS/2 resolves these problems by recognizing that when an application does I/O to an open file the I/O is not really aimed at drive A; it's aimed at a particular floppy disk volume—the one containing the open file. Each disk volume, removable or not, has a volume name stored in its root directory and a unique 32-bit volume identifier stored in its boot sector. Figure 15-1 illustrates the two volume names—one for computer use and one for human use. Each file handle is associated with a particular 32-bit volume ID. When an I/O request is made for a file handle, OS/2 checks to see if the proper volume is in the drive by comparing the 32-bit value of the request with that of the medium currently spinning. If they match, the operation completes. If the mounted volume is different from the requested volume, OS/2 uses the hard error daemon mechanism to prompt the user to insert the correct volume in the drive.

VOLUME LABELS

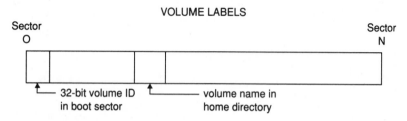

Figure 15-1.
Volume ID and volume name location.

Three problems must be overcome to make this scheme practical. First, checking the volume ID of the medium must be fast. You can't afford to read the boot sector each time you do an I/O operation if doing so halves the speed of disk I/O. Second, you need assurance that volume IDs are unique. Third, you need a plan to deal with a volume that doesn't have a volume ID.

Keeping down the cost of volume verification is easy if you know when a volume is changed; obviously, the ID is read from the boot sector only when a medium has been changed. But how can OS/2 tell that a media change has occurred? It can't; that's a device driver issue.

For starters, if the device contains a nonremovable medium, rechecking its volume ID is never necessary. The device driver understands this, and when it is asked the status of the medium, it responds, "Unchanged." Some removable media drives have a flag bit that warns the driver that the door has been opened. In this case, when asked, the device driver tells OS/2 that the medium is "uncertain." The driver doesn't know for sure that it was really changed, but it may have been; so OS/2 rechecks the volume ID. Rechecking the volume ID is more difficult when a removable media device has no such indicator.

In this case, the author of the device driver uses device-specific knowledge to decide on a minimum possible time to effect a media change. If the device is ready, yet less than the minimum possible time has elapsed since the last operation, the driver knows that the same medium must be in the drive. If more than the minimum possible time has elapsed, the driver returns "medium uncertain," and OS/2 rechecks the volume label. This time interval is typically 2 seconds for floppy disk drives, so effectively an extra disk read is done after every idle period; for any given episode of disk I/O, however, no extra reads are needed.

Ensuring that a volume ID is unique is another problem. Simply lecturing the user on the wisdom of unique IDs is inadequate; the user will still label three disks "temp" or number them all as "10." And even the hypothetical perfect user might borrow from a neighbor a disk whose name is the same as one the user already owns. OS/2 deals with this problem by using a 32-bit randomized value for disk volume IDs. When a disk is formatted, the user enters a supposedly unique name. This name is checksummed, and the result, combined with the number of seconds between the present and 1980, is used to seed a random number generator. This generator returns a 32-bit volume ID. Although accidentally duplicating a volume ID is obviously possible, the four billion possible codes make it quite unlikely.

The name the user enters is used only to prompt the user to insert the volume when necessary, so it need not be truly unique for the volume management system to work. If the user names several disks WORK, OS/2 still sees them as independent volumes because their volume IDs are different. If the user inserts the wrong WORK disk in response to a prompt, OS/2 recognizes it as the wrong disk and reissues the "Insert disk WORK" prompt. After trying each WORK volume in turn, the user will probably decide to relabel the disks!

The thorniest problem arises from unlabeled disks—disks formatted with MS-DOS. Forcing the user to label these disks is unacceptable, as is having OS/2 automatically label them with volume IDs: The disk may be read-only, perhaps permanently so. Even if the disk is not read-only, the problem of low density and high density raises its ugly head. Low-density disks can be read in a high-density drive, but writes made to a low-density disk from a high-density drive can only be read on high-density drives. If a low-density disk is placed in a high-density drive and then labeled by OS/2, its boot sector is no longer readable when the disk is placed in a low-density drive.

For volumes without a proper volume ID, OS/2 attempts to create a unique substitute volume ID by checksumming parts of the volume's root directory and its FAT table. OS/2 uses the existing volume name if one exists; if there is no volume name, OS/2 attempts to describe the disk. None of these techniques is foolproof, and they require extra disk operations every time the medium is identified. Therefore, software distributors and users should make every effort to label disks that OS/2 systems are to use. OS/2 labels are backward compatible with MS-DOS version 3.x labels.

The OS/2 DISKCOPY command makes a byte-by-byte verbatim copy of a floppy disk, *except* that the duplicate disk has a different volume ID value in the boot sector (the volume *label* name is not changed). OS/2 users can't tell this, however, because the DISKCOMP utility lies, and if two disks are identical in every byte *except* for the volume ID, it reports that the disks are identical. However, if the user uses DISKCOPY to duplicate the disk under OS/2 and then compares the two with DISKCOMP under MS-DOS 3.x, a difference is reported.

Our discussion so far has centered on file reads and writes to an open handle. Reads and writes are *volume-oriented* operations because they're aimed at the volume on which the file resides. **DosOpen**s, on the other hand, are *drive oriented* because they search the default or specified drive for the file in question (or create it) regardless of the volume in the drive. All handle operations are volume oriented, and all name-based calls are drive oriented. Currently, you cannot specify that a given file is to be opened on or created on a specific volume. To ensure that a scratch or output file is created on a certain volume, arrange to have a file open on that volume and issue a write to that file immediately before doing the file open. The write operation followed by a **DosBufReset** will ensure that the particular medium is in the drive at that time.

15.3   I/O Efficiency

OS/2 provides full blocking and deblocking services for all disk I/O requests. A program can read or write any number of bytes, and OS/2 will read the proper sectors into internal buffers so that only the specified bytes are affected. Naturally, every **DosRead** or **DosWrite** call takes time to execute, so if your program makes few I/O calls, each for large amounts of data, it will execute faster.

I/O performance can be further improved by making sector aligned calls, that is, by requesting a transfer of an integral multiple of 512 bytes to or from a file seek position that is itself a multiple of 512. OS/2 reads and writes entire disk sectors directly from and to the device hardware without an intermediate copy step through system buffers. Because the file system keeps logically adjacent sectors physically adjacent on the disk, disk seek times and rotational latency are such that one can read or write four sectors of data (2048 bytes) in essentially the same time needed to read or write one sector (512 bytes).

Even if the length or the file position of the request isn't a multiple of 512, OS/2 performs the initial fraction of the request via its buffers, directly transfers any whole sectors out of the middle of the request, and uses the buffers for the fractional remainder. Even if your requests aren't sector aligned, making them as large as feasible is beneficial.

To summarize, I/O is most efficient when requests are large and sector aligned. Even misaligned requests can be almost optimally serviced if they are large. Programs that cannot naturally make aligned requests and that are not I/O intensive should take advantage of the blocking and deblocking services that OS/2 provides. Likewise, programs that need to make large, unaligned requests should use OS/2's blocking management. Programs that need to make frequent, small, nonaligned requests will perform best if they read blocks of sectors into internal buffers and deblock the data themselves, avoiding the overhead of frequent **DosRead** or **DosWrite** calls.

16

Device Monitors, Data Integrity, and Timer Services

In discussing the design goals of OS/2, I mentioned continuing to support the kinds of functionality found in MS-DOS, even when that functionality was obtained by going around the operating system. A good example of such functionality is device data manipulation, a technique that usually involves hooking interrupt vectors and that is used by many application programs. For example, pop-up programs such as SideKick have become very popular. These programs get into memory via the terminate and stay resident mechanism and then edit the keyboard interrupt vector to point to their code. These programs examine each keystroke to see if it is their special activate key. If not, they transfer control to the original interrupt handler. If the keystroke is their special activate key, they retain control of the CPU and display, or "pop up," a message or a menu on the screen. Other programs hook the keyboard vector to provide spell checking or keyboard macro expansion. Some programs also hook the BIOS entry vector that commands the printer, either to substitute alternate printer driver code or to manipulate the data sent to the printer. Programs that turn a spreadsheet's output sideways are an example of this.

In general, these programs edit, or hook, the interrupt vectors that receive device interrupts and communicate with device driver routines in the ROM BIOS. The functions provided by such programs and their evident popularity among users demonstrate a need for programs to be able to monitor and/or modify device data streams. The OS/2 mechanism that does this is called a *device monitor*.

16.1   Device Monitors

The design of device monitors had to meet the general requirements and religion of OS/2. Specifically, the MS-DOS technique of letting applications receive interrupts by editing the interrupt vectors could not be allowed because doing so would destroy the system's ability to provide a stable environment. Furthermore, unlike MS-DOS, OS/2 doesn't use the ROM BIOS as a form of device driver, so hooking the BIOS communication vectors would not provide access to the device data stream. In addition, allowing an application to arbitrarily interfere with a device driver's operation is contrary to OS/2 design principles; the device driver is the architectural embodiment of knowledge about the device, and it must be involved in and "aware" of any external manipulation of the data stream. The result is an OS/2 device monitor mechanism that allows processes, running in their normal ring 3 state, to monitor and edit device data streams with the prior permission and knowledge of the appropriate device driver.

Specifically, a process registers itself as a device monitor by calling the appropriate device driver via a **DosMonReq** call.[1] The process also provides two data buffers, one for incoming monitor data and another for outgoing monitor data. Processes can easily call OS/2, but OS/2 has no way to call processes.[2] OS/2 gets around this by inverting the normal sense of a call and return sequence. When OS/2 needs to "call" a process, it requires that process to call OS/2 beforehand with one of its threads. OS/2 holds this thread captive until the callback event takes place. OS/2 then accomplishes a call to the process by releasing the thread so that it returns from the holding system call and resumes execution within the process. When the process is ready to "return" to OS/2, it recalls the holding entry point (see Figure 16-1).

---

1. Which is a dynlink package that eventually calls the device driver via a **DosDevIOCtl** call.
2. Signals are a partial exception to this, but signals have limitations, as discussed earlier.

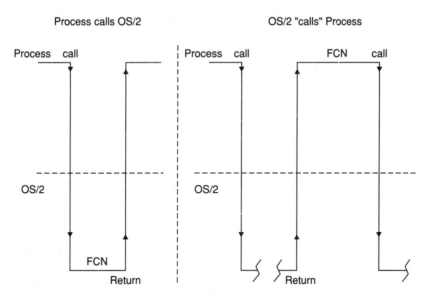

Process calls OS/2   OS/2 "calls" Process

Figure 16-1.
"Calling" a process from OS/2.

OS/2 uses this technique for monitors as well. A monitoring process is required to call the OS/2 entry point directly after registering itself as a device monitor. OS/2 notifies the monitor process of the presence of data in the incoming buffer by allowing this thread to return to the process. Figure 16-2 on the following page illustrates a device with two monitoring processes, X and Y.

But we need to discuss a few additional details. First, because OS/2 strives to make processes see a consistent environment regardless of the presence of other processes, each device can have as many monitors as the device driver allows. OS/2 connects multiple device monitors into a chain so that the device data stream is passed through the first monitor in the chain, then through the second monitor, and so on. When a process registers itself as a monitor, it specifies whether it wants to be first in the chain or last in the chain; some applications are sensitive to this. The first monitor to register itself as first is truly first; the next monitor to ask for first actually becomes second, and so forth. The same algorithm applies to monitors that want to be last: The first to so request becomes the last, the second to request last becomes next to last, and so forth.

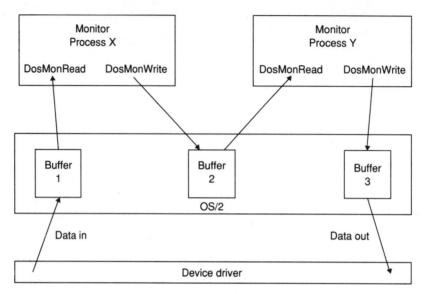

Figure 16-2.
Device monitors.

   The actual format of the monitor data stream is device specific; the device driver decrees the format. Some device drivers have special rules and requirements. For example, the keyboard device driver allows monitoring processes to insert the "screen switch" key sequence into the data stream, whereupon it is recognized as if the user had typed it at the physical keyboard. But the device driver will not pass such sequences that really were typed through the monitor chain; they are directly obeyed instead.

   This approach prevents an amok keyboard monitor from effectively crashing the system by intercepting and consuming all attempts by the user to switch screen groups. The screen device driver does not allow device monitors, not because the performance impact would be too big (as it, in fact, would be) but because the VIO and presentation manager dynlink packages totally circumvent the screen device driver so that it never sees any screen data being written.

   The **DosMonRead** call holds the device's thread until incoming data is available. The **DosMonWrite** call returns the CPU to the process as soon as it is able. The same thread that calls **DosMonRead** need not be the one to call **DosMonWrite** (see below).

Because monitors are an important component of OS/2, an application must be very careful to use them properly; therefore, some caveats are in order. First, monitors are inserted into the device data chain, with obvious effects on the data throughput rate of the device. Each time the user presses a key, for example, a packet must pass through every monitor in the keyboard chain before the application can read the key and obey or echo it. Clearly, any sluggishness on the part of a monitor or the presence of too many monitors in a chain will adversely affect system response. The thread involved in reading, processing, and writing monitor data should be set at a high priority. We recommend the lowest of the force run priority categories. Furthermore, the monitor component of a monitoring application must contain no critical sections or other events that could slow or suspend its operation. In addition, if a monitor data stream will be extensively processed, a normal-priority thread must be used to handle that processing so that the high-priority thread can continue to transfer monitor data in and out without impediment. For example, an auxiliary thread and buffer must be used if a keyboard monitor is to write all keystrokes to a disk buffer.

Finally, if a monitor process terminates abnormally although OS/2 properly unlinks it from the monitor chain, the data in the process's monitor buffers is lost. Clearly, losing an unspecified amount of data without warning from the keyboard data stream or perhaps from printer output will upset the user no little amount. Monitoring processes must be written carefully so that they minimize this risk.

The device monitor feature threatens OS/2's fundamental architectural principles more than any other. Thus, its presence in the system testifies to its importance. Specifically, device monitors violate the design principle of minimizing interference between processes, a.k.a. encapsulation. Clearly, a process that is monitoring a device's data stream can affect the output of or input to a great many processes other than itself. This is sometimes called a feature, not a bug. For example, the printer spooler uses monitors to intercept output aimed at the printer, storing it on disk, and to feed data from those disk files to the actual printer device. Clearly, spooling printer output interferes with another process, but the interference is valuable. Designers of monitoring applications must ensure that their applications damage neither the system's performance nor its stability.

16.2   Data Integrity

I've discussed data integrity in a multitasking environment several times. This section does not review that material in detail but brings together all the elements and introduces a few related system facilities.

The first problem in a multitasking system is that multiple processes, or multiple threads within a process, may try to simultaneously manipulate the same resource—a file, a device, a data structure in memory, or even a single byte of memory. When the manipulation of a resource must be serialized to work correctly, that manipulation is called a *critical section*. This term refers to the act of manipulating the resource, but not particularly to the code that does so. Clearly, if any of four subroutines can manipulate a particular resource, entering any of the four is entering the critical section.

The problem is more pervasive than a programmer unfamiliar with the issue might assume. For example, even the simple act of testing a word to see if it holds the value 4 and incrementing it if it doesn't is a critical section. If only one thread in one process can access this word, then the critical section is serialized. But if more than one thread can access the word, then more than one thread could be in the critical section at the same time, with disastrous results. Specifically, consider the assembly language sequence shown in Listing 16-1. It looks simple enough: Test to see if COUNT holds 4; if it doesn't, increment it; if it does, jump to the label COMPLETE. Listing 16-2 shows what might go wrong in a multithreaded environment: Thread A checks the value to see if it's 4, but it's 3. Right after the compare instruction, a context switch takes place, and thread B is executed. Thread B also performs the compare, sees the value as 3, and increments it. Later, thread A resumes execution, *after the compare instruction,* at a location where it believes the COUNT value to be 3; so it also increments the value of COUNT. The value is now 5 and will continue to be incremented way past the value of 4 that was supposed to be its upper limit. The label COMPLETE may never be reached.

I apologize for again lecturing on this topic, but such problems are very nonobvious, rarely turn up in testing, are nearly impossible to find in the field, and the very possibility of their existence is new with OS/2. Thus, "too much is not enough," caveat-wise. Now that we've reviewed the problems, let's look at the solutions.

```
COUNT        DW      0                 ; Event counter

      .
      .
      CMP       COUNT,4           ; is this the 4th?
      JE        COMPLETE          ; yes, we're done
      INC       COUNT             ; count event
      .
      .
```

Listing 16-1.

```
      Thread A                                    Thread B

      .
      .
      CMP     COUNT,4   [count is now 3]
      ------------------context switch--->
                              CMP       COUNT,4  [count is 3]
                              JE        COMPLETE
                              INC       COUNT    [count is 4]

                                   .
                                   .
      <----------context switch--------
      JE      COMPLETE  [jmp not taken]
      INC     COUNT     [count is now 5]
```

Listing 16-2.

A programmer inexperienced with a multitasking environment
might protest that this scenario is unlikely, and indeed it is. Maybe the
chances are only 1 in 1 million that it would happen. But because a microprocessor executes 1 million instructions a second, it might not be
all that long before the 1-in-1-million unlucky chance comes true. Furthermore, an incorrect program normally has multiple unprotected critical sections, many of which are larger than the 2-instruction window
in our simple example.

The program must identify and protect all critical sections; a program that fails to do so will randomly fail. You can't take solace in
there being only one CPU and assuming that OS/2 probably won't context switch in the critical section. OS/2 can context switch at any time,
and because context switching can be triggered by unpredictable external events, such as serial port I/O and rotational latency on a disk, no
amount of testing can prove that an unprotected critical section is safe.
In reality, a test environment is often relatively simple; context switching tends to occur at consistent intervals, which means that such

problems tend *not* to turn up during program test. Instead, they turn up in the real world, and give your program a reputation for instability.

Naturally, testing has its place, but the only sure way to deal with critical sections is to examine your code carefully while assuming that all threads in the system are executing simultaneously.[3] Furthermore, when examining a code sequence, always assume that the CPU will reschedule in the worst way. If there *is* any possible window, reality will find it.

16.2.1   Semaphores

The traditional solution for protecting critical sections is the semaphore. The two OS/2 semaphores—RAM and system—each have advantages, and the operation of each is guaranteed to be completely immune to critical section problems. In the jargon, their operation is guaranteed *atomic*. Whenever a thread is going to manipulate a critical resource, it first claims the semaphore that protects the resource. Only after it controls the semaphore does it look at the resource because the resource's values may have changed between the time the semaphore was requested and the time it was granted. After the thread completes its manipulation of the resource, it releases the semaphore.

The semaphore mechanism protects well against all cooperating[4] threads, whether they belong to the same process or to different processes. Another OS/2 mechanism, called **DosEnterCritSec**, can be used to protect a critical section that is accessed only by threads belonging to a single process. When a thread issues the **DosEnterCritSec** call, OS/2 suspends execution of all other threads in that process until a subsequent **DosEnterCritSec** call is issued. Naturally, only threads executing in application mode are suspended; threads executing inside the OS/2 kernel are not suspended until they attempt to return to application mode.[5] The use of **DosEnterCritSec** is dangerous because the process's other threads may be suspended while they are holding a critical section. If the thread that issued the **DosEnterCritSec** then also tries to enter that critical section, the process will deadlock. If a dynlink

---

3. This is more than a *Gedankenexperiment*. Multiple processor machines will be built, and when they are, OS/2 will execute multiple threads, even within one process, truly simultaneously.

4. Obviously, if some thread refuses to claim the semaphore, nothing can be done.

5. I leave as an exercise to the reader to explain why the **DosEnterCritSec** call is not safe unless all other threads in the process make use of it for that critical section as well.

package is involved, it may have created extra threads unbeknownst to the client process so that the client may not even be aware that such a critical section exists and might be in use. For this reason, **DosEnterCritSec** is safe only when used to protect short sections of code that can't block or deadlock and that don't call any dynlink modules.

Still another OS/2 critical section facility is file sharing and record locking, which can be used to protect critical sections when they consist of files or parts of files. For example, a database program certainly considers its master database file a critical section, and it doesn't want anyone messing with it while the database application has it open. It can open the file with the file-sharing mode set to "allow no (other) readers, allow no writers." As long as the database application keeps the file open, OS/2 prevents any other process from opening (or deleting!) that file.

The record-locking mechanism can be used to provide a smaller granularity of protection. A process can lock a range of bytes within a file, and while that lock is in effect, OS/2 prevents any other process from reading or writing those bytes. These two specialized forms of critical section protection are unique in that they protect a process against all other processes, even "uncooperating" ones that don't protect their own access to the critical section. Unfortunately, the file-sharing and record-locking mechanisms don't contain any provision for blocking until the conflict is released. Applications that want to wait for the conflict to clear must use a polling loop. Use **DosSleep** to block for at least a half second between each poll.

Unfortunately, although semaphores protect critical sections well, sometimes they bring problems of their own. Specifically, what happens if an asynchronous event, such as program termination or a signal, pulls the CPU away from inside a critical section and the CPU never returns to release the semaphore? The answers range from "moot" to "disaster," depending on the circumstances. The possibilities are so manifold that I'll group some of them.

What can you do if the CPU is pulled away inside a critical section?

■ Ignore it. This is fine if the critical section is wholly accessed by a single process and that process doesn't use signals to modify the normal path of execution and if neither the process nor its dynlink routines attempt to enter the critical section during **DosExitList** processing.

- Clear the semaphore. This is an option if you know that the resource protected by the semaphore has no state, such as a semaphore that protects the right to be writing to the screen. The trick is to ensure that the interrupted thread set the semaphore and that you don't accidentally clear the semaphore when you don't set it. For example, if the semaphore is wholly used within a single process but that process's **DosExitList** handlers may use it, they can force the semaphore clear when they are entered.

- Detect the situation and repair the critical section. This detection can be made for RAM semaphores only during process termination and only if the semaphore is solely used by that process. In such a case, you know that a thread in the process set the semaphore, and you know that the thread is no longer executing the critical section because all threads are terminated. You can test the semaphore by using a nonblocking **DosSemSet;** if it's set, ''recover'' the resource.

    System semaphores are generally better suited for this. When the owning thread of a system semaphore dies, the semaphore is given a special mark. The next attempt to set the semaphore returns with a code that tells the new owner that the previous owner died within the critical section. The new owner has the option of cleaning up the resource.

Another possibility is to try to prevent the CPU from being yanked out of a critical section. Signals can be momentarily delayed with the **DosHoldSignal** mechanism. Process termination that results from an external kill can be postponed by setting up a signal handler for the KILL signal and then using **DosHoldSignal.** This last technique doesn't protect you against termination due to GP fault and the like however.

16.2.2 **DosBufReset**

One remaining data integrity issue—disk data synchronization—is not related to critical sections. Often, when a **DosWrite** call is made, OS/2 holds the data in a buffer rather than writing it immediately to disk. Naturally, any subsequent calls made to read this data are satisfied correctly, so an application cannot see that the data has not yet been written unless the reading application uses direct physical access to the volume (that is, raw media reads). This case explains why CHKDSK may erroneously report errors that run on a volume that has open files.

OS/2 eventually writes the data to the disk, so this buffering is of concern only when the system crashes with unwritten buffered data. Naturally, such crashes are expected to be rare, but some applications may find the possibility so threatening that they want to take protective steps. The two OS/2 functions for this purpose are flushing and write-throughs. The flush operation—**DosBufReset**—writes all dirty buffers—those with changed but unwritten data in them—to the disk. When the call returns, the data is on the disk. Use this call sparingly; although its specification promises only that it will flush buffers associated with the specified file handle(s), for most file systems it writes all dirty buffers in the system to disk. Moreover, if file handles are open to a server machine on the network, most or all of that server's buffers get flushed, even those that were used by other client machines on the network. Because of these costs, applications should use this operation judiciously.

Note that it's not true that a flush operation simply causes a write to be done sooner rather than later. A flush operation may also cause extra disk writes. For example, consider an application that is writing data 10 bytes at a time. In this case, OS/2 buffers the data until it has a full sector's worth. A series of buffer flush operations arriving at this time would cause the assembly buffer to be written to the disk many extra and unnecessary times.

16.2.3   Writethroughs

Buffer flushes are expensive, and unless they are used frequently, they don't guarantee a particular write ordering. Some applications, such as database managers, may want to guarantee that data be written to the disk in exactly the same order in which it was given to OS/2 via **DosWrite.** For example, an application may want to guarantee that the data is in place in a database before the allocation chain is written and that the chain be written before the database directory is updated. Such an ordering may make it easy for the package to recover the database in case of a crash.

The OS/2 mechanism for doing this is called *writethrough*—a status bit that can be set for individual file handles. If a writethrough is in effect for a handle to which the write is issued, OS/2 guarantees that the data will be written to the disk before the **DosWrite** operation returns. Obviously, applications using writethrough should write their data in large chunks; writing many small chunks of data to a file marked for writethrough is very inefficient.

Three caveats are associated with writethroughs:

- If writethrough is set on a file after it is open, all *subsequent* writes are written through, but data from previous writes may still be in dirty buffers.

- If a writethrough file is being shared by multiple processes or is open on multiple handles, all instances of that file should be marked writethrough. Data written to a handle not marked writethrough may go into the buffers.

- The operation of data writethroughs has some nonintuitive surprises when used with the current FAT file system. Specifically, although this feature works as advertised to place the file's data sectors on the disk, it does not update the directory entry that specifies the size of the file. Thus, if you extend a file by 10 sectors and the system crashes before you close the file, the data in those 10 sectors is lost. If you had writethrough set, then those 10 sectors of data were indeed written to the disk; but because the directory entry wasn't updated, CHKDSK will return those sectors to the free list.

  The writethrough operation protects the file's data but not the directory or allocation information. This is not a concern as long as you write over a portion of the file that has been already extended, but any writes that extend the file are not protected. The good news is that the data will be on the disk, as guaranteed, but the bad news is that the directory entry won't be updated; if the system crashes, file extensions cannot be recovered. The recommended solution is to use **DosNewSize** to extend the file as needed, followed by **DosBufReset** to update the directory information on the disk, and then to writethrough the data as needed. Overextending the file size is better than doing too many **NewSize/BufReset** combinations; if you overextend, you can always shrink the file before closing it with a final **DosNewSize**.

16.3 **Timer Services**

Frequently, applications want to keep track of the passage of real time. A game program may want events to occur asynchronously with the user's input; a telecommunications program may want to track how long a response takes and perhaps declare a link timed-out after some interval. Other programs may need to pace the display of a demonstration or assume a default action if the user doesn't respond in a reasonable amount of time. OS/2 provides several facilities to track the passage of real time; applications should use these facilities and shun polling and timing loops because the timing of such loops depends on the system's workload and the CPU's speed and because they totally lock out from execution any thread of a lower priority.

Time intervals in OS/2 are discussed in terms of milliseconds to isolate the concept of a time interval from the physical mechanism (periodic clock interrupts) that measures time intervals. Although you can specify a time interval down to the millisecond, the system does not guarantee any such accuracy.

On most hardware, OS/2 version 1.0 uses a periodic system clock interrupt of 32 Hz (32 times a second). This means that OS/2 measures time intervals with a quantum size of 31.25 milliseconds. As a result, any timeout value is subject to quantization error of this order. For example, if a process asks to sleep for 25 milliseconds, OS/2 knows that the request was made at some time after the most recent clock tick, but it cannot tell how long after, other than that less than 31.25 milliseconds had elapsed between the previous clock tick and the sleep request. After the sleep request is made, another clock tick occurs. Once again, OS/2 can't tell how much time has elapsed since the sleep request and the new clock tick, other than that it was less than 31.25 milliseconds. Lacking this knowledge, OS/2 uses a simple algorithm: At each clock tick, OS/2 decrements each timeout value in the system by the clock tick interval (generally 31.25 milliseconds). Thus, our 25-millisecond sleep request may come back in 1 millisecond or less or in 31.25 milliseconds. A request to block for 33 milliseconds could come back in 32 milliseconds or in 62.5 milliseconds.

Clearly, the OS/2 timer functions are intended for human-scale timing, in which the $1/32$-second quantization error is not noticeable, and not for high-precision timing of fast events. Regardless of the resolution of the timer, the system's preemptive scheduler prevents the implementation of high-accuracy short-interval timing. Even if a timer system call were to time out after a precise interval, the calling thread might not resume execution immediately because a higher-priority thread might be executing elsewhere.

One form of OS/2 timer services is built into some system calls. For example, all semaphore blocking calls support an argument that allows the caller to specify a timeout value. When the specified time has elapsed, the call returns with a "call timed out" error code. Some threads use this facility to guard against being indefinitely locked out; if the semaphore call times out, the thread can give up, display an error message, or try another tactic. Other threads may use the facility expecting to be timed out: They use the timeout facility to perform periodic tasks and use the semaphore just as an emergency flag. Another thread in the system can provide an emergency wakeup for the timer thread simply by clearing the semaphore.

Blocking on a semaphore merely to delay for a specific interval is unnecessary; the **DosSleep** call allows a thread to block unconditionally for an arbitrary length of time, subject, of course, to the timer's quantization error.[6] **DosSleep** measures time intervals in a synchronous fashion: The thread is held inside the operating system until the time interval has elapsed. OS/2 provides an asynchronous timer service that allows timing to take place in parallel with a thread's normal execution. Specifically, the **DosTimerAsync** call is made with a timeout interval, such as **DosSleep,** and also with the handle of a system semaphore.[7] The **DosTimerAsync** call returns immediately; later, when the time interval has elapsed, the system semaphore is cleared. The process can poll the semaphore to see if the time is up, and/or it can block on the semaphore to wait for the time to elapse. Of course, if a process contains multiple threads, some can poll and others can block.

The **DosTimerStart** call is identical to the **DosTimerAsync** call except that the semaphore is repeatedly cleared at the specified interval until a corresponding **DosTimerStop** call is made. **DosTimerStart** clears the semaphore; the process must set it again after it's been cleared.

---

6. And subject to the fact that if thread 1 is doing the **DosSleep**ing the sleep will be interrupted if a signal is taken.

7. Unlike most semaphore applications, the timer functions work only with system semaphores. RAM semaphores may not be used because of the difficulty in posting a RAM semaphore at interrupt time; the RAM that contains the semaphore may be swapped out.

None of the above-mentioned facilities is completely accurate for tracking the time of day or the amount of elapsed time. As we mentioned, if a higher-priority thread is consuming enough CPU time, unpredictable delays occur. Even **DosTimerStart** is susceptible to losing ticks because if the CPU is unavailable for a long enough period the process won't be able to reset the semaphore soon enough to prevent missing its next clearing. Applications that want a precise measurement of elapsed time should use the time values stored in the global infoseg. We also recommend that applications with a critical need to manage timeouts, even if they are executing in the lower-priority background, dedicate a thread to managing the time-critical work and elevate that thread to a higher priority. This will ensure that time-critical events aren't missed because a high-priority foreground thread is going through a period of intensive CPU usage. Of course, such an application must be designed so that the high-priority timer event thread does not itself consume significant CPU time; it should simply log the timer events and rely on its fellow normal-priority threads to handle the major work involved.

17

Device Drivers and Hard Errors

The multitasking nature of OS/2 makes OS/2 device drivers considerably more complex than MS-DOS device drivers. Furthermore, whenever you have devices, you must deal with device failures—the infamous hard errors. The handling of hard errors in a multitasking environment is likewise considerably more complex than it was under MS-DOS.

17.1 Device Drivers

This section gives an overview of device drivers, paying special attention to their key architectural elements. Writing a device driver is a complex task that must be undertaken with considerable care; a great many caveats and "gotchas" lie in wait for the unsuspecting programmer. Many of these "gotchas" are of that most favorite breed: ones that never show up in testing, only in the field. This section is by no means an exhaustive discussion of device drivers, nor is it a how-to guide. Study the OS/2 device driver reference documentation carefully before setting out to write your own.

In Chapter 2 I briefly discussed device independence and the role that device drivers play in bringing it about. I said that a device driver is a package of code that transforms I/O requests made in standard, device-independent fashion into the operations necessary to make a specific piece of hardware fulfill that request. A device driver takes data and status information from the hardware, in the hardware-specific format, and massages that information into the form that the operating system expects to receive.

The device driver architecture has two key elements. First, each hardware device has its own device driver to hide the specific details of the device from the operating system. Second, device drivers are not hard-wired into the operating system when it is manufactured; they are dynamically installed at boot time. This second point is the interesting one. If all device drivers were hard-wired into OS/2, the technique of encapsulating device-dependent code into specific packages would be good engineering practice but of little interest to the user. OS/2 would run only on a system configured with a certain magic set of peripheral devices. But because device drivers are dynamically installable at boot time, OS/2 can work with a variety of devices, even ones that didn't exist when OS/2 was written, as long as a proper device driver for that device is installed at boot time. Note that device drivers can be installed *only* at boot time; they cannot be installed after the system has completed booting up. This is because in a future secure environment the ability to dynamically install a device driver would give any application the ability to violate system security.

Saying that device drivers merely translate between the operating system and the device is a bit of oversimplification; in reality, they are responsible for encapsulating, or owning, nearly all device-specific knowledge about the device. Device drivers service the interrupts that their devices generate, and they work at task time (that is, at noninterrupt time). If a device monitor is necessary for a device, the device driver writer decides that and provides the necessary support. If an application needs direct access to a device's I/O ports or to its special mapped memory,[1] the driver offers those services to processes. The device driver also knows whether multiple processes should simultaneously use the device and either allows or disallows this.

17.1.1 Device Drivers and OS/2 Communication
Because device drivers need to call and be called by OS/2 efficiently and because device drivers must handle hardware interrupts efficiently, they must run at ring 0. This means that device drivers must be trusted and must be trustworthy. A flaky device driver—or worse, a malicious

---

1. For example, the display memory of a CGA or an EGA card.

one—can do unlimited and nearly untraceable damage to any application or data file in the system.

OS/2 can easily call a device driver. Because OS/2 loaded the device driver into memory, it knows the address of its entry point and can call it directly. For the device driver to call OS/2 is trickier because the driver doesn't know the memory locations that OS/2 occupies nor does it have any control over the memory descriptor tables (LDT and GDT). When the device driver is initialized, OS/2 supplies the device driver with the address of the OS/2 **DevHlp** entry point. Device drivers call this address to access a variety of OS/2 services, called **DevHlp** services. The OS/2 **DevHlp** address references a GDT selector so that the **DevHlp** address is valid at all times—in protected mode, in real mode,[2] at interrupt time, and during device driver initialization. Some **DevHlp** functions are only valid in certain modes, but the **DevHlp** facility is always available.

Why don't device drivers simply use dynamic links to access OS/2 services, the way that applications do? The OS/2 kernel dynlink interface is designed for processes running in user mode, at ring 3, to call the ring 0 kernel. In other words, it's designed for outsiders to call in, but device drivers are already inside. They run at ring 0, in kernel mode, and at interrupt time. One, of course, could kludge things so that device drivers make dynlink calls, and then special code at those OS/2 entry points would recognize a device driver request and do all the special handling. But every system call from a normal application would be slowed by this extra code, and every service call from a device driver would likewise be slowed. As a result, device drivers have their own private, high-efficiency "backdoor" entry into OS/2. Figure 17-1 on the following page illustrates the call linkages between OS/2 and a device driver. OS/2 calls only one entry point in the device driver, providing a function code that the device driver uses to address a dispatch table. OS/2 learns the address of this entry point when it loads the device driver. The device driver in turn calls only one OS/2 address, the **DevHlp** entry point. It also supplies a function code that is used to address a dispatch table. The device driver is told this address when it receives its *initialize* call from OS/2. Not shown is the device driver's interrupt entry point.

---

2. A GDT selector cannot literally be valid in real mode because the GDT is not in use. OS/2 uses a technique called tiling so that the selector, when used as a segment address in real mode, addresses the same physical memory as does the protect mode segment.

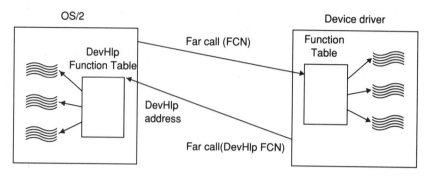

Figure 17-1.
Device driver call linkages.

17.1.2 Device Driver Programming Model

The programming model for device drivers under MS-DOS is simple. Device drivers are called to perform a function, and they return when that function is complete or they encounter an unrecoverable error. If the device is interrupt driven, the CPU hangs in a loop inside the device driver while waiting for the driver's interrupt handler to be entered; when the operation is complete, the interrupt handler sets a private flag to break the task-time CPU out of its wait loop.

The OS/2 device driver model is considerably more complicated because OS/2 is a multitasking system. Even if the thread that calls the device driver with a request has nothing better to do than wait for the operation to complete, other threads in the system could make good use of the time. Another effect of the OS/2 multitasking architecture is that two or more threads can simultaneously call a device driver. To explore this last issue fully, we'll digress for a moment and discuss the OS/2 internal execution model.

By design, OS/2 acts more like a subroutine library than like a process. The only dispatchable entities in the system are threads, and all threads belong to processes. When a process's thread calls OS/2, that thread executes OS/2's code.[3] It's like walking up to the counter at a fast-food restaurant and placing your order. You then slip on an apron, run around behind the counter, and prepare your own order. When the food is ready, you take off the apron, run back around to the front of the counter, and pick up the food. The counter represents the boundary

---

3. The few exceptions to this don't affect the issues discussed here.

between ring 0 (kernel mode) and ring 3 (application mode), and the apron represents the privileged state necessary to work behind the counter.

Naturally, OS/2 is reentrant; at any one time many threads are executing inside OS/2, but each is doing work for only one process—the process to whom that thread belongs. Behind the counter are several folks wearing aprons, but each is working only on his or her own order. This approach simplifies the internals of OS/2: Each instance of a section of code is doing only one thing for one client. If a section of code must wait for something, it simply blocks (analogous to a semaphore wait) as long as it has to and resumes when it can. Threads within the kernel that are competing for a single resource do so by internal semaphores, and they are given access to these semaphores on a priority basis, just as they are when executing in application mode.

OS/2 makes little distinction between a thread running inside the kernel and one running outside, in the application's code itself: The process's LDT remains valid, and the thread, while inside the kernel, can access any memory location that was accessible to the process in application mode, in addition to being able to access restricted ring 0 memory. The only distinction the scheduler makes between threads inside and those outside the kernel is that the scheduler never preempts a thread running inside the kernel. This greatly relaxes the rigor with which kernel code needs to protect its critical sections: When the CPU is executing kernel code, the scheduler performs a context switch only when the CPU voluntarily blocks itself. As long as kernel code doesn't block itself, wait on a semaphore, or call a subroutine that waits on a semaphore, it needn't worry about any other thread entering its critical section.[4]

When OS/2 calls a device driver at task time, it does so with the thread that was executing OS/2—the thread that belongs to the client process and that made the original service call. Thus, the task-time part of a device driver is running, at ring 0, in the client's context. The client's LDT is active, all the client's addresses are active, and the device driver is immune from being preempted by other task-time threads (but not by interrupt service) until it blocks via a **DevHlp** function or returns to OS/2.

---

4. Although hardware interrupts still occur; any critical section modified at interrupt time is still vulnerable.

OS/2 device drivers are divided into two general categories: those for character mode devices and those for block mode devices. This terminology is traditional, but don't take it too literally because character mode operations can be done to block mode devices. The actual distinction is that character mode device drivers do I/O synchronously; that is, they do operations in first in, first out order. Block mode device drivers can be asynchronous; they can perform I/O requests in an order different from the one in which they received them. A traditional serial character device, such as a printer, must not change the order of its requests; doing so scrambles the output. A block device, such as a disk, can reverse the order of two sector reads without problems.

Figure 17-2 shows an algorithm for character mode device drivers.[5] OS/2 calls the device driver with a request, as shown at the top of the figure. If the device driver is busy with another request, the new

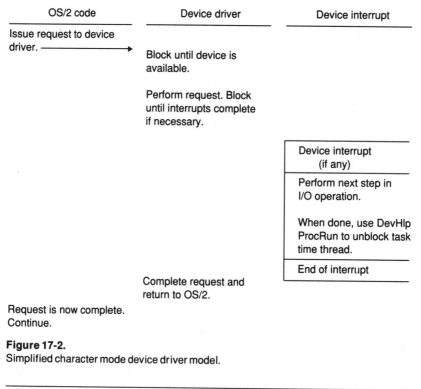

OS/2 code	Device driver	Device interrupt
Issue request to device driver. ⟶	Block until device is available.	
	Perform request. Block until interrupts complete if necessary.	
		Device interrupt (if any)
		Perform next step in I/O operation.
		When done, use DevHlp ProcRun to unblock task time thread.
		End of interrupt
	Complete request and return to OS/2.	
Request is now complete. Continue.		

Figure 17-2.
Simplified character mode device driver model.

---

5. See the device driver reference manual for more details.

requesting thread should block on a RAM semaphore until the device is available. When the device is free, the task-time thread does the requested operation. Sometimes the work can be done at task time (such as an IOCTL call asking about the number of characters in an input buffer), but more frequently the task-time thread initiates the operation, and the work is completed at interrupt time. If the task-time thread needs to wait for interrupt service, it should block on a RAM semaphore[6] that the interrupt-time code will clear. When the last associated device interrupt takes place and the operation is complete, the interrupt code releases the RAM semaphore. The task-time thread awakens and returns to OS/2 with the status bits properly set in the request block.

Figure 17-3 on the following page shows an algorithm for block devices. The general outline is the same as that for character devices but more complicated because of the asynchronous nature of random-access devices. Because requests can be processed in any order, most block device drivers maintain an internal work queue to which they add each new request. They usually use a special **DevHlp** function to sort the work queue in sector number order so that disk head motion is minimized.

The easiest way to understand this figure is to think of a block mode device driver as being made up of N threads: one interrupt-time thread does the actual work, and all the others are task-time threads that queue the work. As each request comes into the driver via a task-time thread, that thread simply puts the request on the queue and *returns to OS/2*. Later, the device driver's interrupt service routine calls the **DevHlp DevDone** function to tell OS/2 that the operation is complete. Returning to OS/2 with the operation incomplete is permissible because the request block status bits show that the operation is incomplete.

Sometimes, OS/2 needs to wait for the operation (such as a read from a directory); so when the device driver returns with the operation incomplete, OS/2 simply waits for it to finish. In other circumstances, such as flushing the cache buffers, OS/2 may not wait around for the operation to complete. It may go on about its business or even issue a new request to the driver, using, of course, a new request block because the old one is still in use. This design gives the system a great deal of parallelism and thereby improves throughput.

---

6. Located in the device driver data area.

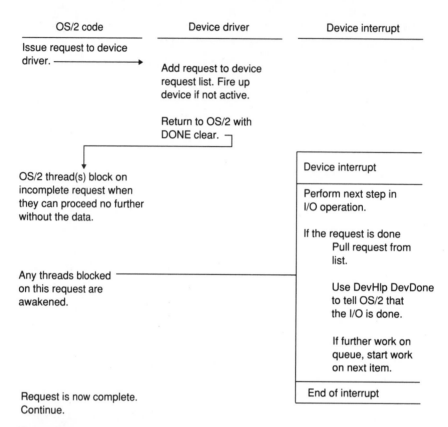

OS/2 code	Device driver	Device interrupt
Issue request to device driver. ⟶	Add request to device request list. Fire up device if not active.	
	Return to OS/2 with DONE clear.	
OS/2 thread(s) block on incomplete request when they can proceed no further without the data.		**Device interrupt**

		Perform next step in I/O operation.
		
		If the request is done
		    Pull request from
		    list.

Any threads blocked on this request are awakened.		Use DevHlp DevDone to tell OS/2 that the I/O is done. If further work on queue, start work on next item.
Request is now complete. Continue.		End of interrupt

Figure 17-3.
Block mode device driver model.

I said that a block mode device driver consists of several task-time threads and one interrupt-time thread. The term *interrupt-time thread* is a bit misleading, however, because it's not a true thread managed by the scheduler but a pseudo thread created by the hardware interrupt mechanism. For example, a disk device driver has four requests queued up, and the READ operation for the first request is in progress. When it completes, the driver's interrupt service routine is entered by the hardware interrupt generated by the disk controller. That interrupt-time thread, executing the driver's interrupt service routine, checks the status, verifies that all is OK, and calls various **DevHlp** routines to post the request as complete and to remove it from the queue. It then notes that requests remain on the queue and starts work on the next one, which involves a seek operation. The driver's interrupt-time code issues the seek command to the hardware and then returns from the interrupt. When the disk stops seeking, another interrupt is generated; the interrupt-time code notes the successful seek, issues the read or write operation to the controller, and exits.

As you can see, the repeated activation of the device driver's interrupt service routine is much like a thread, but with two major differences. First, every time an interrupt service routine is entered, it has a fresh stack. A task-time thread has register contents and a stack that are preserved by the system; neither is preserved for an interrupt service routine between interrupts. A task-time thread keeps track of what it was doing by its CS:IP address, its register contents, and its stack contents. An interrupt service routine must keep track of its work by means of static values stored in the device driver's data segment. Typically, interrupt service routines implement a state machine and maintain the current state in the driver's data segment. Second, a true thread remains in existence until explicitly terminated; an interrupt service thread is an illusion of a thread that is maintained by repeated interrupts. If any one execution of the interrupt service routine fails to give the hardware a command that will generate another interrupt, the interrupt pseudo thread will no longer exist after the interrupt service routine returns.

The block mode driver algorithm description left out a detail. If the disk is idle when a new request comes in, the request is put on the queue, but there is no interrupt-time pseudo thread to service the request. Thus, both the task-time and interrupt-time parts of a device driver must be able to initiate an operation. The recommended approach is to use a software state machine to control the hardware and to ensure that the state machine, at least the start operation part of it, is callable at both task and interrupt time. The algorithm above is then modified so that after the task-time part of a block device driver puts its request on the driver's internal queue it verifies that the device (or state machine or interrupt pseudo thread) is active. If the device has been idle, the task-time thread in the device driver initiates the operation by calling the initial state of the state machine; it then returns to OS/2. This

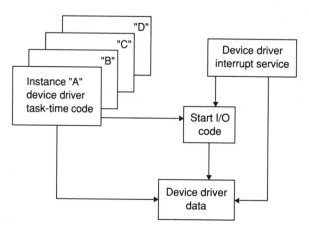

Figure 17-4.
Device driver code structure.

primes the pump; the interrupt pseudo thread now continues to run until the request queue is empty.

Figure 17-4 shows an overview of the OS/2 device driver architecture. Each device driver consists of a task-time part, an interrupt-time part (if the device generates interrupts), and the start-operation code that is executed in either mode. The driver's data area typically contains state information, flags, and semaphores to handle communication between the task-time part and the interrupt. Figure 17-4 also shows that the task-time part of a device driver can have multiple instances. It can be called by several threads at the same time, just as a shared dynlink library routine might be. Unlike a dynlink library, a device driver has no instance data segment; the device driver's data segment is a global data segment, accessible to all execution instances of the device driver's task-time component. Just as a dynlink package uses semaphores to protect critical data areas in its global data segment, a device driver uses semaphores to protect the critical data values in its data segment. Unlike dynlink routines, the device driver has an additional special thread—the interrupt service thread. A device driver can't protect critical sections that are accessed at interrupt time by using semaphores because an interrupt service thread cannot block. It must complete the interrupt service and exit—quickly, at that. When you write device drivers, you must minimize the critical sections that are entered by the interrupt service thread and protect them via the CLI/STI instruction sequence.

17.1.3   Device Management

Device drivers do more than talk to the device; they also manage it for the system. Device drivers are called each time a process opens or closes a device; device drivers determine whether a device can be used by more than one process simultaneously. Likewise, device drivers receive device monitor requests from applications via the IOCTL interface and, when appropriate, call OS/2 via the **DevHlp** interface to perform the bulk of the monitor work. Finally, device drivers can grant processes access to the device's I/O ports, to the device's mapped memory, and/or to special control areas in the device driver's data area itself. Once again, processes ask for these features via IOCTL; the device driver grants the requests via a **DevHlp** dialog with OS/2. Some device drivers are degenerate; they don't actually transfer data but exist solely to manage these other tasks. The screen device driver is an example. Screen data is always written directly to the display buffer by VIO, the application, or the presentation manager. The screen device driver exists to grant direct access, manage screen groups, and so on.

17.1.4   Dual Mode

The last key architectural feature of device drivers is that they are written in *dual mode*: The driver code, both task time and interrupt time, must be able to execute in protected mode and real mode. The process of *mode switching* between protected mode and real mode is quite slow—about 800 microseconds. If we decreed that all device drivers run only in protected mode and that service interrupts run only in protected mode, a disk request from a real mode program might require six or more mode switches—one for the request, and five for the interrupts—for a penalty of almost 5 milliseconds. Consequently, device drivers must run in whatever mode the CPU is in when the request comes along or the interrupt arrives.

At first glance, this seems easy enough: As long as the device driver refrains from computing its own segment selectors, it can execute in either mode. The catch is that OS/2 may switch between modes at every call and/or interrupt, and the addresses of code and data items are different in each mode. A device driver might be called in protected mode with an address in the client process's address space. When the "data ready" interrupt arrives, however, the CPU may be running in real mode, and that client's address is no longer valid—for two reasons.

One, the segment selector part of a memory address has a different meaning in real mode than it does in protected mode; and, two, the client's selector was in the LDT, and the LDT is invalid at interrupt time.[7] OS/2 helps device drivers deal with addressing in a dual mode environment in three ways:

1. Some addresses are the same in both modes and in either protected mode or real mode. The **DevHlp** entry point, the global infoseg address, the request packet address, and any addresses returned via the **DevHlp GetDosVar** function are valid at all times and in both modes.

2. Although the segment selector value for the device driver's code and data segments is different in each mode, OS/2 loads the proper values into CS and DS before it calls the device driver's task-time or interrupt-time entry points. As long as a device driver is careful not to "remember" and reuse these values, it won't notice that they (possibly) change at every call.

3. OS/2 provides a variety of **DevHlp** functions that allow a device driver to convert a selector:offset pair into a physical address and then later convert this physical address back into a selector:offset pair that is valid at that particular time. This allows device drivers to convert addresses that are outside their own segments into physical addresses and then, upon each task-time or interrupt-time call to the driver, convert that physical address back into one that is usable in the current mode. This avoids the problem of recording a selector:offset pair in protect mode and then trying to use it as a segment:offset pair in real mode.

17.2 Hard Errors

Sometimes the system encounters an error that it can neither ignore nor correct but which the user can correct. A classic example is the user leaving ajar the door to the floppy drive; the system can do nothing to access that floppy disk until someone closes the door. Such an error is called a hard error. The term originated to describe an error that won't go away when the operation is retried, but it also aptly describes the effort involved in the design of OS/2 to deal with such errors.

---

7. See the device driver reference manual for more details.

The manner in which MS-DOS handles hard errors is straightforward. In our drive door example, MS-DOS discovers the problem when it is deep inside the bowels of the system, communicating with the disk driver. The driver reports the problem, and MS-DOS displays some text on the screen—the infamous "Abort, Retry, Ignore?" message. Typically, the user fixes the problem and replies; MS-DOS then takes the action specified by the user, finishes its work, and returns to the application. Often, applications didn't want the system to handle hard errors automatically. Perhaps they were concerned about data integrity and wanted to be aware of a disk-writing problem, or they wanted to prevent the user from specifying "Ignore,"[8] or they didn't want MS-DOS to write over their screen display without their knowing. To handle these situations, MS-DOS lets applications store the address of a hard error handler in the INT 24 vector; if a handler is present, MS-DOS calls it instead of its own handler.

The system is in an unusual state while processing an MS-DOS hard error. The application originally calls MS-DOS via the INT 21 vector. MS-DOS then calls several levels deep within itself, whereupon an internal MS-DOS routine calls the hard error handler back in the application. Because MS-DOS is not generally reentrant, the application cannot recall MS-DOS via INT 21 at this point; doing so would mean that it has called MS-DOS twice at the same time. The application probably needs to do screen and keyboard I/O when handling the hard error, so MS-DOS was made partially reentrant. The original call involves disk I/O, so MS-DOS can be reentered via a screen/keyboard I/O call without problem.

Several problems prevented us from adopting a similar scheme for OS/2. First, unlike the single-tasking MS-DOS, OS/2 cannot suspend operations while the operating system calls an application—a call that might not return for a long time. Second, major technical and security problems are involved with calling from ring 0 (the privileged kernel mode) to ring 3 (the application mode). Also, in the MS-DOS environment, deciding which process was responsible for the operation that triggered the hard error is easy: Only one application is running. OS/2 may have a hard time determining which process to alert because more

---

8. This response is classic. Sophisticated users understand the likely consequences of such a reply, but most users would interpret "Ignore" as "Make the problem go away"—an apparently ideal solution!

than one process may have caused a disk FAT sector or a disk directory
to be edited. The improved buffering techniques employed by OS/2
may cause a hard error to occur at a time when no process is doing any
I/O. Finally, even if we solve all these problems, the application that
triggers the hard error may be running in a background screen group
and be unable to display a message or use the keyboard. Even if the application is in the foreground screen group, it can't use the screen and
keyboard if it's not the process currently controlling them.

17.2.1   The Hard Error Daemon

This last problem yields a clue to the solution. OS/2 supports multiple
screen groups, and its screen group mechanism manages multiple simultaneous use of the screen and the keyboard, keeping the current
users—one in each screen group—isolated from one another. Clearly,
we need to use screen groups to allow a hard error dialog to be completed with the user without interfering with the current foreground application. Doing so solves the problem of writing on another
application's screen image and therefore removes most of the need for
notifying an application that a hard error has occurred.

Specifically, OS/2 always has running a process called the hard error daemon. When a hard error occurs, OS/2 doesn't attempt to figure
out which process caused it; instead, it notifies the hard error daemon.
The hard error daemon performs a special form of screen group switch
to the reserved hard error screen group and then displays its message
and reads its input. Because the hard error daemon is the only process
in this screen group, screen and keyboard usage do not conflict. The
previous foreground process is now temporarily in the background; the
screen group mechanism keeps it at bay.

Meanwhile, the process thread that encountered the hard error in the
kernel is blocked there, waiting for the hard error daemon to get a
response from the user. The thread that handles the hard error is never
the thread that caused the hard error, and the kernel is already fully
reentrant for different threads; so the hard error daemon thread is free
to call OS/2 at will. When the user corrects the problem and responds
to the hard error daemon, the hard error daemon sends the response
back to the kernel, which allows the thread that encountered the error to
take the specified action. That thread either retries the operation or produces an error code; the hard error daemon returns the system to the

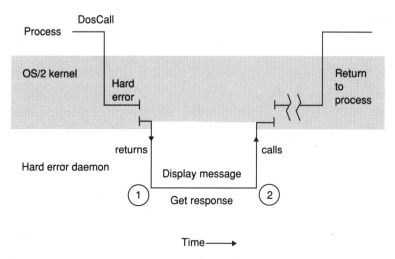

Figure 17-5.
Hard error handling.

original screen group. The screen group code then does its usual trick of restoring the screen image to its previous state. Figure 17-5 illustrates the hard error handling sequence. A process thread encounters a hard error while in the OS/2 kernel. The thread blocks at that point while the hard error daemon's previously captured thread is released. The hard error daemon performs a special modified screen switch at (1), displays its message, gets the user's response, restores the application screen group at (2), and reenters the OS/2 kernel. The response code is then passed to the blocked application thread, which then resumes execution.

Although the most common cause of hard errors is a disk problem — for example, an open drive door or a medium error — other events that require user intervention or user notification use the hard error mechanism. For example, the volume management package (see 15.2 Media Volume Management) uses the hard error mechanism to display its "Insert volume <name>" messages. As I mentioned earlier, MS-DOS applications running in the compatibility box can encounter problems, such as locked files, that they can't understand. Rather than have these applications fail mysteriously, OS/2 uses the hard error daemon mechanism to inform the user of the cause of the real mode application's difficulties. Although the application running in the compatibility box sees an operating system that acts like MS-DOS, the operating system is actually OS/2. Because of this, hard errors encountered by a real mode process are handled by an amalgam of the MS-DOS INT 24 mechanism and the OS/2 hard error daemon. See Chapter 19, The 3X Box.

17.2.2 Application Hard Error Handling

In some cases an application doesn't want the system to handle its hard errors. For example, an application designed for unattended or remote operation, such as a network server, may want to pass notification of hard errors to a remote correspondent rather than hanging up forever with a message on a screen that might not be read for hours. Another example is a database program concerned about the integrity of its master file; it may want to know about hard errors so that it can take some special action or perhaps use an alternative master file on another device. OS/2 allows a process to disable automatic hard error handling on a per file basis. Our network example will want to disable hard error pop-ups for anything the process does; our database example may want to disable hard error pop-ups only for its master file, keeping their convenience for any other files that it might access. When a hard error occurs on behalf of a process or a handle that has hard error pop-ups disabled, OS/2 assumes that a FAIL response was entered to a hypothetical hard error pop-up and returns to the application with a special error code. The application must analyze the code and take the necessary actions.

18

I/O Privilege Mechanism and Debugging/ Ptrace

The earlier chapters of this book focused on the "captains and kings" of the operating system world, the major architectural features. But like any real world operating system, OS/2 contains a variety of miscellaneous facilities that have to be there to get the work done. Although these facilities may not be major elements in some architectural grand scheme, they still have to obey the principles of the design religion. Two of them are the I/O privilege mechanism and the debugging facility.

18.1 I/O Privilege Mechanism

Earlier I discussed the need for a mechanism that allows applications high-speed direct access to devices. But the mechanism must control access in such a way that the system's stability isn't jeopardized and in such a way that applications don't fight over device control. OS/2 meets this requirement with its *I/O privilege* mechanism. This facility allows a process to ask a device driver for direct access to the device's I/O ports and any dedicated or mapped memory locations it has. The I/O privilege mechanism can be used directly by an application, which necessarily makes it device dependent, or indirectly by a dynlink package. The dynlink package can act as a kind of device driver; a new version can be shipped with new hardware to maintain application compatibility. This pseudo device driver is normally much faster than a true device driver because of the customized procedural interface; not entering ring 0 and the OS/2 kernel code saves much time.

Unfortunately, this isn't a free lunch. Dynlink pseudo device drivers can do everything that true device drivers can except handle interrupts. Because hardware interrupts must be handled at ring 0, the handler must be part of a true device driver. Frequently, a compromise is in order: *Both* a dynlink package and a true device driver are provided. The true device driver handles the interrupts, and the dynlink package does the rest of the work. The two typically communicate via shared memory and/or private IOCTLs. An example of such a compromise is the system KBD dynlink package. The system VIO package doesn't need a device driver to handle interrupts because the display device doesn't generate any.

The two components in the OS/2 I/O access model are access to the device's memory and access to its I/O ports. Granting and controlling access to a device's mapped memory is easy because the 80286 protect mode supports powerful memory management facilities. First, a process asks the device driver for access to the device's memory, for example, to the memory buffer of a CGA board. Typically, a dynlink package, rather than an application, does this via the **DosDevIOCtl** call. If the device driver approves the request, it asks OS/2 via the **DevHlp** interface to set up an LDT memory descriptor to the proper physical memory locations. OS/2 returns the resultant selector to the device driver, which returns it to the calling process. This technique isn't limited to memory-mapped device memory; device drivers can use it to allow their companion dynlink packages direct access to a piece of the device driver's data segment. In this way, a combination dynlink/device driver device interface can optimize communication between the dynlink package and the device driver.

Providing I/O port access to a process is more difficult because it is supported more modestly by the 80286 processor. The 80286 uses its ring protection mechanism to control I/O access; the system can grant code running at a certain ring privilege access to *all* I/O ports, but it can't grant access to only some I/O ports. It's too dangerous to grant an application access to all I/O ports simply because it uses VIO and VIO needs direct port access for the display adapter. This solution would mean that OS/2's I/O space is effectively unprotected because almost all programs use VIO or the presentation manager directly or indirectly.

Instead, OS/2 was designed to allow, upon request from the device driver, any code segments marked[1] to execute at ring 2 to have I/O access. The bad news is that access to all I/O ports must be granted indiscriminately, but the good news is that the system is vulnerable to program bugs only when those ring 2 segments are being executed. The capabilities of ring 2 code, as it's called, are restricted: Ring 2 code cannot issue dynlink calls to the system. This is partly a result of ring architecture (supporting ring 2 system calls would require significant additional overhead) and partly to discourage lazy programmers from flagging their entire process as ring 2 to avoid sequestering their I/O routines.

As I said, in OS/2 version 1.0 the ring mechanism can restrict I/O access only to a limited degree. Any malicious program and some buggy programs can still damage system stability by manipulating the system's peripherals. Furthermore, a real mode application can issue any I/O instruction at any time. A future release of OS/2 that runs only on the 80386 processor will solve these problems. The 80386 hardware is specifically designed to allow processes access to some I/O ports but not to others through a bit map the system maintains. This map, which of course the application cannot directly change, tells the 80386 which port addresses may be accessed and which must be refused. This map applies equally to protect mode and real mode applications.[2] OS/2 will use the port addresses supplied by the device driver to allow access only to the I/O ports associated with the device(s) to which the process has been granted access. This release will not support application code segments running at ring 2; any segments so marked will be loaded and run at ring 3. The change will be invisible to all applications that

---

1. This is done via a special command to the linker.
2. Actually, to "virtual real mode" applications. This is functionally the same as real mode on earlier processors.

use only the proper I/O ports. Applications that request access to one device and then use their I/O permissions to program another device will fail.

18.2   Debugging/Ptrace

Because OS/2 goes to a great deal of effort to keep one application from interfering with another, special facilities were built to allow debugging programs to manipulate and examine a debuggee (the process being debugged). Because a debugger is available for OS/2 and writing your own is laborious, we expect few programmers to write debuggers. This discussion is included, nevertheless, because it further illuminates the OS/2 architectural approach.

The first concern of a debugger is that it be able to read and write the debuggee's code and data segments as well as intercept traps, signals, breakpoints, and the like. All these capabilities are strictly in the domain of OS/2, so OS/2 must "export" them to the debugger program. A second concern is system security: Obviously, the debug interface provides a golden opportunity for "cracker" programs to manipulate any other program, thereby circumventing passwords, encryption, or any other protection scheme. OS/2 prevents this by requiring that the debuggee process be flagged as a debug target when it is initially executed; a debugger can't latch onto an already-running process. Furthermore, when secure versions of OS/2 are available, processes executed under control of a debugger will be shorn of any permissions they might have that are in excess of those owned by the debugger.

Before we examine the debugging interface, we should digress for a moment and discuss the OS/2 approach to forcing actions upon threads and processes. Earlier I described the process of kernel execution. I mentioned that when a process thread makes a kernel request that thread itself enters kernel mode and services its own request. This arrangement simplified the design of the kernel because a function is coded to perform one action for one client in a serial, synchronous fashion. Furthermore, nothing is ever forced on a thread that is in kernel mode; any action taken on a thread in kernel mode is taken by that thread itself. For example, if a process is to be killed and one of its threads is in kernel mode, OS/2 doesn't terminate that thread; it sets a flag that says, "Please kill yourself at your earliest convenience."

Consequently, OS/2 doesn't need special code to enumerate and release any internal flags or resources that a killed kernel-mode thread might leave orphaned, and in general no thread need "understand" the state of any other. The thread to be killed cleans itself up, releasing resources, flags, and whatever before it obligingly commits suicide.

But when is the thread's "earliest convenience"? Thread termination is a *forced event,* and all threads check for any pending forced events immediately before they leave kernel mode and reenter application mode. This transition takes place frequently: not only when a system call returns to the calling application, but also each time a context switch takes place.

Although it may appear that forced events might languish unprocessed, they are serviced rapidly. For example, when a process issues a **DosKill** function on its child process, each thread in the child process is marked "kill yourself." Because the parent process had the CPU, obviously, when it issued the **DosKill,** each of the child's threads is in kernel mode, either because the thread is working on a system call or because it was artificially placed in kernel mode when the scheduler preempted it. Before any of those now-marked threads can execute even a single instruction of the child application's code, they must go through OS/2's *dispatch* routine. The "kill yourself" flag is noted, and the thread terminates itself instead of returning to application mode. As you can see, the final effect of this approach is far from slow: The **DosKill** takes effect immediately—not one more instruction of the child process is executed.[3] The only significant delay in recognizing a forced event occurs when a system call takes a long time to process. OS/2 is not very CPU bound, so any call that takes a "long time" (1 second or more) must be blocked for most of that time.

When a kernel thread issues a block call for an event that might take a long time—such as waiting for a keystroke or waiting for a semaphore to clear—it uses a special form of block called an *interruptible block.* When OS/2 posts a force flag against a thread, it checks to see if that thread is blocking interruptibly. If it is, that thread is released from its block with a special code that says, "You were awakened not because the event has come to pass but because a forced event was

---

3. Excepting any **SIGKILL** handlers and **DosExitList** handlers, of course.

posted.'' That thread must then finish the system call quickly (generally by declaring an error) so that the thread can go through the dispatch routine and recognize the force flag. I described this mechanism in Chapter 12 when I talked about another kind of forced event—the OS/2 signal mechanism. An incoming signal is a forced event for a process's thread 1; it therefore receives the same timely response and has the same effect of aborting a slow system call.

I've gone through this long discussion of forced events and how they're processed because the internal debugging facility is based on one giant special forced event. When a process is placed in debug state, a trace force flag is permanently set for the initial thread of that process and for any other threads it creates. When any of those threads are in kernel mode—and they enter kernel mode whenever anything of interest takes place—they execute the debuggee half of the OS/2 trace code. The debugger half is executed by a debugger thread that issues special **DosPtrace** calls; the two halves of the package communicate through a shared memory area built into OS/2.

When the debuggee encounters a special event (for example, a Ctrl-C signal or a GP fault), the trace force event takes precedence over any other, and the debuggee's thread executes the debuggee half of the **DosPtrace** code. This code writes a record describing the event into a communications buffer, wakes up the debugger thread, which is typically blocked in the debugger's part of the **DosPtrace** code, and blocks, awaiting a reply. The debugger's thread wakes up and returns to the debugger with the event information. When the debugger recalls **DosPtrace** with a command, the command is written into the communications area, and the debuggee is awakened to read and obey. The command might be ''Resume normal execution,'' ''Process the event as you normally would,'' or ''Give me the contents of these locations in your address space,'' whereupon the debuggee thread replies and remains in the **DosPtrace** handler.

This approach is simple to implement, does the job well, and takes advantage of existing OS/2 features. For example, no special code is needed to allow the debugger access to the debuggee's address space because the debuggee itself, unwittingly in the **DosPtrace** code, reads and writes its own address space. Credit goes to the UNIX *ptrace* facility, upon which this facility was closely modeled.

Finally, here are a few incidental facts that the readers of this book, being likely users of debugging facilities, should know. OS/2 maintains a linkage between the debugger process and the debuggee process. When the debugger process terminates, the debuggee process also terminates if it has not already done so. The debuggee program need not be a direct child of the debugger; when the debugger process makes its initial **DosPtrace** call, OS/2 connects it to the last process that was executed with the special tracing option. If a process is executed with the tracing option but no debugger process subsequently issues a **DosPtrace** function, the jilted debuggee process is terminated in about two minutes.

19

The 3x Box

It's of critical importance that OS/2 do a good job of running existing MS-DOS applications, but as we've discussed, this is a difficult task. To offer the official MS-DOS interfaces under OS/2 and therefore claim upward compatibility would be easy; unfortunately, few popular applications would run successfully in such an environment. Most sophisticated applications take direct control of the machine environment and use MS-DOS for tasks the application doesn't want to bother with, such as file I/O, keyboard buffering, and so forth. If we're to run existing applications successfully, we must provide a close facsimile to a real mode PC running MS-DOS in all respects, not just the INT 21 program interface.

OS/2 provides such a highly compatible environment, called the real mode screen group, the compatibility box, or simply the 3x box. The 3x box is an environment that emulates an 8086-based PC running MS-DOS version 3.3.[1] MS-DOS programs execute in real mode, and because emulating real mode from within protected mode is prohibitively slow, OS/2 physically switches into real mode to execute MS-DOS applications. Because MS-DOS programs are well aware of the MS-DOS memory layout, this layout is replicated for the OS/2 3x box. The first N bytes (typically 640 KB) are reserved for the exclusive use of the low-memory parts of OS/2 and the 3x box; protected mode applications never use any of this memory. Thus, programs that are careless about memory allocation or that make single-tasking assumptions about the availability of memory can run in a multitasking environment. Figure 19-1 on the following page illustrates the OS/2

---

1. For OS/2 version 1.0, the 3x box is compatible with MS-DOS version 3.3.

memory layout. The low bytes of memory are reserved for the device drivers and portions of OS/2 that must run in real mode. The remainder of the space, up to the RMSIZE value, is dedicated to the 3x box. Memory from 640 KB to 1 MB is reserved for ROMs and video display buffers. Memory above 1 MB holds the remainder of OS/2 and all protect mode applications. Nonswappable, fixed segments are kept at one end of this memory to reduce fragmentation.

OS/2 uses the screen group mechanism to provide a user interface to the 3x box. One screen group is designated the real mode screen group; automatically, OS/2 executes COMMAND.COM in that screen group

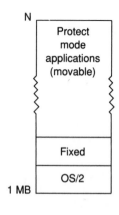

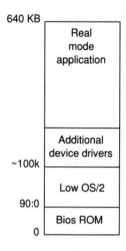

Figure 19-1.
System memory layout.

when it is first selected. The user accesses the real mode environment by selecting that screen group and returns to the protected mode environment by selecting another screen group. OS/2 version 1.0 supports a single real mode screen group because the real mode compatibility is provided by actually running the application in real mode. Thus, only one 640 KB area is reserved for all real mode applications, and adjudicating between the conflicting hardware manipulations of multiple real mode applications without any assistance from the 80286 microprocessor hardware would be prohibitively difficult. The 80386 microprocessor, however, provides a special hardware facility called virtual 8086 mode that will allow a future release of OS/2 to support multiple real mode screen groups, but only on an 80386-based machine.

The operating system that services the 3x application's INT 21 requests is not an exact copy of MS-DOS; it's actually a low-memory extension of OS/2 itself. Because OS/2 is derived from MS-DOS, OS/2 executes MS-DOS functions in a manner identical to that of the real MS-DOS. OS/2 supports the non–MS-DOS functions mentioned above by staying out of the way as much as possible and letting the 3x application "party hearty" with the hardware. For example, hooking most interrupt vectors is supported, as is hooking INT 21 and the ROM BIOS INT vectors. The ROM BIOS calls themselves are fully supported. Frequently, staying out of the way is not as easy as it may sound. For example, OS/2 must intercept and monitor real mode calls made to the disk driver part of the ROM BIOS so that it can prevent conflict with ongoing, asynchronous protect-mode disk I/O. OS/2 may find it necessary to momentarily block a real mode application's BIOS call until the protect mode device driver can release the hardware. Once the real mode application is in the BIOS, the same interlock mechanism prevents the protect mode device driver from entering the disk I/O critical section.

Hard errors encountered by the real mode application are handled by a hybrid of the OS/2 hard error daemon and the 3x box INT 24 mechanism in a three-step process, as follows:

1: Hard error codes caused by events unique to the OS/2 environment—such as a volume manager media change request—activate the hard error daemon so that the user can get an accurate explanation of the problem. The user's response to the hard error is saved but is not yet acted upon. Hard error codes, which are also present in MS-DOS version 3.3, skip this step and start at step 2.

2: If the real mode application has installed its own hard error handler via the INT 24 vector, it is called. If step 1 was skipped, the code should be known to the application, and it is presented unchanged. If step 1 was taken, the error code is transformed to ERROR_I24_GEN_FAILURE for this step. The response returned by the program, if valid for this class of hard error, is acted upon. This means that hard errors new to OS/2 can actually generate two pop-ups—one from the hard error daemon with an accurate message and one from the application itself with a General Failure message. This allows the user to understand the true cause of the hard error and yet notifies the application that a hard error has occurred. In such a case, the action specified by the application when it returned from its own hard error handler is the one taken, not the action specified by the user to the initial hard error daemon pop-up.

3: If the real mode application has not registered its hard error handler via the INT 24 mechanism, OS/2 provides a default handler that uses the hard error daemon. If step 1 was taken and the hard error daemon has already run, it is not run again; OS/2 takes the action specified in response to the hard error pop-up that was displayed. If step 1 was not taken because the hard error code is MS-DOS 3.x compatible and if step 2 was not taken because the application did not provide its own handler, then OS/2 activates the hard error daemon in step 3 to present the message and receive a reply.

The 3x box supports only MS-DOS functionality; no new OS/2 features are available to 3x box applications—no new API, no multiple threads, no IPC, no semaphores, and so on.[2] This decision was made for two reasons. First, although any real mode application can damage the system's stability, allowing real mode applications to access some

2. There are two exceptions. The **OPEN** function was extended, and an INT 2F multiplex function was added to notify real mode applications of screen switches.

protect mode features may aggravate the problem. For example, terminate and stay resident programs may manipulate the CPU in such a way as to make it impossible for a real mode application to protect a critical section with semaphores and yet guarantee that it won't leave the semaphore orphaned. Second, because OS/2 has only one real mode box and it labors under a 640 KB memory ceiling, it doesn't make sense to develop new real mode applications that use new OS/2 functions and thus require OS/2.

The 3x box emulation extends to interrupts. OS/2 continues to context switch the CPU when the 3x box is active; that is, the 3x box application is the foreground application. Because the foreground process receives a favorable priority, its CPU is preempted only when a time-critical protect mode application needs to run or when the real mode application blocks. If the CPU is running a protect mode application when a device interrupt comes in, OS/2 switches to real mode so that a real mode application that is hooking the interrupt vectors can receive the interrupt in real mode. When the interrupt is complete, OS/2 switches back to protected mode and resumes the protected application.

Although protected mode applications can continue to run when the 3x box is in the foreground, the reverse is not true. When the 3x box screen group is in the background, all 3x box execution is suspended, including interrupts. Unlike protected mode applications, real mode applications cannot be trusted to refrain from manipulating the screen hardware when they are in a background screen group. Normally, a real mode application doesn't notice its suspension when it's in background mode; the only thing it might notice is that the system time-of-day has apparently "jumped forward." Because mode switching is a slow process and leaves interrupts disabled for almost 1 millisecond, mode switching can cause interrupt overruns on fast devices such as serial ports. The best way to deal with this is to switch the real mode application into a background screen group; with no more real mode programs to execute, OS/2 does no further mode switching.

Some OS/2 utility programs such as FIND are packaged as Family API applications. A single binary can run in both protected mode and real mode, and the user is saved the inconvenience of switching from real mode to protected mode to do simple utility functions. This works well for simple utility programs without full screen or graphical interfaces and for programs that have modest memory demands and that in other ways have little need of OS/2's extended capabilities. Obviously, if an application can make good use of OS/2's protect mode features, it should be written to be protect mode only so that it can take advantage of those features.

20

Family API

When a new release of a PC operating system is announced, application writers face a decision: Should they write a new application to use some of the new features or should they use only the features in earlier releases? If they go for the sexy new features, their product might do more, be easier to write, or be more efficient; but when the program hits the market, only 10 percent of existing PCs may be running the new release. Not all of the existing machines have the proper processor to be able to run the new system, and, of those, many of their users haven't seen the need to go to the expense and endure the hassle of upgrading their operating system. If it's viable to write the new application so that it requires only the old operating system (and therefore runs in compatibility mode under the new operating system), then it's tempting to do so. Even though the product is not as good as it might be, it can sell to 100 percent of the installed base of machines — 10 times as many as it would if it required the new operating system.

And here you have the classic "catch-22" of software standards: If users don't see a need, they won't use the new system. If they don't use the new system, applications will not be written explicitly for it; so the users never see a need. Without some way to prime the pump, it will be a long time before a comprehensive set of applications are available that use the new system's features.

OS/2 tackles this problem in several ways. The software bundled with OS/2 runs in protected mode, and OS/2 attempts to include as much additional user function as possible to increase its value to a user who initially owns no protected mode applications. The most important user acceptance feature of OS/2, however, is called *Family API*.

Family API is a special subset of the OS/2 protected mode API. Using special tools included in the OS/2 developer's kit, you can build applications that use only the Family API. The resultant .EXE file(s) run unchanged in OS/2 protect mode or on an 8086 running MS-DOS 2.x or 3.x.[1] Thus, developers don't have to choose between writing applications that are OS/2 protect mode and writing applications that are MS-DOS compatible; they can use the Family API mechanism and do both. Your applications will run as protected mode applications under OS/2 and as MS-DOS applications under a true MS-DOS system.

Clearly, the Family API is a noteworthy feature. It offers some OS/2 functions, together with the dynamic link system interface, to programs that run under MS-DOS without a copy of OS/2 anywhere in sight. It does this by providing an OS/2 compatibility library that accepts the OS/2 system interface calls and implements them itself, calling the underlying MS-DOS system via INT 21 as necessary. This information should give you a big head start in figuring out which OS/2 functions are included in the Family API: Clearly all functions that have similar INT 21 functions—such as **DosOpen, DosRead,** and **DosAllocSeg**— are supported. Also present are functions, such as **DosSubAlloc,** that can be supported directly by the special Family API library. Features that are extremely difficult to support in a true MS-DOS environment, such as multiple threads and asynchronous I/O, are not present in the Family API.

Where does this library come from? And how does it get loaded by MS-DOS to satisfy the OS/2 executable's dynlink requests? It's all done with mirrors, as the expression goes, and the "mirrors" must be built into the application's .EXE file because that file is all that's present when a Family API application is executed under MS-DOS. Figure 20-1 shows the layout of a Family API .EXE file.

OS/2 needed to define a new .EXE file because the existing MS-DOS .EXE file format contained too little information for the OS/2 protect mode segmented environment. Because, as we've discussed, the 8086 memory architecture is—despite the terminology normally used—a linear memory architecture, the MS-DOS .EXE format described only a single hunk of memory that was to be loaded

---

1. Of course, they also run in the MS-DOS 3.x compatible screen group under OS/2; but except for convenience utilities, it's generally a waste to dedicate the one real mode screen group to running an application that could run in any of the many protect mode screen groups.

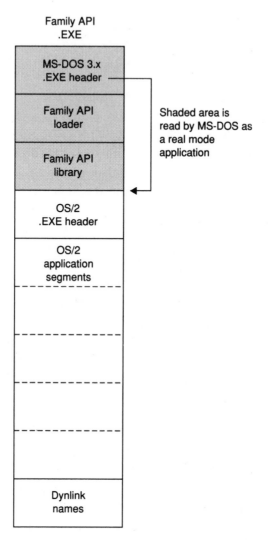

Figure 20-1.
Family API executable (.EXE) format.

contiguously. OS/2 needs each segment described separately, with information on its status: read only, code or data, demand load or preload, and so on. Naturally, OS/2 also needs a .EXE format with special records to describe loadtime dynamic links. This new .EXE format was defined so that its initial bytes look exactly like those of the old MS-DOS .EXE file header. A special flag bit is set in this fake .EXE header that is ignored by all releases of MS-DOS but that OS/2 recognizes to mean "It's not true. I'm really an OS/2 .EXE file. Seek to this location to find the *true,* new-style .EXE header."

When an MS-DOS system is told to load this .EXE file, it sees and believes the old .EXE file header. This header does not describe the application itself but a body of special code built into the .EXE file before the actual application's code: the Family API loader and library. In other words, to MS-DOS this .EXE file looks like a valid, executable program, and that program is the Family API loader and library. The Family API loader and library are loaded into memory, and execution begins. MS-DOS doesn't load in the body of the application itself because it wasn't described as part of the load image in the special MS-DOS .EXE file header. As soon as it starts to execute, the Family API loader begins reading in the application's segments, performs a loader's general relocation chores, and fixes up dynlink references to the proper entry points in the Family API library package. When the application is loaded, the Family API loader block moves the application to its final execution address, which overlays most of the Family API loader to reclaim that space, and execution begins.

All OS/2 .EXE files have this fake MS-DOS .EXE format header. In non–Family API executables, the Family API loader and library are missing, and by default the header describes an impossibly big MS-DOS executable. Should the application be accidentally run under a non–OS/2 system or in the OS/2 compatibility screen group, MS-DOS will refuse to load the program. Optionally, the programmer can link in a small stub program that goes where the Family API loader would and that prints a more meaningful error message. As we said earlier, the old-style .EXE headers on the front of the file contain a flag bit to alert OS/2 to the presence of a new-style .EXE header further into the file. Because this header doesn't describe the Family API loader and library parts of the file, OS/2 ignores their presence when it loads a Family API application in protected mode; the application's dynlink references are fixed up to the normal dynlink libraries, and the Family API versions of those libraries are ignored.

There Ain't No Such Thing As A Free Lunch, and the same unfortunately applies to the Family API mechanism. First, although the

Family API allows dynlink calls to be used in an MS-DOS environment, this is not true dynlinking; it's quasi dynlinking. Obviously, runtime dynlinking is not supported, but even loadtime dynlinking is special because the dynlink target library is bound into the .EXE file. One of the advantages of dynlinks is that the target code is not part of the .EXE file and can therefore be changed and upgraded without changing the .EXE file. This is not true of the dynlink emulation library used by the Family API because it *is* built into the .EXE file. Fortunately, this disadvantage isn't normally a problem. Dynlink libraries are updated either to improve their implementation or to add new features. The Family API library can't be improved very much because its environment—MS-DOS—is limited and unchanging. If new Family API features were added, loading that new library with preexisting Family API .EXE files would make no sense; those programs wouldn't be calling the new features.

A more significant drawback is the size and speed hit that the Family API introduces. Clearly, the size of a Family API .EXE file is extended by the size of the Family API loader and the support library. The tools used to build Family API executables include only those library routines used by the program, but even so the library and the loader add up to a nontrivial amount of memory—typically 10 KB to 14 KB in the .EXE file and perhaps 9 KB (the loader is not included) in RAM. Finally, loading a Family API application under MS-DOS is slower than loading a true MS-DOS .EXE file. Comparing loadtime against the loadtime of MS-DOS is tough for any operating system because loading faster than MS-DOS is difficult. The .EXE file consists of a single lump of contiguous data that can be read into memory in a single disk read operation. A relocation table must also be read, but it's typically very small. It's hard for any system to be faster than this. Clearly, loading a Family API application is slower because the loader and library must be loaded, and then they must, a segment at a time, bring in the body of the application.

Although the Family API makes dual environment applications possible, it can't totally hide from an application the difference between the MS-DOS 3.x and the OS/2 execution environment. For example, the Family API supports only the **DosFindFirst** function for a single search handle at a time. An application that wants to perform multiple directory searches simultaneously should use **DosGetMachineMode** to determine its environment and then use the unrestricted **DosFindFirst** function if running in protect mode or use the INT 21 functions if running in real mode. Likewise, an application that wants to manipulate printer data needs to contain version-specific code to hook INT 17 or to use device monitors, depending on the environment.

Part III

The Future

21

The Future

This chapter is difficult to write because describing the second version of OS/2 becomes uninteresting when that version is released. Furthermore, preannouncing products is bad practice; the trade-offs between schedule and customer demand can accelerate the inclusion of some features and postpone others, often late in the development cycle. If we talk explicitly about future features, developers may plan their work around the availability of those features and be left high and dry if said features are postponed. As a result, this chapter is necessarily vague about both the functional details and the release schedule, discussing future goals for features rather than the features themselves. Design your application, not so that it *depends* on the features described here, but so that it is *compatible* with them.

OS/2 version 1.0 is the first standard MS-DOS–compatible operating system that unlocks the memory-addressing potential of the 80286—a "train" that will "pull" a great many APIs into the standard. On the other hand, foreseeable future releases cannot expect such penetration, so the designers of OS/2 version 1.0 focused primarily on including a full set of APIs. Major performance improvements were postponed for future releases simply because such improvements can be easily added later, whereas new APIs cannot. Most of the planned work is to take further advantage of existing interfaces, not to create new ones.

21.1 File System

Clearly, the heart of the office automation environment is data—lots of data—searching for it, reading it, and, less frequently, writing it. A machine's raw number-crunching capacity is relatively uninteresting in this milieu; the important issue is how fast the machine can get the data and manipulate it. Certainly, raw CPU power is advantageous; it allows the use of a relatively compute bound graphical user interface, for example. But I/O performance is becoming the limiting factor, especially in a multitasking environment. Where does this data come from? If it's from the keyboard, no problem; human typing speeds are glacially slow to a computer. If the data is from a non-mass-storage device, OS/2's direct device access facilities should provide sufficient throughput. That leaves the file system for local disks and the network for remote data. The file system is a natural for a future release upgrade. Its interface is generic so that applications written for the first release will work compatibly with new file systems in subsequent releases.

Talking about pending file system improvements is relatively easy because the weaknesses in the current FAT file system are obvious.

■ Large Disk Support

Clearly, a new file system will support arbitrarily large disks without introducing prohibitive allocation fragmentation. Allocation fragmentation refers to the minimum amount of disk space that a file system can allocate to a small file—the allocation unit. If the allocation unit is size N, the average file on the disk is expected to waste N/2 bytes of disk space because each file has a last allocation unit and on the average that unit will be only half filled. Actually, if the allocation unit is large, say more than 2 KB, the average fragmentation loss is greater than this estimate because a disproportionate number of files are small.

The existing MS-DOS FAT file system can handle large disks, but at the cost of using very large allocation units. Depending on the number and the size of the files, a 100 MB disk might be as much as 50 percent wasted by this fragmentation. The new Microsoft file system will support a very small allocation unit— probably 512 bytes—to reduce this fragmentation, and this small allocation unit size will not adversely affect the performance of the file system.

■ File Protection

A new file system also must support file access protection as part of the move toward a fully secure environment. File protection is typically a feature of multiuser operating systems; the MS-DOS FAT file system was designed for a single-user environment and contains no protection facilities. So why do we need them now? One reason is that a networked PC is *physically* a single-user machine, but *logically* it's a multiuser machine because multiple users can access the same files over the network. Also, as we shall see, it is sometimes useful to be able to protect your own files from access by yourself.

Today, most network installations consist of server machines and client machines, with client machines able to access only files on server machines. MSNET and PCNET servers have a rudimentary form of file protection, but it needs improvement (see below). In the future, as machines become bigger and as products improve, files on client machines will also be available across the network. Clearly, a strong protection mechanism is needed to eliminate risks to a client machine's files. Finally, a file protection mechanism can be useful even on a single-user machine that is not accessible from a network. Today a variety of "Trojan" programs claim to be one thing but actually are another. In a non-networked environment, these programs are generally examples of mindless vandalism; typically, they purge the contents of the victim's hard disk. In a future office environment, they might edit payroll files or send sensitive data to someone waiting across the network. If you, as a user, can put sensitive files under password protection, they are safe even from yourself when you unwittingly run a Trojan program. That program doesn't know the password, and you certainly will decline to supply it. Self-protection also prevents someone from sitting down at your PC while you are at lunch or on vacation and wreaking havoc with your files.

Protection mechanisms take two general forms: *capability tokens* and *access lists*. A capability token gives access to an object if the requestor can supply the proper token, which itself can take a variety of forms. A per-file or per-directory password, such as is available on existing MSNET and PCNET products, is a kind of capability token: If you can present the password, you can access the file. Note that the password is associated with the *item,* not the *user.* The front door key to your house is a good example of a capability token, and it shows the features and limitations of the approach very well. Access to your house depends on owning the capability token—the key—and not on who you are. If you don't have your key, you can't get in, even if it's your own house. Anybody that *does* have the key *can* get in, no matter who they are. A key can sometimes be handy: You can loan it to someone for a day and then get it back. You can give it to the plumber's office, for example, and the office can give it to the plumber, who can in turn give it to an assistant. Capability tokens are flexible because you can pass them around without notifying the owner of the protected object.

This benefit is also the major drawback of capability token systems: The capabilities can be passed around willy-nilly and, like a key, can be duplicated. Once you give your key out, you never know if you've gotten ''them'' back again. You can't enumerate who has access to your house, and if they refuse to return a key or if they've duplicated it, you can't withdraw access to your house. The only way to regain control over your house is to change the lock, which means that you have to reissue keys to everybody who *should* get access. In the world of houses and keys, this isn't much of a problem because keys aren't given out that much and it's easy to contact the few people who should have them. Changing the capability ''lock'' on a computer file is much more difficult, however, because it may mean updating a great many programs that are allowed access, and they all have to be updated simultaneously so that none is accidentally locked out. And, of course, the distribution of the new capability token must be carried out securely; you must ensure that no ''bad guy'' gets a chance to see and copy the token.

And, finally, because a separate capability token, or password, needs to be kept for each file or directory, you can't possibly memorize them all. Instead, they get built into programs, stored in files, entered into batch scripts, and so on. All these passwords—

the ones that are difficult to change because of the hassle of updating everybody—are being kept around in "plain text" in standardized locations, an invitation for pilferage. And just as the lock on your door won't tell you how many keys exist, a capability token system won't be able to warn you that someone has stolen a copy of the capability token.

An alternative approach is the access list mechanism. It is equivalent to the guard at the movie studio gate who has a list of people on his clipboard. Each protected object is associated with a list of who is allowed what kind of access. It's easy to see who has access—simply look at the list. It's easy to give or take away access—simply edit the list. Maintaining the list is easy because no change is made unless someone is to be added or removed, and the list can contain group names, such as "anyone from the production department" or "all vice presidents."

The fly in this particular ointment—and the reason that MSNET didn't use this approach—is in authenticating the identification of the person who wants access. In our movie studio, a picture badge is probably sufficient.[1] With the computer, we use a personal password. This password doesn't show that you have access to a particular file; it shows that you are who you claim to be. Also, because you have only one password, you can memorize it; it needn't be written on any list. Finally, you can change the password frequently because only one person—the one changing it, you—needs to be notified. Once the computer system knows that you're truly Hiram G. Hornswoggle, it grants or refuses access based on whether you're on an access list or belong to a group that is on an access list. MS-DOS can't use this approach because it's an unprotected system; whatever flag it sets in memory to say that you have properly authenticated yourself can be set by a cheater program. OS/2 is a protect mode operating system and is secure from such manipulation provided that no untrusted real mode applications are executed.[2] A networking environment provides an extra challenge because you can write a program—perhaps

---

1. Note that the photo on the badge, together with a hard-to-duplicate design, keeps the badge from being just another capability token.
2. A future OS/2 release will take advantage of the 80386 processor's virtual real mode facility to make it safe to run untrusted real mode programs on an 80386.

running on an MS-DOS machine to avoid protection mechanisms—that "sniffs" the network, examining every communication. A client machine can't send a plain-text password over the network to authenticate its user because a sniffer could see it. And it certainly can't send a message saying, "I'm satisfied that this is really Hiram." The client machine may be running bogus software that will lie and say that when it isn't true. In other words, a network authentication protocol must assume that "bad guys" can read all net transmissions and can generate any transmission they wish.

As should be clear by now, a future OS/2 file system will support per-object permission lists. OS/2 will be enhanced to support users' identifying themselves by means of personal passwords. Future network software will support a secure network authentication protocol.

A new file system will do more than support access lists; it will also support filenames longer than the FAT 8.3 convention, and it will support *extended file attributes*. The FAT file system supports a very limited set of attributes, each of which are binary flags—system, hidden, read-only, and so on. Extended attributes allow an arbitrary set of attributes, represented as text strings, to be associated with each file. Individual applications will be able to define specific attributes, set them on files, and later query their values. Extended attributes can be used, for example, to name the application that created the file. This would allow a user to click the mouse over the filename on a directory display and have the presentation manager bring up the proper application on that file.

Finally, although this file system wish list looks pretty good, how do we know that we've covered all the bases? And will our new file system work well with CD-ROM[3] disks and WORM drives? The answers are "We don't" and "It doesn't," so a future OS/2 release will support *installable file systems*. An installable file system is similar to an installable device driver. When the system is initialized, not only device drivers but new file system management packages can be installed into OS/2. This will allow specialized file systems to handle specialized

3. Special versions of compact discs that contain digital data instead of digitized music. When accessed via a modified CD player, they provide approximately 600 MB of read-only storage.

devices such as CD-ROMs and WORM, as well as providing an easy interface to media written on foreign file systems that are on non–MS-DOS or non–OS/2 systems.

21.2   The 80386

Throughout this book, the name 80386 keeps cropping up, almost as a kind of magical incantation. To a system designer, it *is* a magical device. It provides the protection facilities of the 80286, but it also provides three other key features.

21.2.1   Large Segments

The 80386 has a segmented architecture very much like that of the 80286, but 80286 segments are limited to 64 KB. On the 80386, segments can be as large as 4 million KB; segments can be so large that an entire program can run in 2 segments (one code and one data) and essentially ignore the segmentation facilities of the processor. This is called *flat model*. Writing programs that deal with large structures is easier using flat model, and because compilers have a hard time generating optimal segmented code, converting 8086/80286 large model programs to 80386 flat model can produce dramatic increases in execution speed.

Although a future release of OS/2 will certainly support large segments and applications that use flat model internally, OS/2 will not necessarily provide a flat model API. The system API for 32-bit applications may continue to use segmented (that is, 48-bit) addresses.

21.2.2   Multiple Real Mode Boxes

The 80386 provides a mode of execution called virtual real mode. Processes that run in this mode execute instructions exactly as they would in real mode, but they are not truly in real mode; they are in a special 8086-compatible protected mode. The additional memory management and protection facilities that this mode provides allow a future version of OS/2 to support more than one real mode box at the same time; multiple real mode applications will be able to execute simultaneously and to continue executing while in background mode. The virtual real mode eliminates the need for mode switching; thus, the user can execute real mode applications while running communications applications that have a high interrupt rate.

21.2.3 Full Protection Capability

The virtual real mode capability, coupled with the 80386's ability to allow/disallow I/O access on a port-by-port basis, provides the hardware foundation for a future OS/2 that is fully secure. In a fully secure OS/2, the modules loaded in during bootup—the operating system itself, device drivers, installable file systems, and so on—must be trusted, but no other program can accidentally or deliberately damage others, read protected files, or otherwise access or damage restricted data. The only damage an aberrant or malicious program will be able to do is to slow down the machine by hogging the resources, such as consuming most of the RAM or CPU time. This is relatively harmless; the user can simply kill the offending program and not run it anymore.

21.2.4 Other Features

The 80386 contains other significant features besides speed, such as paged virtual memory, that don't appear in an API or in a specific user benefit. For this reason, we won't discuss them here other than to state the obvious: An 80386 machine is generally considerably faster than an 80286-based one.

So what do these 80386 features mean for the 80286? What role will it play in the near and far future? Should a developer write for the 80286 or the 80386? First, OS/2 for the 80386[4] is the same operating system, essentially, as OS/2 for the 80286. The only new API in 80386 OS/2 will be the 32-bit wide one for 32-bit mode 80386-only binaries. The other features—such as virtual memory, I/O permission mapping, and multiple real mode boxes—are of value to the user but don't present any new APIs and therefore are compatible with all applications. Certainly, taking advantage of the 80386's new instruction order codes and 2^{32}-byte-length segments will require a new API; in fact, a program must be specially written and compiled for that environment. Only applications that can't function at all using the smaller 80286-compatible segments need to become 80386 dependent; 80286 protect mode programs will run without change and without any disadvantage on the 80386, taking advantage of its improved speed.

To summarize, there is only one operating system, OS/2. OS/2 supports 16-bit protected mode applications that run on all machines, and

---

4. A product still under development at the time of this writing. All releases of OS/2 will run on the 80386, but the initial OS/2 release treats the 80386 as a ''fast 80286.'' The only 80386 feature it uses is the faster mode-switching capability.

OS/2 will support 32-bit protected mode applications that will run only on 80386 machines. A developer should consider writing an application for the 32-bit model[5] only if the application performs so poorly in the 16-bit model that a 16-bit version is worthless. Otherwise, one should develop applications for the 16-bit model; such applications will run well on all existing OS/2-compatible machines and on all OS/2 releases. Later, when the 80386 and OS/2-386 have sufficient market penetration, you may want to release higher-performance upgrades to products that require the 80386.

21.3 The Next Ten Years

Microsoft believes that OS/2 will be a major influence in the personal computer industry for roughly the next ten years. The standardization of computing environments that mass market software brings about gives such standards abnormal longevity, while the incredible rate of hardware improvements brings on great pressure to change. As a result, we expect OS/2 to live long and prosper, where *long* is a relative term in an industry in which nothing can survive more than a decade. What might OS/2's successor system look like? If we could answer that today, a successor system would be unnecessary. Clearly, the increases in CPU performance will continue. Personal computers will undoubtedly follow in the footsteps of their supercomputer brethren and become used for more than calculation, but also for simulation, modeling, and expert systems, not only in the workplace but also in the home. The future will become clearer, over time, as this most wonderful of tools continues to change its users.

The development of OS/2 is, to date, the largest project that Microsoft has ever taken on. From an initially very small group of Microsoft engineers, to a still small joint Microsoft-IBM design team, to finally a great many developers, builders, testers, and documenters from both Microsoft and IBM, the project became known affectionately as the ''Black Hole.''

As I write this, OS/2 is just weeks away from retail sale. It's been a great pleasure for me and for the people who worked with me to see our black hole begin to give back to our customers the fruits of the labors that were poured into it.

---

5. When it is announced and documented.

Glossary

anonymous pipe
a data storage buffer that OS/2 maintains in RAM; used for inter-process communications.

Applications Program Interface (API)
the set of calls a program uses to obtain services from the operating system. The term *API* denotes a service interface, whatever its form.

background category
a classification of processes that consists of those associated with a screen group not currently being displayed.

call gate
a special LDT or GDT entry that describes a subroutine entry point rather than a memory segment. A far call to a call gate selector will cause a transfer to the entry point specified in the call gate. This is a feature of the 80286/80386 hardware and is normally used to provide a transition from a lower privilege state to a higher one.

captive thread
a thread that has been created by a dynlink package and that stays within the dynlink code, never transferring back to the client process's code; also a thread that is used to call a service entry point and that will never return or that will return only if some specific event occurs.

child process
a process created by another process (its parent process).

closed system
hardware or software design that cannot be enhanced in the field by third-party suppliers.

command subtree
a process and all its descendants.

context switch

the act of switching the CPU from the execution of one thread to another, which may belong to the same process or to a different one.

cooked mode

a mode established by programs for keyboard input. In cooked mode, OS/2 handles the line-editing characters such as the back space.

critical section

a body of code that manipulates a data resource in a non-reentrant way.

daemon program

a process that performs a utility function without interaction with the user. For example, the swapper process is a daemon program.

debuggee

the program being debugged.

debugger

a program that helps the programmer locate the source of problems found during runtime testing of a program.

device driver

a program that transforms I/O requests made in a standard, device-independent fashion into the operations necessary to make a specific piece of hardware fulfill that request.

device monitor

a mechanism that allows processes to track and/or modify device data streams.

disjoint LDT space

the LDT selectors reserved for memory objects that are shared or that may be shared among processes.

dynamic link
a method of postponing the resolution of external references until load-time or runtime. A dynamic link allows the called subroutines to be packaged, distributed, and maintained independently of their callers. OS/2 extends the dynamic link (or dynlink) mechanism to serve as the primary method by which all system and nonsystem services are obtained.

dynlink
see **dynamic link.**

dynlink library
a file, in a special format, that contains the binary code for a group of dynamically linked subroutines.

dynlink routine
see **dynamic link.**

dynlink subsystem
a dynlink module that provides a set of services built around a resource.

encapsulation
the principle of hiding the internal implementation of a program, function, or service so that its clients can tell what it does but not how it does it.

environment strings
a series of user-definable and program-definable strings that are associated with each process. The initial values of environment strings are established by a process's parent.

exitlist
a list of subroutines that OS/2 calls when a process has terminated. The exitlist is executed after process termination but before the process is actually destroyed.

Family Applications Program Interface (Family API)
a standard execution environment under MS-DOS versions 2.x and 3.x and OS/2. The programmer can use the Family API to create an application that uses a subset of OS/2 functions (but a superset of MS-DOS 3.x functions) and that runs in a binary-compatible fashion under MS-DOS versions 2.x and 3.x and OS/2.

file handle
a binary value that represents an open file; used in all file I/O calls.

file locking
an OS/2 facility that allows one program to temporarily prevent other programs from reading and/or writing a particular file.

file system name space
names that have the format of filenames. All such names will eventually represent disk "files"—data or special. Initially, some of these names are kept in internal OS/2 RAM tables and are not present on any disk volume.

forced event
an event or action that is forced upon a thread or a process from an external source; for example, a Ctrl-C or a **DosKill** command.

foreground category
a classification of processes that consists of those associated with the currently active screen group.

GDT
see **global descriptor table.**

general priority category
the OS/2 classification of threads that consists of three subcategories: background, foreground, and interactive.

general protection (GP) fault
an error that occurs when a program accesses invalid memory locations or accesses valid locations in an invalid way (such as writing into read-only memory areas).

giveaway shared memory

a shared memory mechanism in which a process that already has access to the segment can grant access to another process. Processes cannot obtain access for themselves; access must be granted by another process that already has access.

global data segment

a data segment that is shared among all instances of a dynlink routine; in other words, a single segment that is accessible to all processes that call a particular dynlink routine.

global descriptor table (GDT)

an element of the 80286/80386 memory management hardware. The GDT holds the descriptions of as many as 4095 global segments. A global segment is accessible to all processes.

global subsystem initialization

a facility that allows a dynlink routine to specify that its *initialize* entry point should be called when the dynlink package is loaded on behalf of its first client.

grandparent process

the parent process of a process that created a process.

handle

an arbitrary integer value that OS/2 returns to a process so that the process can return it to OS/2 on subsequent calls; known to programmers as a magic cookie.

hard error

an error that the system detects but which it cannot correct without user intervention.

hard error daemon

a daemon process that services hard errors. The hard error daemon may be an independent process, or it may be a thread that belongs to the session manager or to the presentation manager.

huge segments
a software technique that allows the creation and use of pseudo segments larger than 65 KB.

installable file system (IFS)
a body of code that OS/2 loads at boot time and that provides the software to manage a file system on a storage device, including the ability to create and maintain directories, allocate disk space, and so on.

instance data segment
a memory segment that holds data specific to each instance of the dynlink routine.

instance subsystem initialization
a service that dynlink routines can request. A dynlink routine's *initialize* entry point is called each time a new client is linked to the routine.

interactive category
a classification of processes that consists of the process currently interacting with the keyboard.

interactive program
a program whose function is to obey commands from a user, such as an editor or a spreadsheet program. Programs such as compilers may literally interact by asking for filenames and compilation options, but they are considered noninteractive because their function is to compile a source program, not to provide answers to user-entered commands.

interprocess communications (IPC)
the ability of processes and threads to transfer data and messages among themselves; used to offer services to and receive services from other programs.

interruptible block
a special form of a blocking operation used inside the OS/2 kernel so that events such as process kill and Ctrl-C can interrupt a thread that is waiting, inside OS/2, for an event.

I/O privilege mechanism
a facility that allows a process to ask a device driver for direct access to the device's I/O ports and any dedicated or mapped memory locations it has. The I/O privilege mechanism can be used directly by an application or indirectly by a dynlink package.

IPC
see **interprocess communications.**

KBD
an abbreviated name for the dynlink package that manages the keyboard device. All its entry points start with **Kbd.**

kernel
the central part of OS/2. It resides permanently in fixed memory locations and executes in the privileged ring 0 state.

LDT
see **local descriptor table.**

loadtime dynamic linking
the act of connecting a client process to dynamic link libraries when the process is first loaded into memory.

local descriptor table (LDT)
an element of the 80286/80386 memory management hardware. The LDT holds the descriptions of as many as 4095 local segments. Each process has its own LDT and cannot access the LDTs of other processes.

logical device
a symbolic name for a device that the user can cause to be mapped to any physical (actual) device.

logical directory
a symbolic name for a directory that the user can cause to be mapped to any actual drive and directory.

low priority category
a classification of processes that consists of processes that get CPU time only when no other thread in the other categories needs it; this category is lower in priority than the general priority category.

magic cookie
see **handle.**

memory manager
the section of OS/2 that allocates both physical memory and virtual memory.

memory overcommit
allocating more memory to the running program than physically exists.

memory suballocation
the OS/2 facility that allocates pieces of memory from within an application's segment.

MOU
an abbreviated name for the dynlink package that manages the mouse device. All its entry points start with **Mou.**

multitasking operating system
an operating system in which two or more programs/threads can execute simultaneously.

named pipe
a data storage buffer that OS/2 maintains in RAM; used for interprocess communication.

named shared memory
a memory segment that can be accessed simultaneously by more than one process. Its name allows processes to request access to it.

open system
hardware or software design that allows third-party additions and upgrades in the field.

object name buffer
the area in which OS/2 returns a character string if the **DosExecPgm**
function fails.

parallel multitasking
the process whereby programs execute simultaneously.

parent process
a process that creates another process, which is called the child process.

physical memory
the RAM (Random Access Memory) physically present inside the
machine.

PID (Process Identification Number)
a unique code that OS/2 assigns to a process when the process is
created. The PID may be any value except 0.

pipe
see **anonymous pipe; named pipe.**

presentation manager
the graphical user interface for OS/2.

priority
(also known as CPU priority) the numeric value assigned to each runnable thread in the system. Threads with a higher priority are assigned
the CPU in preference to those with a lower priority.

privilege mode
a special execution mode (also known as ring 0) supported by the
80286/80386 hardware. Code executing in this mode can execute
restricted instructions that are used to manipulate key system structures and tables. Only the OS/2 kernel and device drivers run in this
mode.

process
the executing instance of a binary file. In OS/2, the terms *task* and *process* are used interchangeably. A process is the unit of ownership, and processes own resources such as memory, open files, dynlink libraries, and semaphores.

protect mode
the operating mode of the 80286 microprocessor that allows the operating system to use features that protect one application from another; also called protected mode.

queue
an orderly list of elements waiting for processing.

RAM semaphore
a kind of semaphore that is based in memory accessible to a thread; fast, but with limited functionality. See **system semaphore.**

raw mode
a mode established by programs for keyboard input. In raw mode OS/2 passes to the caller each character typed immediately as it is typed. The caller is responsible for handling line-editing characters such as the back space.

real mode
the operating mode of the 80286 microprocessor that runs programs designed for the 8086/8088 microprocessor.

record locking
the mechanism that allows a process to lock a range of bytes within a file. While the lock is in effect, no other process can read or write those bytes.

ring 3
the privilege level that is used to run applications. Code executing at this level cannot modify critical system structures.

runtime dynamic linking

the act of establishing a dynamic link after a process has begun execution. This is done by providing OS/2 with the module and entry point names; OS/2 returns the address of the routine.

scheduler

the part of OS/2 that decides which thread to run and how long to run it before assigning the CPU to another thread; also, the part of OS/2 that determines the priority value for each thread.

screen group

a group of one or more processes that share (generally in a serial fashion) a single logical screen and keyboard.

semaphore

a software flag or signal used to coordinate the activities of two or more threads; commonly used to protect a critical section.

serial multitasking

the process whereby multiple programs execute, but only one at a time.

session manager

a system utility that manages screen group switching. The session manager is used only in the absence of the presentation manager; the presentation manager replaces the session manager.

shared memory

a memory segment that can be accessed simultaneously by more than one process.

signaling

using semaphores to notify threads that certain events or activities have taken place.

signals

notification mechanisms implemented in software that operate in a fashion analogous to hardware interrupts.

software tools approach
a design philosophy in which each program and application in a package is dedicated to performing a specific task and doing that task very well. See also **encapsulation.**

stack frame
a portion of a thread's stack that contains a procedure's local variables and parameters.

static linking
the combining of multiple compilands into a single executable file, thereby resolving undefined external references.

single-tasking
a computer environment in which only one program runs at a time.

swapping
the technique by which some code or data in memory is written to a disk file, thus allowing the memory it was using to be reused for another purpose.

system semaphore
a semaphore that is implemented in OS/2's internal memory area; somewhat slower than RAM semaphores, but providing more features.

System File Table (SFT)
an internal OS/2 table that contains an entry for every file currently open.

task
see **process.**

thread
the OS/2 mechanism that allows more than one path of execution through the same instance of an application program.

thread ID
the handle of a particular thread within a process.

thread of execution

the passage of the CPU through the instruction sequence.

time-critical priority

a classification of processes that may be interactive or noninteractive, in the foreground or background screen group, which have a higher priority than any non-time-critical thread in the system.

time slice

the amount of execution time that the scheduler will give a thread before reassigning the CPU to another thread of equal priority.

VIO

an abbreviated name of the dynlink package that manages the display device. All its entry points start with **Vio.**

virtual memory

the memory space allocated to and used by a process. At the time it is being referenced, the virtual memory must be present in physical memory, but otherwise it may be swapped to a disk file.

virtualization

the general technique of hiding a complicated actual situation behind a simple, standard interface.

writethrough

an option available when a file write operation is performed which specifies that the normal caching mechanism is to be sidestepped and the data is to be written through to the disk surface immediately.

3x box

the OS/2 environment that emulates an 8086-based PC running MS-DOS versions 2.x or 3.x.

INDEX

The manuscript for this book was prepared and submitted to Microsoft Press in electronic form. Text files were processed and formatted using Microsoft Word.

Cover design by Greg Hickman
Interior text design by the staff of Microsoft Press
Illustrations by Nick Gregoric
Principal typographer: Carol Luke
Principal production artist: Peggy Herman

Text composition by Microsoft Press in Times Roman with display in Helvetica Bold, using the Magna composition system and the Linotronic 300 laser imagesetter.